The aim of this series is to interest the general reader in the wildlife of Britain by recapturing the enquiring spirit of the old naturalists. The editors believe that the natural pride of the British public in the native flora and fauna, to which must be added concern for their conservation, is best fostered by maintaining a high standard of accuracy combined with clarity of exposition in presenting the results of modern scientific research.

The New Naturalist

WILD & GARDEN PLANTS

Max Walters
Sc.D., V.M.H

With sixteen pages of colour plates and
over 60 black and white photographs and
drawings

HarperCollins*Publishers*

HarperCollins*Publishers*
London Glasgow Sydney Auckland
Toronto Johannesburg

To Humphrey Gilbert-Carter and John Gilmour,
my predecessors as Director of the Cambridge University Botanic Garden

First published 1993

ISBN 0 00219376 0 (Hardback)
ISBN 0 00219889 4 (Paperback)

Printed and bound by Butler & Tanner, Frome, Somerset, UK

Contents

Colour Plates

Editors' Preface

Throughout its long and, we like to think, distinguished history, the New Naturalist series has sought to provide a survey of British natural history that is scholarly, informed and up to date, but most importantly accessible to all with an interest in our countryside and its wildlife, both plant and animal. In the first half dozen volumes in the series the Editors set the pattern of how they saw this philosophy being realised. At a time when ecology was not the household word and object of international conventions that it now is, its practitioners tended to approach the subject from either a habitat or a species point of view. This dichotomy of approach was reflected in that first list of titles which included *Butterflies* and *Natural History in the Highlands and Islands*. Our predecessors also appreciated, years before urban conservation became such an important element on the environmentalists' agenda, that natural history was not confined to the countryside and *London's Natural History* still stands as the pioneer work on urban natural history.

That first list of half a dozen titles also includes one of the most successful and enduring volumes in the series – John Gilmour's and Max Walters' *Wild Flowers* first published in 1954. At the time John Gilmour was Director of the University Botanic Garden at Cambridge and botanical editor of the series whilst in the words of the Editors, "his able and learned colleague", Max Walters, was Director of the University Herbarium. Two years later Max Walters was to co-author with John Raven *Mountain Flowers* which so evocatively describes the magic of our mountains and their alpine flora.

Given the huge area of our country that is occupied by gardens and their importance as wildlife habitats and the astonishing numbers of people who are either active gardeners themselves or visitors to our great gardens it is perhaps surprising that the New Naturalist series has not produced a volume on garden natural history before. In this, his third contribution to the series, Max Walters redresses the deficiency and describes the nature and origins of the largely alien flora that constitutes our garden vegetation. As the reader will discover, it is a story that is intimately bound up with the history of field botany and medicine and with the search for new and exotic plants in the eighteenth and nineteenth centuries. Here also are described the ways in which the science of genetics is used to transform wild species and hybrids into familiar and spectacular garden cultivars. As Dr Walters points out, most gardeners are not trained as botanists and this book bridges the gap between science and practice with great clarity even to the extent of explaining the modern contribution of molecular biology and biotechnology to horticulture.

The concluding chapters deal with the influence of recent developments in ecology on gardens and the role that they are increasingly coming to play in the conservation of wild plants, together with a review of the 'green movement' and its significance. Finally, and not unexpectedly, Dr Walters returns to the theme of education that he introduced in the opening chapter. Having

spent his career as a University teacher he is especially well-placed to empha-
sise the central role of education in conservation and he closes by posing the
question, "Where does a nature reserve end and a garden begin?".

It is with particular pleasure that we introduce *Wild & Garden Plants* to the
series, a book in the true New Naturalist tradition, by our editorial colleague.

Author's Foreword

Blessed with an equable climate, the English are a nation of gardeners. Indeed, it seems that one of the main factors in the obvious reluctance of English people to live in flats arises from our need for a garden, however small, around the home, and urban planners are belatedly adapting their thinking to cope with this natural resistance. But side by side with the love of gardens in the English tradition is a love of 'wild nature' outside the enclosed garden. How far are these two passions linked and how far are they opposed?

Many books have been written on aspects of this subject, and I shall have occasion to mention some of these which have helped and influenced me; but few have approached the topic from the angle of the plants themselves, and it is this gap in the literature that my book modestly aims to fill. More important than books, however, are the influences of my friends and teachers, to whom I owe much of my interest in the interplay of botany and horticulture. A brief reference to these influences would not only be a seemly tribute to my fellow-authors in the New Naturalist series, but would also enable me to explain how my own thoughts on wild and garden plants have developed over the years.

A childhood spent in industrial South Yorkshire, where even the open moorland was soot-covered, is about the worst training-ground for a future plantsman, whether botanist or gardener. Looking back on that childhood, I can remember the thrill of finding primroses on rare visits to the rich limestone country of the Derbyshire Dales, and on the other hand I can recall the few hardy flowers of our small front garden on the hard millstone grit: London Pride, that remarkable tough saxifrage, and *Dicentra spectabilis* which we called Love-lies-bleeding or Bleeding Heart. (Neither of these plants, incidentally, takes too kindly to the soft, lime-rich soils of Cambridge which became my home.) From this background I could have been a 'hard' scientist interested only in physics and chemistry: but very fortunately early influences conspired to turn me to field botany, around which I was eventually able to shape my main career. The earliest of all came from my maternal grandfather, whom I remember dimly as a kindly old man (he had, as I learned later, suffered a stroke and was recuperating) who took me out for walks and showed me bluebells and other wild flowers. Following this stimulus, I recall my simple childhood enjoyment of a whole steep bank covered with what we called 'aniseed' – that abundant, charming early summer umbel called sweet cicely *Myrrhis odorata* – and other early delights of discovery. By the time I reached the Grammar School at Penistone I was ready for 'real biology', and happily found good, enthusiastic teachers there who knew the value of field studies.

In this way I started with a strong bias towards native plants which was strengthened by my University undergraduate courses. It is true that the man who inspired in me a particular love of trees, Humphrey Gilbert-Carter, practised no 'apartheid' between wild and garden trees – indeed, he called his book on the woody plants of our countryside and gardens *British Trees and Shrubs* – but the general flavour of all our courses caused us to avert our eyes from the wealth of plant material in horticulture as if this remarkable display were somehow unsuitable for scientific study. My teaching career in botany largely reinforced this concentration on the wild flora, though I gradually became aware and ashamed of my ignorance of garden plants and, eventually, began to question the strict division between field botanist and plantsman. This process was aided by the influence of personal friends, who had in general been fortunate enough to have been brought up in circumstances where they picked up without effort some knowledge of the names and horticultural preferences of many familiar garden genera. One of these earliest influences was John Raven, who shared with me a passion for the British flora which culminated in our writing the New Naturalist *Mountain Flowers* together. It is true that our book on British mountain plants says little or nothing about alpine gardening; but increasingly John's interest in his own gardens (in two highly contrasting areas of the British Isles, namely Cambridgeshire and West Scotland) began to rub off on me. Eventually, much of John's special enthusiasm for plants in gardens came to be recorded in his own inimitable style in *A Botanist's Garden* (Raven, J. 1971, reprinted 1992).

Another group of botanical friends who effectively educated me were the authors of the standard work on the British Flora: Clapham, Tutin and Warburg. Edmund Warburg in particular, to whom I owe my devotion to the lady's mantle genus *Alchemilla*, greatly impressed me because he could name garden plants with the same apparent confidence as the 'critical' brambles and whitebeams of the wild British flora. As for Clapham and Tutin, botanising with them showed no uneasy avoidance of puzzling specimens in hotel gardens or 'gentlemen's seats'. This happy teaching process expanded in the mid 1950s when I was invited to join the team of *Flora Europaea* for, although our *raison d'être* was to write a wild Flora of Europe as an international cooperative project, members of the Editorial and Organising Committee, acting as host in turn in their University cities, offered, as suitable relaxation, visits to botanically interesting gardens in the vicinity. In this way, for example, I saw something of the remarkable gardens of Ireland when David Webb was host in Dublin, and began to feel that I knew my way about the garden flora even if I dismally failed at the technical level of *Rhododendron* cultivars. I still do, in fact: we must all accept our limitations!

I have reserved to the last some comments on John Gilmour's influence. Partly this is justified chronologically – I really came to know John well only after his appointment as Director of the University Botanic Garden in Cambridge in 1951 – but I make this tribute separately because my friendship with John taught me much about the gap between botany and horticulture, and how it might be bridged. Several ideas I derived from John Gilmour bore fruit when I came to succeed him in 1973, and some strands, particularly those associated with the conservation of garden plants, I have been able to develop a little since my own retirement in 1983. It would be wholly inappropriate for me to try to pay full tribute here to the benevolent influence John had on my career (for those interested, the obituary I wrote for the Memorial Volume might fill this gap (Walters, 1989)): but I must explain that John, as a founder-editor of the New Naturalist, had kindly invited me to be co-author with him of *Wild Flowers*, an early book in the series happily still in print. From John I gained an interest in the history of my subject which has increasingly fascinated me, and, quite differently, a realisation of the importance of scientific horticulture to botanical science and *vice versa*. John succeeded more than anyone else I have known in interpreting the often mysterious ways of professional botanists to the interested amateur gardener. Nowhere was this more useful than in the vexed question of the names of plants. He really took to heart the *cri de coeur* of the keen gardener struggling, as he saw it, to cope with 'these outlandish scientific names': 'Why do they keep on changing the name?' I sincerely hope that John's pragmatic approach will be evident in my treatment of the subject of names in this book.

This is enough about my colleagues and teachers. Now I must turn to my reasons for writing the book. First, I believe there is a new market for a book which consciously sets out to be about the garden as in a special sense a part of nature. Perhaps I should explain this a little. Forty years ago, when I read Part II Botany in the Natural Sciences Tripos in Cambridge, we were still taught that the Norfolk Broads, the Breckland and Wicken Fen were all to differing degrees natural plant communities, and that the task of the ecologist was mainly to unravel the dynamics of the vegetation in terms of present-day factors of climate, soil and competition. It is true that Godwin's early pioneer work had thrown much light on the influence of man's recent activities at Wicken in particular and, of course, his monumental achievement in building the new science of palynology was rapidly changing the climate of opinion: but curiously enough (though I was a pupil of Godwin) the time-lag in interpretation was surprisingly long. Hand in hand with this insistence on naturalness went ignorance of what lay between the traditional vegetation types of boulder clay woods, chalk grassland, fen and breckland sand. The only exception we allowed was the study of weeds, which were in the British Flora and therefore respectable.

Forty years on, it seems that a different attitude is common. We still teach Botany as distinct from Zoology, Horticulture or Agriculture, but there is far more willingness to set aside the traditional divisions of the Universities, and pure Botany is assailed ever more strongly by a unified Biology in which genetics, molecular biology and biochemistry unite the study of plants and animals. We are also prepared to interpret vegetation in terms of archaeological and historical factors, and even to take a cool look at classification of the natural world in its historical and philosophical perspectives. The modern student is not so compartmentalised as we were, and the taste and interests of the amateur are changing *pari passu*.

Not only are the rigid divisions breaking down, but there is at the same time an enormous expansion of popular interest in natural history, and two technical terms of my University education, namely 'ecology' and 'environment' are now household words. We even have a Ministry of the Environment, and all major political parties assure the voters that they are committed to something called 'conservation' of the environment. Natural history has a new look, and a potentially enormous clientele, and to many new recruits the old divisions seem inappropriate. Included amongst those outmoded divisions, it seems to me, is that between what is popularly taken to be wild nature and the landscapes created by man, whether they be the treeless moorlands of upland Britain, or the small compact gardens of suburbia. In the grim deserts of our inner cities we are beginning to create 'wild gardens' or 'educational nature reserves' whose ethos and contents differ radically both from the formal parks of Victorian England and from the semi-natural nature reserves.

The second reason for writing this book for the New Naturalist series is almost a sentimental one. When I succeeded John Gilmour as a member of the Editorial Board, the whole future of the series was in doubt. Partly this was due to the mysterious economics of publishing, which lay outside my area of knowledge: but partly, I felt, there was a crisis of re-appraisal affecting both the form and content of the books. I believe we are now through this crisis, and am confident that the 'New Naturalist' of today will buy in sufficient numbers a modestly-priced and attractively-presented volume on British Natural History. What interests this 'New Naturalist' of today, and can I cater for it in my specialist field? Inevitably, my book therefore takes as a starting-point the volume on *Wild Flowers* which John Gilmour and I wrote in the early fifties. What is new since 1950? Equally inevitably, the shape of 'what is new' is in terms of my own personal experience, so that the book is somewhat self-indulgent, and I must now try to justify omissions that may disappoint some readers.

A most important question I had to face was: 'What is a garden?'. There are several possible definitions and, for the purposes of this book, I am adopting the narrowest one, namely, to use current jargon, a garden is an amenity area adjacent to a house in which a range of decorative plants can be grown. In this way I largely exclude from consideration vegetables and fruit trees and shrubs. We are, of course, still left with an uneasy border-zone illustrated, for example, by a mixed row of scarlet and white-flowered runner beans (*Phaseolus*). Rightly, in my opinion, many people with small gardens decide that such vegetables can be treated as amenity garden plants and they can thereby kill two birds with one stone: but the broad distinction is clear enough.

Where we are in real difficulty is in the matter of the herb garden. My decision not to exclude herbs in the modern, largely culinary sense arises mainly from the fact that the story of 'herbs' (in a wider sense) is so much part of the story of gardens, that I could hardly write this book if I interpreted amenity too literally. A perfect example is the place of rosemary *Rosmarinus officinalis* in our gardens. In fact we grow rosemary for three purposes: for the attractive flowers, for its aromatic foliage used in herb sachets, and increasingly for culinary use. Is this an 'amenity plant'? I have come down in its favour, but I have not devoted, as I might have done, a separate chapter to herbs, and I hope it will become clear why I have not done so.

My decision to include trees and shrubs except those grown for their edible fruit seems unavoidable. Much of our aesthetic appreciation of landscape is dependent on the presence of woody plants, and the great landscape architects of the eighteenth century used this fact for our continuing delight. Moreover, the history of gardens in general, and Botanic Gardens in particular, is so bound up with our knowledge and appreciation of trees and shrubs that it would not be possible to tell the story I want to relate without including them. Having said this, I must stress that my choice of material is very restricted; and more than marginal comment on either forestry or native woodland – both 'New Naturalist' topics worth a separate book – is obviously out of the question.

A final word on the Botanic Garden, and its place in my general theme.

Had I not been fortunate enough to direct for ten years (and live in for thirty-five years) one of the best Botanic Gardens in Britain, my interests and expert knowledge would obviously not have developed to enable me to write the book at all. So Botanic Gardens in general, and the Cambridge University Botanic Garden in particular, must feature in these pages. But, of course, this is not a book about gardens as such: it is about garden *plants*, and in this broad theme the Botanic Garden plays a contributory role along with other powerful influences.

Acknowledgements

Many people have helped me directly in the writing and illustrating of this book, but to some I owe a considerable debt and must make personal acknowledgement. To Arthur Chater and Ruth Stungo, who have patiently read and criticised the whole of the text; to David Webb, with whom I discussed on holiday in the West of Ireland the project in embryo, and whose critical support I always value; to Andrew Gagg and my son Martin, both of whom have taken pictures destined for the book on very pleasant botanical-photographic outings; and to Anne James who has turned my often partly illegible script into disk, and compiled much of the index. A special word of thanks is also due to Isobel Smales at Collins, who combines cheerfulness and efficiency in her dealings with authors and editors.

In addition to Andrew Gagg and Martin Walters, who supplied the numerous photographs credited to them, I am greatly indebted to several colleagues for individual photographs: Frank Perring (Plate 39); Chris Preston (Plate 23); Michael Proctor (Plate 32 & Fig. 36); Peter Sell (Fig. 32), and Ray Woods (Plate 4). Michael Hickey specially drew Figure 33, and he and Clive King made available from their joint book (1988) the material for Figures 28 & 30. Ted Cocking kindly supplied the two photographs used in Figure 45, Chris Cook the material for Figure 37, Laurie Friday the photograph used in Figure 42 and Ruth Stungo and the Chelsea Physic Garden Figures 20 & 46.

For permission to use material already published, I am grateful to Cambridge University Press, who lent me the originals of many photographs used in my own books, and to the following for individual Figures: Academic Press, London (Fig. 37); Blackwell Scientific Publications, Oxford (Fig. 42); Botanical Society of the British Isles (Figs. 10, 24, 40, 51); Country Life, London (Fig. 44); Lehmanns Verlag, Munich (Fig. 26); Macmillan, London (Fig. 11); Royal Horticultural Society (Fig. 45); Societas Biologica Fennica Vanamo, Helsinki (Fig. 21); and the artist John Wilkinson (Fig. 15).

My final thanks, as always, are reserved for my wife: not content with cheerful moral and physical support, Lorna has also read proofs and helped with the index, and it is literally true that without her loving care the book would not have been completed.

Part I

General

"But let it be remembered, that the principles of a science are to be taught as truly with reference to the commonest forms as to the rarest. And have we not the fields and the rivers? But besides this, is not the whole suburb of this metropolis one magnificent botanic garden?"

John Lindley, in his Inaugural Address as Professor of Botany in London University, 1827.

In the first four chapters some botanical themes are considered as they relate to wild and garden plants. They mainly centre round the following questions: where do they come from, what is the pattern of their variety of form, and what do we know of the causes of this variation both in nature and at the hand of man? Inevitably, some rather complicated botanical subjects have been condensed and, at times, over-simplified. My hope is that some interested readers may feel it worth while to take the questions futher, and suitable reading is suggested; but for those who may find parts rather heavy going I would stress that the book is not all like this, and ask for their forbearance.

1

The Sources of Wild and Garden Plants

Most garden plants are exotics

If you visit the University Botanic Garden in Cambridge you will, I hope, enjoy the rich and varied collections spread out around you; but there is one special display you must see – the so-called Chronological Bed. This was the brain-child of the second scientific Director of the Garden, John Gilmour. John learned over the years from his experience of gardeners, horticulturists and the general public at Kew and Wisley how little most people knew of the extraordinary history of many of the commonest and most loved garden plants – tulips and rhododendrons, lupins and the like, which are the gardener's stock-in-trade – and he had a brilliant idea. He made a long, thin bed running alongside one of the public paths, and divided it attractively into suitable lengths of a few metres; in each of these units he planted, in time sequence, a selection of familiar garden plants which were introduced into our English gardens at a particular period. So from left to right, starting with ancient mediaeval herbal plants introduced before 1550, and proceeding in twenty-year units, we have laid out before us a potted history of how and when we obtained our garden plants. An accompanying booklet fills in the picture.

The Chronological Bed reminds us, in the best possible way, of how over the centuries our gardens have been continually enriched by new and unfamiliar plants. Broadly we can say that many early garden flowers were taken from the wild in Asia and Europe; then after Columbus and the rise of the American colonies came a great burst of New World plants, and then, some two centuries ago, began the discovery of the Australian and New Zealand floras, and most recently the floral riches of the Himalayas and the Far East. Of course, this process is still going on, and indeed we still extend the Chronological Bed.

Why are our gardens planted with trees, shrubs and flowers taken from the ends of the earth? Of course, fashion and the excitement of novelty have something to do with it, but not as much as you might think. Scientifically, two factors are involved. The first one concerns our stock of native plants. Gardeners do not readily appreciate a fact well known to botanists – that the British flora is remarkably poor in species. How many native British trees and shrubs find any place in our gardens? Remarkably few: yew hedges and holly bushes are very much the exception to the general rule that our woody garden plants are exotics. One of the purposes of this book is to explore this remarkable imbalance between the native and the introduced trees in our gardens, and much of Chapter 5 is devoted to this subject. But the generalisation, though most obvious in the case of trees, actually holds for all our garden flowers. The wild flowers of our hedgerows and woods have contributed relatively little to the traditional English garden.

The second factor concerns our present-day climate and recent climatic history. Owing to a regular warm current popularly known as the Gulf Stream (though purists tell us it is strictly the 'North Atlantic Drift'), practically the whole of the British Isles is milder than it has right to be judging from our latitude. We can, as every gardener knows, expect to be able to be out and about in the garden in every season. Of course we suffer the occasional hard winter – though what we call a hard winter is mild by the standards of, say, Sweden or Michigan, U.S.A. – and we may have to replant our Mediterranean *Cistus*, our New Zealand *Hebe* or our Australian *Eucalyptus*, but with reasonable statistical certainty this will not happen every winter, so on the whole we grumble and re-plant.

Of course, these two factors, namely the composition of our native flora and the quality of our climate, are inter-related, though not in as straightforward a way as one might think. Perhaps we should explain this relationship.

Why our native flora is impoverished

Fifteen thousand years ago, what we now call the British Isles were part of the Continent of Europe, much of which was covered by vast sheets of ice. It was the end of the last of the successive Ice Ages, and our climate was much like that of Greenland and Spitsbergen today. Old Stone Age man eked out a precarious living on the tundra at the edge of the ice-sheets, and large animals, both carnivores and herbivores, roamed freely. Geologically speaking, since the retreat of the ice, the period we call 'Recent' can be thought of as the last minute of time compared with the inconceivably long time scale of geological and biological evolution on Earth. So every artefact of man – his roads, cities, industries and gardens – is very new and sudden in its impact.

Of course, we find this difficult to comprehend, because we see so much change enshrined in human history; and indeed, until quite recently, our knowledge of what we now call the post-glacial history of the vegetation and flora was only very sketchy. In my lifetime, however, that knowledge has enormously increased, mainly due, in Britain, to that pioneer ecologist who became Professor of Botany in Cambridge, Sir Harry Godwin. Godwin's great work, *History of the British Flora*, first published in 1956 with a second edition in 1975, is now reprinted as a 'Science Classic' by Cambridge University Press, and available to all (Godwin 1984). Another work of the Cambridge School – a 'pollen atlas' of Europe over the last 13,000 years (Huntley & Birks 1983) – now provides us with a detailed chronology for the spread of our modern temperate vegetation, and in particular the familiar native trees, across Europe and eventually into the British Isles. Many simplified, more popular accounts of this story now exist: the one by Pennington (1969) is highly recommended to the interested student, and at a very simplified level my own Chapter 4 in *Wild Flowers* in the New Naturalist Series (Gilmour & Walters, ed.5, 1973) is still valid.

The first thing to grasp is how *recent* everything is. It is not just man who is new to the scene, and 'spoiling nature' everywhere. Rather we are being forced more and more to think of both man and nature faced with similar problems as immigrants in a hostile but improving environment. There was no 'Garden of Eden' in what we now call Britain, and human beings were just one of many immigrant species of plants and animals as the ice finally re-

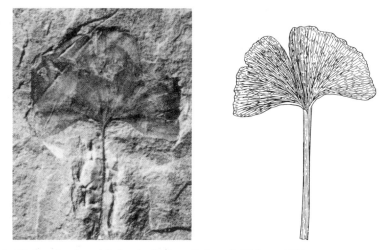

Fig. 1 Ginkgo: fossil and living leaf. From Briggs & Walters 1984

treated north. If we think about it, the 'Garden of Eden' and 'Paradise' are Biblical ideas which were brought with Christianity from the Eastern Mediterranean. Would they have been so deep in our view of nature if we still worshipped the Norse Gods of our ancestors? Obviously not: our idea of nature could have been very different indeed.

Though man and nature are both immigrants into Northern Europe, there is an interesting biological difference. Many, perhaps most, of our wild plant (and animal) species have probably been there before, in so-called pre-glacial and inter-glacial periods. If anything we could call *Homo sapiens* was here before, we have little or no trace of him. So technically we tend to speak of a re-immigrant rather than an immigrant flora. But clearly this subject, however intrinsically interesting, lies outside the theme of our book. The only point we might note is that most kinds of plants are much older than man: the beech tree *Fagus*, the plane tree *Platanus* and many others look recognisably the same as they do today when we find them as Tertiary fossils living long before man has evolved. Some indeed are 'living fossils' in our gardens, like the famous maidenhair tree *Ginkgo* (Fig. 1).

We now see why our stock of native plants is so poor. It looks as if the original much richer flora was wiped out by the Ice Ages, and many of these plants have not re-immigrated. Of course we do not know in more than a very few cases whether their absence from present-day Britain is due to inefficient re-immigration or to more subtle ecological factors, and biogeographers who study the past and present distributions of wild plants and animals are inclined to speculate and to argue on these topics. But the collective experience of gardeners supports the view that many plants no longer native in the British Isles since the Ice Ages are perfectly hardy here, and some, like *Rhododendron ponticum*, are spectacularly successful even in competition with our native woodland. When we bring them, or their descendants, back into our countryside they often do very well. So we can only conclude that there is a serious time-lag in natural re-immigration and, when man consciously or unconsciously takes a hand in the process, many hardy plants feel at home here and settle down. Whether they remain in our gardens and planted estates, or whether they escape and become wild is, of course, one of the main themes of this book. Before that, we must look rather more closely at some features of the post-glacial history of our vegetation.

The concept of hardiness

Of all the common horticultural concepts, that of hardiness presents real problems to the scientist. In the extreme case we all agree with the cause and the effect. After a hard winter (over the British Isles as a whole these seem to have occurred every fifteen years or so in the present century) we see defoliated *Eucalyptus*, and we know that many of these young trees will, if they survive at all, have to start again from ground level. We wait until the next summer, then accept the inevitable and cut them down to the ground. A hard winter can be defined in terms of temperature (the January or February minimum, for example), but whether a particular tender plant dies or survives is, as every gardener knows, a very complicated matter, in which other variables, such as soil and shelter, obviously enter. Nevertheless, we can make important generalisations about the hardiness of wild and garden plants based upon accumulated facts.

With regard to the wild flora, there is no doubt about the overall importance of climate in determining, for example, that oxlips *Primula elatior* grow wild only in what is climatically the most 'continental' part of Britain, whilst the red campion *Silene dioica* avoids almost exactly the same area. In fact, a most important generalisation about plants and climate is based upon the idea of a 'continental' versus an 'oceanic' climate. A continental climate, such as holds for much of Northern Europe, is characterised by hot summers, cold winters and relatively low total rainfall: the climate of Cambridgeshire or Essex. The opposite, oceanic climate, has much less temperature contrast between summer and winter, and a relatively high rainfall, such as we find in Devon, the Lake District or South-west Ireland. Every botanist knows that wild ferns, for example, are abundant in the west and rare or local, choosing damp shady sheltered habitats, in the east; and every gardener knows that the richest and most luxuriant gardens in England are outside the East Anglian area.

It is, of course, one thing to point to a correlation between plant distribution and climate, and quite another to argue scientifically that climate determines plant distribution. To demonstrate scientifically that oxlips grow only within the most continental part of the British Isles because this area has the combination of extreme temperature and low rainfall is beyond our competence. It is reasonable, however, to take all the facts of plant distribution together, and make generalisations: this group of species is a 'continental' one, and this group is 'oceanic'. That is how the patterns look, and much of science has to proceed by intelligent guesswork. If we demand rigorous proof, we shall soon be out of business in biology!

Another factor of obvious importance for the wild flora is the effect of altitude. No-one who has tried to botanise, as I have, on the summit of the highest mountain in the Cairngorms in a horizontal blizzard on a July day can be under any illusion about this. So certain generalisations are inescapable. They are mainly about what botanists call life-form. Those tightly-packed cushion-plants so cherished by alpine gardeners are the product of extreme natural selection, which eliminates anything trying to grow upright in the way that many lowland plants can do. Of course, several different influences are at work on the top of an exposed Scottish mountain, of which wind speed and temperature are only two, but this is not the place to discuss the adaptations of mountain plants in detail. (The interested reader is referred to the volume I wrote with John Raven in the New Naturalist series entitled *Mountain Flowers*, (1956, reprinted 1965, 1984)). There is, however, a very special reason why mountain plants play a part in our story, which we can now discuss.

The zonation of vegetation

Britain, as every geographical student knows, lies in the North Temperate zone, characterised by broad-leaved (deciduous) woodland. Further north, as in much of Scandinavia, evergreen coniferous forest covers the countryside where man has not cleared it, and north of that, in a belt around the Pole, we find the treeless arctic tundra. Of course, these zones or belts of vegetation have irregularities in them, and in particular there are transitional areas; but the broad generalisation is very obvious, and holds for all the main land masses in the Northern Hemisphere: Europe, Asia and North America. So vegetation types are determined by climate, and the latitudinal belts constitute the basic pattern. It has, however, been realised by plant geographers from the beginnings of that science in the early nineteenth century that there is a remarkable repetition of the pattern wherever in the North Temperate Zone a mountain range interrupts the plain. In Europe the great chain of mountains stretching from the Pyrenees in the West to the Carpathians and Balkans in the East show an altitudinal zonation of essentially the same elements, namely coniferous forest, then scrub, then treeless alpine 'tundra' and, finally, permanent snow and ice (Fig. 2).

Fig. 2 Mountain zonation: *Pinus heldreichii* at the tree limit on Mt. Olympus, Greece. Photo Martin Walters

This is remarkable enough, but what is even more remarkable is that it is not just the general appearance of the vegetation cover that is similar, but in very many cases the plant communities are actually made up of many of the same species. This is true of trees such as the Scots pine *Pinus sylvestris*, of shrubs such as the birch *Betula pubescens* and even of many dwarf 'alpines' such as the moss campion *Silene acaulis*. What this means is that each separate mountain range repeats, as it were, the post-glacial history of the vegetation. Not long ago – some 12,000 years, experts tell us – much of lowland Europe was a tree-less tundra covered with a rather sparse, open vegetation. As the ice retreated, the zones of trees invaded from the south: first the dwarf birches and willows *Salix*, then the coniferous trees like pine, and finally our familiar native deciduous trees like oak *Quercus* and ash *Fraxinus*. The main movements over centuries of gradually warming climate were northwards; but wherever there was a mountain, the zones moved upwards in the same approximate order. So the reason that you can admire mountain avens *Dryas octopetala* in the Arctic tundra, on a Scottish hillside or high up on a mountain in the Alps – and it looks remarkably similar wherever you see it – is that the surviving populations on mountains are the remains, or relics, of a formerly more continuous population over much of Europe south of the main ice-sheet.

In this northward and upward immigration, some species were more successful than others which were left behind. The early post-glacial spread into what is now the British Isles was relatively easy because, as we have already said, our islands did not exist as such, but were attached to the main European Continent by wide land bridges where the North Sea, the Channel and the Irish Sea are today. In the middle of this process, however, changes in the relative levels of land and sea created first the North Sea and the Channel, and then the Irish Sea, and natural colonisation across a sea barrier was greatly impeded. Only a special selection of plants, therefore, successfully re-immigrated to present-day Britain, and an even more restricted selection to Ireland. The present-day flora of France contains some 5,000 vascular plants, that of Britain only roughly half that number, and that of Ireland roughly one third (Webb 1978). Too much should not be read into these figures because, of course, France is much larger than Britain, with a much greater climatic range; but the correlation is there. We must also remember the question of extinction. We know, from identified sub-fossil remains, that there were some species of plants (e.g. *Ephedra*) growing in present-day Britain and Ireland in post-glacial periods which are totally extinct in the British Isles today. But a surprisingly large number of 'late-glacial relics', as they are sometimes called, survive in reduced populations in our mountains. Indeed, the remnants of the Caledonian Scots pine forests around the Cairngorms in Scotland are clearly part of this story, which is repeated for many other less conspicuous plants. We are justified in concluding that the relative poverty of our native flora reflects our isolated position at the edge of Europe during the re-immigration after the ice.

Man's role in the post-glacial re-immigration

It seems reasonable to assume that primitive man himself had little or no effect on the late-glacial countryside, though the large wild herbivorous mammals like the extinct Irish deer must have had important grazing effects. As the forest re-clothed the countryside, however, we can assume an ever-increasing role for man. By the time of Neolithic man, some 4000 to 5000 years ago, parts of the English countryside such as the East Anglian Breckland had already lost the continuous forest cover under the complicated pressures of human societies. From that time on, it has been an increasingly complex story of human interference with the vegetative cover – a story which we are only just beginning to unravel a little.

One thing at least we can begin to appreciate: it is not easy to define exactly what we mean by a 'native plant'. A wild plant we can easily define: it is the opposite to a cultivated plant, a plant that looks after itself in the countryside as opposed to being actively encouraged in a garden. (Even that idea may leave us with difficulties in particular cases: 'weeds' are the most obvious ones.) But what can we say is a native plant? Since all, or virtually all, our flora is re-immigrant, how long does a plant have to be growing here to qualify? And does it matter by what agency it arrived here? This is not mere playing with words. If we claim that our gardens contain very few native plants, we must all agree what is a native plant in order to substantiate the claim.

It is probably true to say that, until recently, the only way we could answer this question was by reference to the records made by the early field botanists such as John Ray who made pioneer studies of the wild flora of Britain in the seventeenth century (Fig. 3). Any plant Ray found growing wild we tend to

Fig. 3 John Ray. From Walters 1981

assume was native, unless he (or we) had good reason to doubt the conclusion. An example might illustrate this. On what was his last great botanising trip in the North of England in 1671, Ray went to see *Polemonium coeruleum* the Jacob's ladder, growing around Malham Cove, and the newly-discovered shrubby cinquefoil *Potentilla fruticosa*, growing on the banks of the River Tees. Both of these remarkable wild flowers – and many more – can still be visited and admired today in the same places where Ray first recorded them more than three hundred years ago. Moreover, both these plants are more familiar to us today as garden plants, and without Ray's evidence we might reasonably question which way these familiar plants had gone. Did we take them in from the wild and domesticate them? Or were they brought from abroad into gardens and escaped? We shall talk about these interesting problems and the different lines of evidence we can use to try to solve them in later chapters. For the moment we can just make the point, as Godwin did when he subtitled his great work *A Factual Basis for Plant Geography* (Godwin 1956), that we now have incontrovertible evidence in many cases from peat and pollen studies that a particular plant is 'truly native'. If we can show, as is the case for *Polemonium*, that the plant was growing wild in what is now England at least 10,000 years ago, then even the most stringent criterion for native status would be satisfied. A native plant would be one which arrived here independently of man, and has been here for at least 2000 years.

Where our difficulties are most obvious, perhaps, is in assessing the native status of our trees. Chapter 5 of this book is devoted to this and related themes but, again, a single example might whet the appetite. When Julius Caesar's scientific advisers made their famous report on the trees they saw in conquered Britain, they said they saw all the expected and familiar trees except *Abies* and *Fagus*. (The report – in Latin of course! – actually uses these two names.) Now *Abies* (probably *Picea abies*, the spruce tree) does not surprise us: most people realise that what they often call 'Christmas trees' are not wild in England. But what about *Fagus*, the beech? Could Caesar's reporters fail to see a beech tree in England? Can such negative evidence be used to decide that all our beech trees have come into England since the Romans? The answer we now have is, interestingly enough, 'Yes' and 'No'! The beech tree is native, because we have undoubted sub-fossil finds from long before the Roman invasion; but Caesar's men were probably correct in saying that they saw no beech woods where they are today – on chalk downs, for example. So we have not only the problem of how long a particular species has been in Britain, but also increasing evidence that the fortunes of a particular species have oscillated quite rapidly during human history. Increasingly we see the vegetation today as the product of very complex interactions between man and his environment, and in that process man the gardener plays a remarkably interesting role. This is one of the main themes of this book.

Man as creator and improver

So far we have talked almost exclusively about garden plants as if they were wild plants cared for by man. To some extent this simple picture remains true, but the number of garden plants that are more or less the same as their wild ancestors is relatively small and could well be diminishing rapidly. To gardeners, especially if they are experts in particular groups such as 'Geraniums', wild-type plants cultivated by them are often called 'species' – even with the spurious singular form 'a specie' – to distinguish them from the numerous varieties raised and named by them. Technically, garden varieties not described and named as wild plants are called 'cultivars', and generally have vernacular (English) names, not Latin ones. All this will be explained in the next chapters, when we talk about kinds and relationships of wild and garden plants and how they get their names.

We do not, of course, have any accurate account of how primitive man first began the domestication of plants and animals, but we do know that quite sophisticated pleasure-gardens existed, in Egypt and Mesopotamia for example, long before the Christian era. Indeed, our very word 'Paradise' is a Persian word meaning a garden. This means that some familiar flowers, amongst them roses and lilies, have an ancient, complex history of cultivation which goes back into pre-history and is in detail unknown to us. Whether we shall ever know exactly which wild ancestral stocks went into the pedigree of a modern rose seems very doubtful but, as in all areas of knowledge, speculation on circumstantial evidence cannot be prevented and, indeed, if those who speculate make clear what their evidence is, can be an integral part of the advance of knowledge. So, in what follows in this book, there will be some hard knowledge based on fact, and some speculation. Any historical treatment has to be like that.

2

The Kinds of Plants

The origin of plant names

Everyone who has occasion to deal with plants, from the professional botanist at Kew to the gardener growing vegetables and flowers, has to use names for the different plants they grow or study. The naming of plants is a necessary activity, for we could not talk or write about them unless we were reasonably confident, for example, that 'oak tree', 'rose bush' or 'primrose' meant in each case roughly the same thing to any other English-speaking person. So our starting point is clear: we need names for plants as for any other objects, whether natural or man-made. Centuries ago, our ancestors believed in the fixity of kinds of plants and animals, created by God and unchanged since the act of Creation. This is how people understood the world of nature in Mediaeval Europe, and the idea is enshrined for us in the first chapters of Genesis (from the Authorised Version of 1662):

> "In the day that the Lord made the earth and the heavens, and every plant of the field before it was in the earth .... And out of the ground the Lord God formed every beast of the field .... and brought them to Adam to see what he would call them: *and whatsoever Adam called every living creature, that was the name thereof.*"

In this marvellous creation myth God makes the diversity of living things, and man (Adam) gives them names. Although we no longer believe that the Genesis stories are to be taken literally, and although we might argue about the nature of a 'creator God', most of us would accept this essential truth about the living world and our description of it.

If names are man-made, they will be subject to change, misuse and decay. How then shall we answer the question: "What is the name of this plant?" It is no exaggeration to say that many seventeenth-century naturalists saw this as their most important task. Listen to the great English naturalist John Ray explaining how, once he was seized with enthusiasm for 'field botany', he found he had to cope with this problem. The quotation here is translated from the original Latin of the Preface to Ray's famous Flora of Cambridge-shire published in 1660, as given in Ewen and Prime's edition, 1975 (Fig. 4):

> "... I untiringly pressed on with my enterprise by seeking out the different kinds of [herbs] and planting them in my garden, then I made long walks of exploration in the countryside in the vicinity of Cambridge ... and, led on by an impatient longing for novelty, eagerly searched for strange plants in foreign lands."

So Ray's first task was to look for different plants and assemble them together just as we might do today, and he knew that growing plants together

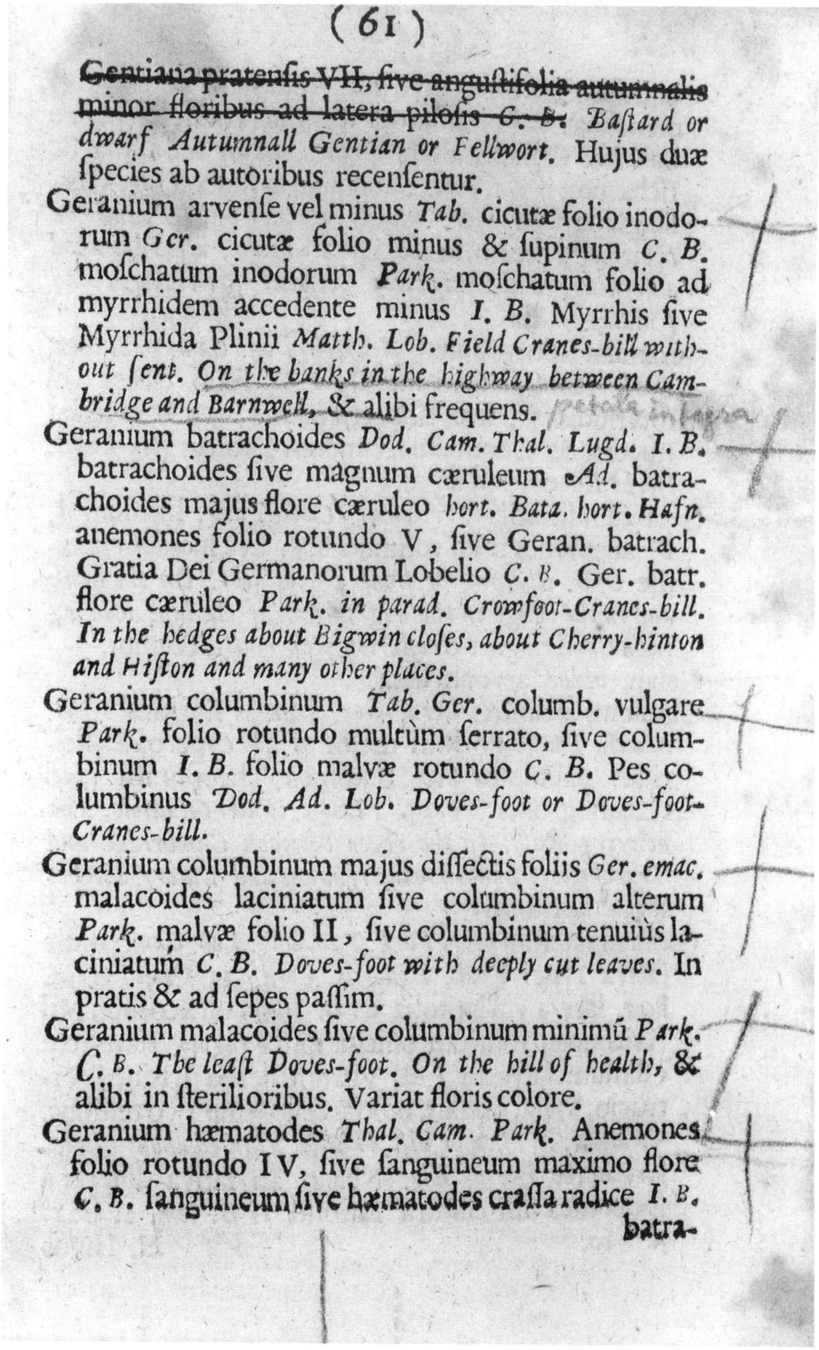

(61)

~~Gentiana pratenfis VII, five anguftifolia autumnalis minor floribus ad latera pilofis~~ G. B. *Baſtard or dwarf Autumnall Gentian or Fellwort.* Hujus duæ ſpecies ab autoribus recenſentur.

Geranium arvenſe vel minus *Tab.* cicutæ folio inodorum *Ger.* cicutæ folio minus & ſupinum *C. B.* moſchatum inodorum *Park.* moſchatum folio ad myrrhidem accedente minus *I. B.* Myrrhis five Myrrhida Plinii *Matth. Lob. Field Cranes-bill without ſent. On the banks in the highway between Cambridge and Barnwell,* & alibi frequens.

Geranium batrachoides *Dod. Cam. Thal. Lugd. I. B.* batrachoides five magnum cæruleum *Ad.* batrachoides majus flore cæruleo *hort. Bata. hort. Hafn.* anemones folio rotundo V, five Geran. batrach. Gratia Dei Germanorum Lobelio *C. B.* Ger. batr. flore cæruleo *Park. in parad. Crowfoot-Cranes-bill. In the hedges about Bigwin cloſes, about Cherry-hinton and Hiſton and many other places.*

Geranium columbinum *Tab. Ger.* columb. vulgare *Park.* folio rotundo multùm ſerrato, five columbinum *I. B.* folio malvæ rotundo *C. B.* Pes columbinus *Dod. Ad. Lob. Doves-foot or Doves-foot-Cranes-bill.*

Geranium columbinum majus diſſectis foliis *Ger. emac.* malacoides laciniatum five columbinum alterum *Park.* malvæ folio II, five columbinum tenuiùs laciniatum *C. B. Doves-foot with deeply cut leaves.* In pratis & ad ſepes paſſim.

Geranium malacoides five columbinum minimũ *Park. C. B. The leaſt Doves-foot. On the hill of health,* & alibi in ſterilioribus. Variat floris colore.

Geranium hæmatodes *Thal. Cam. Park.* Anemones folio rotundo IV, five ſanguineum maximo flore *C. B.* ſanguineum five hæmatodes craſſa radice *I. B.* **batra-**

Fig. 4 Page from John Ray's Flora of Cambridgeshire. Note Latin text, with some English for local use. From Walters 1981

in a garden was a great help in getting to know them and seeing which were truly different. He was in fact frustrated in later life, when writing his great three-volume work on the plants of the world, *Historia Plantarum*, by the fact that he had no convenient access to a botanic garden (see C.E. Raven's biography of Ray, reprinted 1986, pp. 226-7).

Having decided that a plant was distinct from all others he already knew, what was his next step? We probably tend to think that the great pioneer naturalists of earlier times were, like Adam, free agents, naming their plants and animals for the first time. This picture is quite untrue. Ray and his contemporaries were working in a long tradition of European botanical writing which in fact goes back to at least Classical Greece, in the fourth century before Christ. As Ray explains:

"First of all I had to familiarise myself with the literature of the subject, and then compare the plants that I had found in the countryside with the pictures in the books; then when I found any similarity between them, I had to study the descriptions more closely."

Ray often found that his predecessors knew the plant he had collected, and had already named and described it, sometimes with an illustration. Here is an example, taken from Ray's Cambridge Flora:
"Rubus *Bramble-bush or Black-berry Bush*"
There is no problem here. In fact *Rubus*, the bramble or blackberry, is beautifully illustrated in a very famous sixth-century edition of the works of the Greek physician Dioscorides, a book usually referred to as the *Codex Vindobonensis*, over a thousand years before Ray. There is also a fine coloured illustration in a twelfth-century Herbal made at Bury St.Edmunds, probably in the monastery there, and now in the Bodleian Library, Oxford (Plate 2). So Ray does not hesitate to use the Latin name. After the Latin name he gives the two English names by which we still know this familiar hedgerow plant. But Ray was a keen observer who had learned many common plants as a child from his mother in the village of Black Notley in Essex, so he knows that there are *two* kinds of brambles in East Anglia, and next to the ordinary bramble he gives the following:
"Rubus minor fructu coeruleo   *Small Bramble, Dewberries*"
This corresponds to the knowledge of any countryman today: there are blackberries and dewberries, and although when ripe they are both good to eat, it is the blackberry and its garden relatives that are worth picking in August and September.

In this example we can see some essential points in the history of the names of plants. The first is that the ideal situation of the Garden of Eden story in Genesis, where Adam gives *the* name for everyone to use, did not last long. Indeed, those who study the development of human language and culture would say that each isolated tribe must have had its own name for each plant they knew and used, so that from the first (whatever we think that means) translation of names from one language to another was necessary as soon as there was any contact between different tribes. We seriously underestimate the age and complexity of this process. Even before books were written on paper, quite sophisticated dictionaries existed giving the equivalent names of plants, animals and other objects in two or more ancient languages. The most famous of these dates from the seventh century BC and was written down on stone tablets, surviving the destruction of the city of Ninevah in 610 BC. This remarkable 'book' was commissioned by the King in Ninevah to cope with a linguistic problem very comparable to that which faced John Ray and still faces us today. For us the problem is Latin versus English: the Babylonian equivalent was Sumerian, the classical language, and Akkadian, the everyday language used by ordinary people. This Babylonian plant dictionary lists some 400 Sumerian plant names, equated with about 800 Akkadian names as applicable to about 200 distinct kinds of plants. (For more information on this and other areas of ancient plant knowledge, see the early chapters of A.G. Morton's *History of Botanical Science* 1981.)

Ray does not hesitate about the use of Latin names, for the very good reason that all his botanical books were written in Latin. All higher education in fact was conducted in Latin, and the rapid rise of modern science in which Ray played an important part was rendered much easier in Europe by the fact that all educated men could write and converse in their *lingua franca*, Latin.

Unlike botanists, gardeners regularly use many English names. It would be pedantic to insist on saying '*Rubus idaeus*' when we referred to garden raspberries, and in the case of garden blackberries, which are actually quite diverse and complicated, we do not have a convenient Latin name at all. (Linnaeus would have called them all *Rubus fruticosus* and left it at that.) Even the botanists themselves are not averse to the occasional English name: how many of us speak of *Quercus* when we want to refer to an oak tree? So one way of looking at plant names is that we should be tolerant of different names in different circumstances. If we need to be quite precise, or if we need to talk to a colleague who does not speak English, we would use the scientific name. If, on the other hand, we take our family for a picnic in a bluebell wood, we do not speak of *Hyacinthoides non-scripta* when we show them glorious sheets of bluebells in flower – though we might remind them that the 'bluebells of Scotland' are actually quite different plants.

Genus and species

So *Rubus* was the name for the bramble or blackberry and it still is. But what about the dewberry? Here we find Ray using a little descriptive phrase as a name. He recognises (as everybody does) that it is a sort of bramble, but a different sort. In fact the Latin name he uses tells you how it differs: literally it means 'the small *Rubus* with a bluish fruit'. In this example we can see how our modern scientific names came about. It was a quite natural process: first we had the name or noun (these words are in origin the same: Latin 'nomen'), and then, as our knowledge of plants grew, several related kinds were distinguished by descriptive words (adjectives in Latin), the whole phrase eventually making a new name. Of course the process is not always so smooth and easy as in our *Rubus* case, but there are a surprisingly large number of names used by gardener and botanist alike today which come down to us unambiguously from classical times, such as *Crocus*, *Iris*, *Lilium* and *Rosa*. In the case of *Crocus* and *Iris* the Latin name is exactly the same as the common English name; in the case of 'lily' and 'rose' we have very slightly changed the name, but it is still immediately recognisable. These names are what botanists called *genera* (plural of *genus*). The different kinds of *Rubus*,

Crocus, Iris etc. distinguished originally by some descriptive word or words are what botanists call *species* (plural and singular are the same).

By choosing the example of *Rubus*, I have intentionally risked making Ray's task sound too easy. In fact, equating British plants with those of classical and mediaeval texts was very difficult and often, by the nature of the case, impossible. Ray was a child of his time: whilst his whole approach to the study of the natural world was 'modern', in that he insists that you should actually go and look at the plant and not just take as true what the ancients had written, he nevertheless spent a great deal of time trying to find a name and a description of every plant in the existing literature. As we now see it, some of this painstaking study might look excessive, and we naturally wonder whether he would not have done better to start from scratch in many cases. What we have to remember is that there was virtually no knowledge of where plants grow or why they only grow where they do – what we would now call plant geography and plant ecology – so that Ray only gradually came to realise that some plants might be, as we would say, new to science and never previously described. The fact that his botany began and developed in East Anglia was a contributory factor: there are few wild plants in lowland England that are not widespread in the adjacent parts of the European Continent, so that Ray was often right in equating what he found with the plants described by his illustrious predecessors in Holland, Germany, France and Switzerland in particular. The wonder is not that he sometimes got the wrong answer but rather that in the vast majority of cases he got it right.

To the botanist John Ray, interested as he was in all plants whether wild or cultivated, the terms 'genus' and 'species' were totally familiar. They are in fact terms that would be used by all educated men of his day, and they came down from Aristotelian logic. In the history of botany they become standardised exactly in the way we use them today after the death of Ray, by the great Swedish naturalist Linnaeus in the middle of the eighteenth century. Linnaeus' great contribution was to reduce all the phrase-names for species like *Rubus minor fructo coeruleo* to a pair of words, so that, in the example we have chosen, the scientific name for dewberry becomes *Rubus caesius* ('caesius' means 'lavender-blue') and the ordinary blackberry becomes *Rubus fruticosus* ('fruticosus' means 'shrubby'). There are many other standardised Linnaean names that are the names we use today: they appear for the first time in this standard 'binomial' form in the *Species Plantarum* which Linnaeus published in 1753.

The reason why Linnaeus' work became so greatly acclaimed was that it brought order out of an increasingly bewildering mass of unwieldly phrase-names. During the period between Ray and Linnaeus – Ray's main works were published in the second half of the seventeenth century – the exploration and colonisation of newly-discovered lands, especially North America, yielded large numbers of plants and animals new to science. To catalogue all this new information science needed an agreed, standard system of naming and classification. Linnaeus' binomial system, in which the first name or noun is the genus and the binomial of noun + adjective is the species within the genus, provided that standard system. But Linnaeus did something else. He provided a simple, formal system of comparing the flower and fruit characters of genera to arrange them into higher groups which he called Classes ('Classis') and Orders ('Ordo'). To these higher groups he gave Greek-based names. Counting the floral parts, it was possible to decide in which higher group any given genus should be included. This piece of Linnaeus' system has not survived, and perhaps need not further concern us here, except that it can serve as an introduction to our next subject, namely the families of plants, and the idea of classification.

Plant classification

Two of the most successful modern reference-books for botanists and gardeners are alphabetically-arranged dictionaries or encyclopaedias. The botanists have a very convenient practical successor to a standard work by Willis which ran through many editions and is now entitled *The Plant Book* (Mabberley 1987). Here you can look up the main facts about any genus of flowering plant, presented in a concise, standard abbreviated form. Turn to *Rubus* and you will find half a page of text beginning 'Rosaceae. 250 (+ apomictic lines) cosmop. es. N.' Translated, this means that *Rubus* is in the Rose family, Rosaceae, that there are about 250 different species (together with innumerable 'apomictic lines' – see p. 62) and that they occur throughout the world, but especially in the northern hemisphere. If you are a gardener interested in *Rubus* you are quite likely to turn to that excellent cooperative *Encyclopaedia of Garden Plants and Flowers* published by Readers Digest (Hay and Beckett, (eds.) ed.3 1985). You will find a page of text and 4 colour plates devoted to the *Rubus* we grow in our gardens, and cross-references under their English names to the soft fruit we call blackberry, raspberry, etc. which deserve separate entries. The Readers Digest entry begins, like Mabberley's, with the family Rosaceae and the number of species in the genus (250 + the apomictic microspecies).

Gardeners and botanists alike, then, use the standard system to order their information. The names are international, and they are used strictly according to an agreed 'Code of Botanical Nomenclature' which is subject to revision every few years at the International Botanical Congress. The system is a hierarchical one, which means that each family of flowering plants contains one or more genera, and each genus contains one or more species. *Rubus* is a large genus containing some 250 species, and the Rosaceae to which the genus *Rubus* belongs is a large family containing 107 genera. Although the complete hierarchical classification contains other higher groups, for most purposes it is sufficient to know the genus, the family to which it belongs, and some at least of the species which it contains. The genus is thus the keystone of our so-called natural classification of plants.

Gardeners who are not trained as botanists (the vast majority) do not on the whole use the word genus much. I used to think this must be because the word is awkward, with its unfamiliar plural 'genera', but more recently, reading more widely the early horticultural literature, I realised that there is a deeper, and much more interesting, reason. Gardeners do not call 'rose' a genus because they do not feel they need the term: the *name* of the plant is 'rose' (or 'Rosa'), and what interests them is the different kinds of rose which, as we have seen, arise naturally as descriptive terms. So whether the kind of rose is a botanical species (eg *Rosa rubrifolia*, the 'purple-leaved rose') or a garden cultivar (eg Rose 'Peace') does not matter much in ordinary horticultural talk or writing.

Genera are grouped into larger units called families, producing what is technically called a hierarchical classification. For most purposes, this is a classification containing three steps or ranks, namely family, genus and species. Some of the plant families we recognise can be found, described and named, in mediaeval 'herbals' written several centuries before Linnaeus. Among these are the Cruciferae, a large family of familiar plants containing cabbages, wallflowers and many common weeds; the Labiatae or mint family with many familiar wild and garden plants; and the Compositae, the family containing the daisy and the dandelion. These few very long-established families stand out as names in our classification because they are allowed to have non-standard endings different from the '–aceae' ending of the Rose family, Rosaceae, for example. Associating related groups of genera into families is thus an old idea. It received a new impetus at the time of Ray when Pierre Magnol, a contemporary of Ray working in Montpellier, France, whose name is perpetuated in the genus *Magnolia*, standardised a number of families with the French ending '–aceae'. For some time after Linnaeus there was a struggle between these so-called 'natural families' of the French school and Linnaeus' 'sexual system' of classes and orders – and the 'natural system' won. Today we look back at this controversy as a piece of history, but the battle of ideas is still with us. The 'natural families' we are using today are essentially those of the French botanists of two centuries ago, and we do not dispute their validity, though every so often someone will write a learned paper purporting to show that a particular genus is 'in the wrong family' and should be transferred to another.

There are two quite different ways of looking at the relative stability of flowering plant classification. One, which has been widespread since Charles Darwin wrote *On the Origin of Species* in 1859, is that the 'natural families' are stable because they correspond to what has happened in evolution. On this interpretation, which was essentially the view that Darwin expressed, all genera of Rosaceae have descended from a common ancestor (a sort of original 'rose') and they are all therefore more closely related to each other than any one of them is to, say, a genus of the pea family Leguminosae. Indeed, when we say that apples (*Malus*) and pears (*Pyrus*) are closely related, we mean not just that the trees, their leaves, flowers and fruit are rather similar, but that we think they must have originated from some common stock. We feel, however, that we are on much shakier ground when we presume a common ancestor, much further back in time, for apples and roses. The alternative interpretation of the stability of plant families is that there has been no great pressure to change them, not because they are, in some indefinable sense, 'correct', but because they prove to be convenient. I incline to this view, and set down some of the relevant facts and inferences about our flowering plant families and genera in a technical paper (Walters 1986). It is, of course, possible to adopt a middle view which, whilst recognising that our 'natural classifications' are the work of botanists, would nevertheless expect them to bear some relation to the patterns which are themselves the product of evolutionary processes.

So much for plant families, but what of the higher groupings? How do we associate our families of plants together to talk about them? Ever since the time of Theophrastus in Ancient Greece one obvious grouping has been important, naming the distinction between trees and shrubs (or woody plants) on the one hand, and herbs without persistent woody stems. This is now the most important practical grouping in our gardens, and much horticultural literature accepts that trees and shrubs can most conveniently be treated separately from other garden plants. It was in fact abandoned by the scientists between the classifications of Ray and Linnaeus, because more and more examples became known where flower and fruit characters showed that two or more plants were quite closely related, though some were woody and other herbaceous. The pea family Leguminosae is perhaps the most familiar case: most gardens contain both woody and herbaceous members and, in fact, this example was often discussed by Ray and his contemporaries when they faced the problem. Even today we find eminent botanists clinging to this main ancient division: see, for example, the work of the Kew taxonomist Hutchinson (eg. 1969).

One very important higher group deserves special mention, namely the distinction between monocotyledons (represented by the lily) and dicotyledons (represented by the rose). Roses and lilies are so important in our European art and culture that groups of 'rose-like' and 'lily-like' flowers naturally grew up in descriptive writing, and one striking difference in floral symmetry could not escape notice. It was not until the time of Ray, however, that the full significance of this difference was appreciated. To Ray goes the credit for being the first botanist to show conclusively that 'lily-like plants' with thin, parallel-veined leaves, and 'rose-like plants' often with broad, net-veined leaves, differed also in their seed-leaves or cotyledons. He gave these two main groups the names we still use: the lily relatives have a single seed-leaf, and are called monocotyledons, and the rose relatives, with two seed-leaves, are the dicotyledons. The gardener is familiar with this seed-leaf difference in, say, seedling cabbages (where two broad seed-leaves are obvious) and seedling onions (where there is a single, narrow seed-leaf). Dicotyledons greatly outnumber monocotyledons in the world's flora: roughly we can say that of the 350 families of flowering plants, about 300 are dicotyledons. The most important monocotyledonous families in the wild floras of the world are the grasses (Gramineae) and the palms (Palmae), and in our gardens and greenhouses the orchids (Orchidaceae) are also a large and important family.

Finally, a word about 'lower plants'. The flowering plants (technically Angiospermae) are by far the most important group of plants both in the wild and in our gardens, and so far what we have said applies almost entirely to them. However, the other seed plants (Gymnospermae), mainly familiar to us as the cone-bearing trees such as the pines, are also important, and the ferns and fern-allies (Pteridophyta) play a part in our modern flora. In terms of evolutionary history both these major groups preceded the flowering plants and were, in their turn, the dominant land plants. They can all be grouped together as vascular plants, with well-developed vascular conducting tissue in their stems and leaves. All the more humble green lower plants – mosses, liverworts, algae – are outside the subject of this book.

This has taken us a long way from our simple survey of plant names and classification, but I have risked a mention of the historical background, if only because many people who use plant names may be interested in their antiquity, and in the complex story of how classification arose.

Variation and its effect on naming

In one sense, much of this book is concerned with plant variation, so I am perhaps anticipating in particular the next chapter by introducing the topic here. My excuse is that we must now discuss an area explicitly concerned with the naming of cultivated plants, for which indeed a special Code exists to regulate naming.

Any ordinary wild species which is reproducing sexually by seed set following fertilisation shows variation within or between populations. Flower-colour is a very obvious case: almost any bluebell wood will have a few white-flowered examples differing from the typical bluebell only in the colour of the flower. We are familiar with such variation, and it may intrigue us by its rarity. The ordinary botanical classification supplies an extended hierarchy of what we call 'infra-specific' classification which we can use as appropriate. Where a species occurs over a wide geographical range we often find that whole populations in one part of the range look different from populations in another other part; such differences, especially if there are intermediate populations where the two variants meet, are often distinguished as subspecies. A good example, familiar in our gardens and planted forests, is the European pine *Pinus nigra*. Foresters distinguish between the Austrian pine, which is the European subspecies called subsp. *nigra*, and the Corsican pine, native in Corsica, which is called subsp. *laricio*. It is this latter tree that is widely planted for forestry. If the variation is on a more local scale, or occurs sporadically, it will usually be recognised by botanists as a variety (varietas) or form (forma). In each case it can be given a Latin name.

All this natural variation is available to plant collectors to bring into our gardens. Most wild species are introduced into cultivation from a very restricted sample – often, in the case of trees and shrubs, from a single individual or small population – so it is not surprising that what we grow is a very biased representation of the wild species. We shall see examples of this later in the book. But there is a further complication shown by cultivated plants, namely that the introduced plant does not remain the same as its wild progenitor. Several things may happen. The plant may cross with an allied species in cultivation to produce a hybrid, and many of our garden plants are such hybrids. Now the ordinary botanical rules allow for the naming of species hybrids (and even the much rarer intergeneric hybrids), so that, for example, the popular border plant called *Geranium* × *magnificum* is a hybrid between two other species, *G.ibericum* and *G. platypetalum*. A hybrid can be named either by giving the name of its parents joined by '× ', or by giving a binomial in which the second word is preceded by '× '. Increasingly, as we shall explain in the book, new garden plants are made by hybridisation, so that the simple situation where we have the wild 'unimproved' species in cultivation becomes the exception, not the rule. For species hybrids, then, we can follow the botanical rules. But gardeners have for centuries given names to their favourite 'strains' of cultivated plants and many of these are in wide use. Indeed, any ordinary horticultural catalogue is likely to be using at least as many of these English names for cultivated plants (abbreviated to 'cultivars') as they are Latin names of species. What usually happens is that the genus is specified, then followed by the cultivar name: eg. *Rosa* (or Rose) 'Peace'.

Since 1953, when the first 'Cultivated Code' of rules was published with international agreement, such names have been regulated in an attempt to bring order out of chaos. The most important rule is that a cultivated plant *can* be named in English (or some other modern language), but that this special cultivar name must be attached to the scientific name of either the species or the genus. The reason why the cultivar need not be attached to any particular species is that many cultivars have a very complex ancestry involving several species, so that the only practicable solution is to refer it only to the genus, as in the case of our rose example.

There are other differences between the rules for naming wild plants and cultivars, but they mostly concern the specialists who select new cultivars and need not concern us here. Perhaps we should mention one interesting rule: since 1959 it has actually been *forbidden* to use a Latin name for any new cultivar, although this rule cannot be enforced retrospectively. The reasoning behind this is that cultivar names should be readily distinguishable from names of botanical varieties, which must refer to plants growing in the wild. If you are interested in taking this subject further, there is a short chapter in Gledhill (1985) which deals with the Cultivated Code.

Names and authorities

Strictly speaking, the scientific name for any plant is not complete without the citation of the 'authority' or name of the author at the end of the Latin name. The commonest 'authority' for European plants is Linnaeus himself (usually abbreviated to the single letter 'L.'). Thus the correct name for the dewberry is *Rubus caesius* L. This does *not* mean that Linnaeus was the first person to christen the dewberry in Latin – we saw that Ray named it a hundred years earlier. It does not even guarantee that Linnaeus was the first botanist who used the exact Latin words as a binomial for every species bearing his authority. It simply means that we have made an international agreement to use Linnaeus' *Species Plantarum* as the starting-point for botanical names, and to ignore all earlier names. It is a sensible decision, although it inevitably inflates Linnaeus' reputation as the 'giver of names'.

In practice, and for most purposes, the authority can be omitted, because most people using names are following some particular standard work, in which the authority for the particular name can be found if it is important (to decide questions of synonymy, for example). Very few horticultural works burden their text with authorities. It is, however, most important for the stability of names that key standard works such as *Flora Europaea* (1964-1980) and the *European Garden Flora* (1984→) do give authorities.

3

The Variation of Plants

Identification

Naming can be thought of as the formal recognition of variation. This is as true for inanimate objects as it is for plants and animals. So, logically, we ought to have started out with a discussion of how and why plants vary before we talked about their names and how we classify them. But there is a strong argument against doing this. As we have appreciated, human beings could not communicate and build on their knowledge of the world of nature without naming and classifying what they saw as different 'kinds'. Knowledge of how and why plants vary actually arises, in the history of our science as in our personal experience, from an accumulation of individual pieces of information, using different names for different plants. This is so self-evident that we perhaps find it difficult to stand aside and see its implications.

Let me try to illustrate the importance of this process by taking a very familiar word central to many of our thoughts and writings as botanists or gardeners – the *flower*. What is a flower? If you ask a trained botanist, a gardener or the proverbial 'man in the street' you will find they give rather different answers. We tend to say that one of these answers is the correct one and the others are at least partly wrong, but that is only because quite recently in the growth of our knowledge of plants we have agreed formal definitions of technical terms which themselves grew up without any definition. It would be better to say that no one of these possible definitions is the correct one, simply that for different purposes and in different contexts we are using the same word somewhat differently. Is the dandelion a flower? "Yes", says the man in the street (if he is not a keen gardener). "No", says the gardener, "it is a weed". "No" (perhaps surprisingly!) says the botanist, "it is a head of many small flowers" – technically a "capitulum of florets".

This example may help to explain why botanists, gardeners and others do not always manage to talk to each other as usefully as they might. What is needed is a little tolerance on all sides, and a recognition that for the purposes of science we need more rigorous and more explicit definitions than we do for the varied purposes of ordinary conversation. Yet it is quite wrong to assume that throughout science we actually operate all the time with explicit definitions. We try to do so, partly because obscurely we feel that we ought, but we are prevented from behaving as logical thinking machines, some would say by the limitations of our powers of thought.

Nowhere is this limitation more obvious than in the way biologists see and describe the world of nature. Our review of the way plant names grew as our knowledge increased over the centuries has, I hope, brought home to us the very important fact that, for example, when John Ray named a 'new' plant, he usually did it as we do today. We look in the books and try to match it with a description or an illustration attached to a name. (We might even, as Ray could occasionally do, find an expert who will name it for us.) What we are doing is matching or *identifying* the plant, a process of recognition that the new specimen is the same as a named reference specimen or specimens. How far is this process of identification of wild or garden plants something that we do without conscious thought, and how far is it a laborious, careful, even scientific process?

When we meet our friend John on the street we do not in most cases consciously identify him. Indeed, we may find that, if a third person asks us for a description of John, we are quite surprisingly bad at giving it! The way we operate in describing the natural world is not very different. I remember being irritated as a student when one of my teachers would tell me the name of some flower and I asked why it was not some other, to be told 'I don't know – go and look up the characters in a Flora!'. The fact is we do not necessarily carry in our heads all the technical information: we just get to know by experience what is what. The reason why this recognition process is important is that it actually happened in the history of botany. The name of the rose preceded its definition. Indeed, we could say that formal diagnosis and description of the kinds of plants only gradually became standardised, mainly between the sixteenth and the eighteenth centuries, long after we had agreed on undisputed names for many of our commonest European plants.

Returning to our friend John, we can operate confidently without knowing in detail what he looks like because we are sure there *is* only one John Smith who is our friend. In other words, he is a single individual. But this is not the case with most naming, whether of plants, animals or even motor-cars. Here we are stretching the point when we identify something. We are really saying that to all intents and purposes the plant or object we have is 'the same as' something else already named. It is practically never the case that what we have is the same individual. We are all obscurely aware of this difficulty, and I feel we should not sweep it under the carpet in thinking about identification. It is a very important complication that deserves some further attention.

Species and populations

Since Charles Darwin wrote his famous book entitled *On the Origin of Species* published in 1859, the way we look at variation in plants and animals has changed fundamentally. The mediaeval world view had encouraged a belief that all the different kinds of living beings had been created by God 'in the beginning', and that they all had their fixed place in hierarchical order with Man at the top. The kinds of plants and animals were fixed and invariable, made by the Creator in the forms we now know. Darwin's view was very different. He saw nature as being in a process of continual change, with plant and animal species themselves changing over a time-span that was difficult to appreciate because we cannot imaginatively think of the world as millions of years old. Of course, here and now, species look 'fixed' – a lion is a lion, not a tiger – but they were not so from the dawn of creation, nor will they remain so till the end of time.

We are now so used to the idea of organic evolution that it may surprise us to realise how recently – little more than a century ago – this idea became widely accepted. Of course it was not completely unheralded. Indeed, ideas of evolution can be found in the writings of the ancient Greeks and in many other places, long before the Darwinian controversy. What Darwin did, with great effect, was to assemble and present all the evidence for organic evolution, and, even more importantly, to present a plausible explanation of this remarkable process in the idea of *natural selection*. If you have never read the *Origin*, do try it. This Victorian best-seller (it ran to six editions before the author's death) is quite fascinating – a sort of scientific detective story, using masses of observations from all branches of natural history to present an overwhelming case. Through it all shines Charles Darwin's extraordinary qualities as an acute observer of the world of nature – qualities that make the English natural history tradition so remarkable.

But Darwin was more than a naturalist studying wild nature. He was also, like many other English naturalists before and since, a lover of the man-made countryside, aware of man's role in taming and modifying nature. One of his most interesting books (published in 1868) is in fact devoted to the theme of the variation of plants and animals under domestication. Here all was grist to Darwin's mill – cats and dogs, fancy pigeons and poultry, 'double' roses, cabbages and cauliflowers. He rightly considered that these man-made varieties of domesticated animals and cultivated plants provided some of the most important evidence for understanding the natural world. Darwin's main theme is often presented as a series of steps in an argument:

1. Plants and animals vary.

2. Because all organisms reproduce abundantly, there will be a geometrical increase in their numbers unless checked.

3. In nature, checks operate (as disease, famine, war, etc.), and only those individuals survive that have some inherent advantage over others.

4. These better-fitted individuals, surviving this process of 'natural selection', pass on their advantage to their offspring.

5. This process over thousands of generations gradually produces new variants to take the place of the original organisms.

Not all these statements are equally acceptable without qualification, though acceptance of the basic idea of organic evolution through natural selection could be said to be implicit, if not explicit, in most biological work today. But much has happened since Darwin and, in particular, one area of which Darwin confessed his almost complete ignorance – the nature of variation and the mechanisms of inheritance – is now a developed biological science, namely genetics. Plant and animal genetics studies the reproduction of individuals in populations, and aims to elucidate basic laws that enable us to predict to a large extent the result of mating or crossing between different individuals. So far as higher plants are concerned, what interests us here is the findings of 'classical' genetics, not the more modern 'cell biology' or 'molecular biology', though we shall have cause to mention some implications of fundamental research in these fields.

The genetic understanding of variation

Genetics could be said to be the first really integrated branch of biology, dealing equally with all living things. As a scientific discipline it appears remarkably late on the scene, and is not yet a hundred years old, though the work of the pioneer Mendel, lost for many years, was first published in 1865. This fascinating story can be found in many books, for example, in Briggs & Walters (ed.2 1984).

The basic ideas we derive from genetics can be simply stated for our requirements. It is true that all organisms vary (as Darwin noted, to begin his famous argument), but not all variation can be inherited. Of course all gardeners know this, in a general way. If we grow a crop of cabbages on poor soil, the yield will usually be less, sometimes dramatically so, than if we grow them on rich, well-manured soil. We know by experience that that sort of difference in size and vigour of a plant population is nothing to do with heredity (all the seed was 'the same', we say), and everything to do with the environment – the gardening skill and the quality of the soil. So this idea of 'nature *versus* nurture' – that some variation is hereditary, and some is environmentally-induced – is one that we all derive from experience. The important advance in genetics in the early years of this century was to produce some kind of general explanation of why variation is like this.

We now know that much variation within higher plant and animal populations is caused by differences on the minute paired structures called chromosomes, a set of which is present in nearly every cell of the body of every individual. Years before the acceptance of what became known as the 'chromosome theory of heredity', Mendel had investigated pairs of contrasting characters in experiments with garden peas, such as, for example, green versus yellow colour of peas in the pod, and showed that the proportion of each colour in the offspring of crosses was fixed and predictable. From such crossing experiments he deduced important rules for the behaviour of the 'factors', as he called them, responsible for the differences shown in the adult plant. A remarkable feature of the history of genetics was that the physical explanation of why these rules worked, in terms of the observable behaviour of chromosomes in cells, only came some 40 years after Mendel's experiments. Once the study of chromosomes in cells (cytology in the strict sense) became allied to the study of heredity in crossing experiments, scientific plant and animal breeding became possible, with all the twentieth century development that we have witnessed in the growth of plant breeding institutes and laboratories, the production of new crop plants and part of the modern agricultural revolution. It is important to keep a sense of perspective when we hear the term 'genetic engineering', and to remember that the real breakthrough was being made a hundred years ago.

How does all this affect our understanding of the variation of plants in wild populations and in gardens? Most wild plants and animals reproduce sexually: that is, in the production of offspring, fusion takes place between a male cell and a female cell (called 'sperm' and 'egg') and a fertilised egg or zygote is formed. In higher animals populations consist of male and female individuals, often in roughly equal proportions. Whilst this is true of some flowering plants, such as the willow tree *Salix* or the common nettle *Urtica dioica*, it is not true of most. We know this because a typical flower contains both male parts (stamens producing pollen) and female parts (the carpels or ovary containing the seeds). Although both male and female organs are often present together in a single flower – both the lily and the (wild) rose are good examples – it is by no means always true that pollen from the stamens transferred to the stigmas of the same flower can result in sexual fertilisation and the production of good seed. If a plant's own pollen will work (as in the case of garden peas or cultivated wheat) we say the plant is self-pollinating or 'self-fertile'; but, as most gardeners know, self-sterile plants requiring a different pollinator are quite common. Knowing which cultivars are self-sterile can be very important, as in the case of one of the most important apples in Britain, Cox's Orange Pippin, where other pollinating varieties must be planted nearby.

Why is cross-pollination (more generally, cross-breeding) so widespread? This was a great mystery to Darwin, who rightly saw that there must be some selective advantage to those plant and animal species in which cross-fertilisation is the rule. After all, a hermaphrodite plant can set seed to establish the next generation most certainly by self-pollination, like our peas in the vegetable garden. Why therefore should there be many devices in flowering plants which prevent or reduce self-pollination and favour cross-pollination?

Darwin had no general explanation for this obvious tendency in nature, and was humble enough to admit that he was ignorant. It is surely one of the successes of genetics that we do now have a general theory. The starting point is Darwin's, namely, that in any population of organisms there is variation. As we have seen, much of this variation is a direct response to conditions of the environment and is not directly inherited. But underneath this surface variation there is the deeply-significant genetically-based variation which can, at least in simple cases, be investigated by crossing experiments, as the pioneer Mendel did.

Genetics and statistics

Given this double component in the variation within a population, we can now enquire more closely how each factor operates. At this point in the argument we must introduce some very simple statistics. It is a remarkable fact in the history of science that that branch of applied mathematics we call statistics did not develop far until the geneticists asked questions that needed statistical methods to solve them. So statistics and genetics have grown hand in hand in the present century, and some of the most famous figures in the history of genetics, such as Sir Ronald Fisher, have been statisticians.

It is very easy to see why the geneticists needed the mathematicians to help them if we think of Mendel's experiment with peas. It is, incidentally, one of the reasons why our subject is of such intrinsic interest to the layman, since anyone who has a garden, however small, can actually make simple observations and perform simple experiments, just as Darwin and Mendel did, and thereby understand from practical experience the main ideas of modern evolutionary theory. What Mendel did was to make a series of crossing experiments taking the pollen of a pea plant with, say, purple flowers and pollinating a white-flowered plant with it. He then, like many a gardener before him, sowed the seed and counted how many purple-flowered and how many white-flowered plants he had in the 'F_1', or first filial generation. Repeating the experiments the following season, but this time allowing open pollination between the F_1 individuals, he followed the pattern of inheritance into the 'second filial generation' or 'F_2'. (For a simple account of Mendel's experiments see Briggs & Walters (ed.2 1984).) Using a pure line of purple-flowered peas, he found that *all* the F_1 generation was purple-flowered, but that in the F_2 generation purple- and white-flowered pea plants appeared in the approximate ratio of 3:1 (Fig. 5). These and similar experiments using different characters enabled Mendel to enunciate his two simple laws on which all genetics was founded. But note that what Mendel actually got from his experiments was, in each case, what we would now call a set of raw data. How did he decide what was happening? If *all* the flowers turn out to be

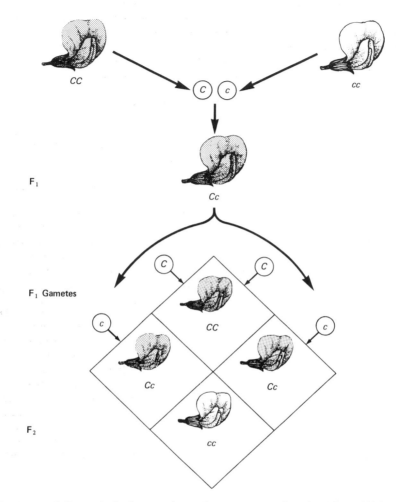

Fig. 5 Mendelian ratio in flower-colour of peas. From Briggs & Walters 1984

purple, as in the F_1, there is, of course, no problem: but with hundreds of F_2 plants what he got was *about* three-quarters purple-flowered and one quarter white-flowered. Now common-sense would probably tell him that he would not get *exactly* 3:1. What seemed to have happened is that Mendel had a simple, elegant theory about what was happening. He knew what the result 'ought' to be, and tolerated some departure from an exact predicted ratio. This story has a bizarre final twist: as Fisher was able to show by statistical analysis many years later, Mendel's actual results are too good, and Fisher concluded that either Mendel himself had 'cooked' his results or (much more likely, it seems) his gardeners in the monastery garden, knowing the ratio the old man was hoping for, made sure that he got something very near to it! (See Fisher in Bennett (ed.) 1965.)

At the heart of the problem, then, is this question. How do we deal with a set of data derived from a variable population? Statistics provides us with a number of procedures, one of which is designed to answer Mendel's question, namely how good is the fit between an actual experimental ratio and an expected ratio? If we want to do this for ourselves, tossing a penny is the easiest way. We think that it is a random event, equally likely to be heads or tails, but if we actually toss a coin what happens? Two heads out of two would not surprise us and certainly would not make us decide that we had a biased (or even a two-headed!) penny. But would five out of five, ten out of ten, or a hundred out of a hundred, force us to conclude that our original hypothesis – that heads and tails were equally likely – must be wrong? Clearly *at some point* we abandon the original idea. A statistical test of goodness of fit will enable us to evaluate the data, and test our original hypothesis.

There is one other essential element in any understanding of variation, namely the 'normal curve of variation'. In Mendel's experiments with peas, the difference between the purple and white flowers was a clear-cut, qualitative one. But most variation is not like that. Take height, for example. If you measure the height of individuals in any population, whether of plants or human beings, the majority of heights will be 'in the middle range' and there will be a few exceptionally tall and a few exceptionally short individuals. If the population is large enough and we measure them all, the result will be, approximately, what is called a *normal curve* when we present the figures graphically. Here is an actual example of data published by the famous botanist De Vries, one of the pioneers of genetics, in 1894. It relates to the length of the fruiting capsules in a population of evening primrose *Oenothera erythrosepala*, and is presented in the form of a histogram (block diagram) (Fig. 6).

Though Mendel's experiments using simple, qualitative characters provided the essential basis of our understanding the laws of heredity, most variation presents itself in a more continuous form represented by the normal curve. We can easily see why that should be so, once we realise that a character like individual height is one of many characters profoundly affected by the environment. We can, by cutting off the leading shoot of a plant, change a potentially tall individual into a short one. (It is worth noting here that most

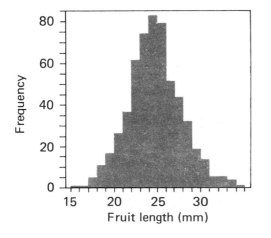

Fig. 6 Fruit length in evening primrose *Oenothera*. From Briggs & Walters 1984

plants differ in this respect from the higher animals, for in animals like ourselves the amount of pruning tolerated is very limited indeed!) So many characters directly affected by environmental factors will tend not to show clear-cut qualitative differences between individuals. But there is more involved. So-called 'Mendelian segregation', in which we can predict in what simple ratio the two variants will appear in the F_2 generation, applies to what we would now call a single gene (Mendel called them factors), located at one of vast numbers of possible positions on a particular chromosome. Variation between individuals in a population is the result of the separate or coordinated behaviour of very large numbers of genes, so even if (as we think) they are separately segregating according to Mendel's rules, we could not usually recognise this fact in all but the simplest planned experiment.

The environment

So far we have spoken of the environment in a rather vague, general way. Perhaps we should now enquire more closely into this idea. Environment is now a very familiar word – we even have a whole Government Ministry devoted to it – and like many familiar words, it can lose its edge. In German the word is 'Umwelt' ('the world around us') and this expresses the technical, biological meaning very well. Now, 'the world around us' – our environment – shapes what we are like from the cradle to the grave, and we are often told that the earliest influences are the most significant. What is true of human beings seems also to be true of plants, and most gardeners can attest from their own experience that, for example, a pot of overcrowded seedling cabbage plants may never catch up from their bad early development, however favourable the conditions are after planting out. One obvious difference between a plant in the wild and the same plant in a garden is that the garden plant is specially shielded from competition from other plants or animals – competition with other plants for soil moisture, for mineral salts, for light, and with animals who would eat them or tread on them. The term environment then includes both the inorganic and the organic world about us, and very often it is the *organic* world that is of paramount importance. Indeed, we could say that much Darwinian natural selection involves the response of individuals in wild populations to environmental pressures caused by other organisms, including their own kind, and that much of the 'selection pressure' endured by wild plants or animals is removed when we domesticate them. This idea is of great importance in explaining a lot of the variation that our garden plants show, variation that is not or hardly visible in their ancestors in the wild, and we must look more closely at this difference in the next chapter.

Another aspect of the environment is important: its stability. Of course no environment remains totally unchanged, and some change, such as seasonal change in our temperate climates, is predictable and cyclical. Even here, however, we can see the importance of this roughly predictable succession of summer and winter, because in our gardens we are always 'tempting Providence' by growing, for example, tender woody plants like *Eucalyptus* and getting away with it for a few successive years with mild winters. Our native plants have to be hardier, because for them survival through the occasional hard winter is a long-term necessity. In a hard winter, individuals who, for whatever reason, are less well protected will be eliminated from the population and fail to contribute to the next generation. In terms of a normal curve of adaptive characters, what happens under hard winter selection can be thought of as a chopping off from the curve of the individuals making up one of the tails of the extreme variation. The majority of hardy plants survive in the middle region of the curve. But suppose our winters become significantly harder in a general shift in climate. What then happens? The theory is that under 'directional selection' the whole population will move over as we progressively lose the ill-adapted individuals. After many years of such a climatic shift, a new, hardier population will have been selected.

On this theory, the stability of the environment is of crucial importance to populations of plants and animals in the wild. If they are in a stable environment, exceptional individuals, occupying both tails of the normal curve, will be preferentially eliminated, and the populations will remain roughly constant. Any instability will cause fluctuations, and directional change will gradually change the whole genetic structure of the population. Put in very simple terms, a wild population need not contain much genetic variation provided the environment remains constant, for it is already adapted. Change the environment, however, and the reservoir of genetic variation comes to the rescue, and without that variation the whole population could be wiped out. Here is the answer that modern selection theory gives to Darwin's problem as to why crossing rather than selfing seems to be promoted in nature. Crossing, because of the nature of the genetic mechanism, promotes new variation – technically, the recombination of genes in new arrangements. Without it, sooner or later, the population will fail to adapt, and the whole species will become extinct. The idea of a wild species containing a large reservoir of genetic variation, much of it hidden for most of the time, is a very important one. It explains much of what we find when we bring wild plants into cultivation, and we shall be discussing what happens in terms of examples in the succeeding chapters. But, like all important generalisations, we ought to be prepared to find that it does not always apply. Some wild plants are much more obviously variable than others, and we have to ask ourselves whether the theory can be modified to fit all the facts. If we are honest, I think the answer ought to be negative. There are plenty of things we do not yet understand. One is the nature and causes of what we call mutation – the really new genetic material. The next chapter faces some of these questions.

Adaptive variation

We have already seen that some kinds of variation shown by wild and garden plants can be inherited by their offspring and that, at least in the simplest cases, we can even predict in what proportion the different variants will appear in later generations. We have also made the point that the direct effect of the environment can cause individuals or whole populations to differ greatly from the normal variants, but that we know that many such environmentally-induced variants, such as variants with stunted growth, are not heritable. These so-called acquired characters disappear in the next generation if the particular environmental effect is not operating. Gardeners know this in their experience with growing plants. But the idea that acquired characters can be inherited persists, and we must now enquire a little more closely into the reactions of individuals and of populations to environmental factors.

One of the most obvious pressures exerted on plants by the environment is the degree of exposure. A sheltered site will carry a very different set of plants from an exposed site, and we know this is true in a general way both in the wild and in our gardens. In Britain, where the prevailing winds tend to be westerly, isolated trees will generally show an asymmetrical outline (Fig. 7) with more growth on the sheltered, east side. The extreme effect of exposure can be found on mountain tops and coastal cliffs, where woodland cannot grow, and the nearest thing to trees present will be tortuous, more or less prostrate shrubs. In many cases, the plants characteristic of such exposed communities will be very distinct species, perhaps with no close relatives of more erect growth habit, and gardeners grow many such plants as 'alpines' in their rock-gardens. The mountain avens, *Dryas octopetala* (Plate 3), a choice woody prostrate 'alpine', is an excellent example. But in other cases we find that the dwarf plants present in these exposed sites are variants of more widespread species that grow taller in less exposed habitats. In the case of *Dryas* we know that it remains prostrate even in our sheltered lowland gardens, and moreover that when we grow it from seed the next generation will also be prostrate. But what of other plants in exposed habitats? Should we assume that, given a chance, they will grow into erect individuals?

Botanists, in fact, were surprisingly slow to investigate this by controlled experiments, and it was well into the present century before we had any proper information about the heritability of natural adaptive variation. The subject was greatly illuminated in the 1920's by the Swedish botanist Turesson who demonstrated for several common plants that adaptive characters like height are in many wild populations actually fixed genetically and can even be inherited. He coined the word 'ecotype' to denote such genetically-fixed adaptive variants within species. Extreme ecotypes are sometimes im-

Fig. 7 Effect of wind exposure. The tree on the left is a Siberian crab-apple, that on the right a pollarded willow. Willow may be broken by gales, but is not permanently bent. Photo Martin Walters

pressively different from typical individuals of their species. An excellent example is provided by the wild juniper *Juniperus communis*, which can be an erect shrub reaching 3 or 4 metres on sheltered inland sites but which is represented on mountains and on some coastal headlands by prostrate variants. In the Cambridge Botanic Garden there is a remarkable collection of individual juniper bushes all propagated vegetatively from populations growing wild in different parts of the British Isles (Fig. 8). The existence in

Fig. 8 Juniper bed in the Cambridge Botanic Garden. Photo Martin Walters

the wild of such genetically dwarf variants explains at least in part the dwarf conifers of our gardens. Some of this variation has come to us directly from the wild, and is ecotypic in nature. We shall say more about this in Chapters 5 and 6, when we look at garden trees and shrubs.

How are we to explain heritable adaptive variation? In the history of our subject the problem of the inheritance of acquired characters has caused much argument and even polemics. The idea that any and every acquired character, even the distortion of the tree affected by the prevailing wind, can be to some extent directly inherited was championed by the biologist Lamarck at the end of the eighteenth century. In this way he explained to his own satisfaction how all the remarkable adaptations shown by plants and animals must have come about in evolution. Darwin himself, many years later, preserved an open mind on the question, but, as we have seen, presented a much more plausible explanation of organic evolution by natural selection. In Darwin's view, a population of dwarf plants growing on an exposed mountain top had changed gradually in the direction of genetic dwarfness by the differential loss of individuals with the innate tendency to grow upright. There is nothing in Darwin's explanation that rules out the inheritance of acquired characters to explain adaptation: it is simply not necessary to assume any such direct effect given that organisms vary and transmit, neutrally as it were, such variation to their offspring.

Some of the argument, the reader might now be thinking, turns on what is meant by 'the inheritance of acquired characters'. A variable population that changes gradually from an erect to a more prostrate form under extreme environmental pressure could be said to have acquired adaptive characters which are inherited. The crux of the matter is how the inherited variation arises in the first place.

Mutation and the gene

When I was a student in Cambridge in the late thirties, the then Director of the Botanic Garden, Humphrey Gilbert-Carter, a great enthusiast for trees, used to take us to see a particular specimen of the Californian coast redwood *Sequoia sempervirens*, growing in the Garden. From the side of one of the main trunks of this tree was growing out a very peculiar horizontal, stumpy branch on which the needle-leaves looked shorter and blunter than those on the rest of the tree. This branch, he explained, was a 'bud-sport', genetically different from the tree on which it originated, and from it all the dwarf conifers called *Sequoia sempervirens* 'Prostrata' had been propagated. This remarkable prostrate variant we now grow, as free-living plants, in our collection of 'Cantab plants' (garden plants known to have been produced or first described in the Cambridge Botanic Garden) but the original branch is no longer to be seen on the parent tree, having been killed when the whole tree suffered in the exceptionally hard winter of 1962-3.

The phenomenon of 'sports' is very familiar to gardeners. Unpredictably, a single shoot of some garden plant will produce a branch on which leaf or flower may look remarkably different. Sometimes the difference is so striking that the gardener is tempted to try to strike cuttings from this different shoot or, more likely, to propagate it by grafting on to a parent stock so that the 'sport' is growing on the root of the original parental type. In this way many common cultivars must have been developed and are, indeed, still arising.

Familiar examples of garden plants showing this kind of variation are *Pelargonium* (the gardener's 'geraniums'), potatoes and fruit trees.

In most cases where the gardener propagates such a new variant, there is little or no information about the hereditary nature of the change. This is because it is horticultural practice to perpetuate 'new' plants wherever possible by vegetative means, often, in the case of woody plants, by grafting on to stocks of the wild or parental type. Botanically, the phenomenon can be called mutation, the new variant is a mutant and the population that arises through vegetative propagation is a genetically uniform clone.

The word 'mutation', like many other modern technical terms, has a long history. It originally simply meant 'change' and can be found in the writings of Chaucer in the fourteenth century. It was first used in the technical biological sense by the botanist de Vries, whose work with the evening primrose, *Oenothera*, we have already mentioned. We now know that the odd appearance of small numbers of 'mutant' variants in de Vries' breeding experiments with evening primroses arises from a remarkable and quite atypical peculiarity in the genetical make-up of these particular plants, and we restrict the use of the term 'mutation' to the origin of the character-differences which show Mendelian inheritance. We now talk of the genes or factors causing the particular genetic effect mutating to other types (technically 'alleles') showing the contrasting character. In the case of Mendel's peas (Fig. 5), we say that there is a gene controlling flower-colour, with one allele conferring purple flowers and another white flowers. In a mixed population, individual plants carry pairs of these alleles, which may be both 'coloured' (CC), mixed 'coloured' and 'white' (Cc) or both 'white' (cc). The 'pure coloured' individuals (CC) with two 'doses' of C breed true for coloured flower, as do the 'pure white' ones (cc) for white, but the mixed (Cc) individuals, though they show the coloured flower themselves, do not breed true, and fixed proportions of coloured and white appear in later generations. In this example, the coloured allele is said to be dominant, and the white allele recessive; an individual with two 'doses' of the same allele (CC or cc) is called homozygous, and one with both alleles (Cc) is called heterozygous. Not all genes exhibit clear dominance however, so that in different cases the heterozygotes can show simply the character of the dominant, or they can show an intermediate character, so that they can be seen to be different from either parent. All genes, we believe, can mutate: that is, they are subject to change from one allele to another, and we can in some cases actually measure the rate of mutation and show that certain environmental factors (such as radiation) can increase this rate.

Modern population genetics, then, envisages three essential processes: *mutation* to produce the basic heritable variation, *recombination* of the gene alleles to produce a range of variation, and *selection* acting on that range of variation to produce the particular variability we actually see in nature. Geneticists see gene mutation as a process that is random with respect to changes in the environment and, although there have been remarkable advances in recent years in our understanding of the chemical basis of gene action and mutation, there is still much that we do not understand. Like Darwin we should be prepared to avoid being too dogmatic about fundamental questions of heredity. But the picture holds together well enough to explain how populations of sexually-reproducing plants and animals adapt themselves to their niches in an ever-changing environment. Since, however, much of the thinking about population genetics is based on animal populations, we must ask ourselves at this point in the discussion whether this picture applies equally to the plant world. When we do this, we are forced to answer at best a hesitant and qualified 'Yes'.

Plant populations

Higher plants are very different from higher animals in several important ways. A good point to start thinking about these differences is the idea of the individual. If we walk out into our garden or into open country, and look at the range of plants about us, how often can we point to any *individual* plant? A little thought will soon reveal that only two important kinds of plant populations consist of large numbers of separate individuals: these are, interestingly enough, at the two extreme ends of the spectrum of variation in size, namely trees and annual 'weeds'. In a piece of oak-ash woodland we see individual trees of oak and ash towering above most other plants and we can speak confidently of a population of individual trees. In our garden, if we have been negligent with weeding, we can find whole populations of short-lived annual (more accurately ephemeral) plants of several different weed species such as groundsel *Senecio vulgaris* and shepherd's purse *Capsella bursa-pastoris*. But between these two extremes there are very many plant populations in which we cannot easily distinguish separate individuals – the clump of daisies on the lawn, the stand of reed-grass by the river and even the Michaelmas daisy in the neglected herbaceous border. All these common perennial plants spread freely by vegetative means, creating local populations that are genetically uniform clones whether the parts are still physically connected or not. So the 'interbreeding local population' required by genetical theory to be the material on which natural selection works is *not* the commonest situation in the wild plant communities we see around us, and we have to ask of each plant population what is its structure and how large a part does vegetative spread play? On the whole, it seems that we have few cases where the detailed analysis enables us to answer that sort of question. All we can say is that our view of how natural selection operates would tempt us to conclude that a genetically uniform population may be safe in the short term but doomed to extinction in the long term because it lacks the capacity to respond to change. But what is short-term and what is long-term? Are we thinking of thousands or millions of years? Evolution is a long process!

A second way in which flowering plants differ importantly from higher animals is in their possession of the protected device that we call a seed. On the whole the higher animals, even those laying eggs, do not use the reproduction of their kind to solve the problem of surviving unfavourable conditions or of colonising new ground. The seed of the average flowering plant, on the other hand, often serves both these purposes. One reason why this is an important difference is that, because seeds are normally the product of sexual fusion, they carry within them collectively a large part of the genetical variation within the population. Dormant seed, then, surviving in the soil, acts as a sort of reservoir of variation, much of which may not be apparent in the growing population. We are only recently becoming aware of how important this may be for wild plants, but the published studies of dormant seed deal mainly with agricultural weeds. In a very careful series of experiments, quoted in Harper's excellent text-book on the population biology of plants (1977), the famous Broadbalk field at Rothamsted Agricultural Station, which has been planted to winter wheat annually since 1843, was used to sample the size of the underground reservoir. The experiments produced the staggering estimate that every square metre of the field had, buried in the soil, some 39,000 seeds belonging to 47 species, and more than two-thirds of this seed-bank consisted of poppies *Papaver*! In the case of arable weeds, this reservoir of seed is obviously important: it enables the weed species to survive bad years – or even decades – when arable cultivation ceases or when the farmer's weed control measures are effective, and to flourish when conditions become again favourable. We are all familiar with this in the English countryside where, from time to time, poppies suddenly appear in a field where none have been visible for many years. What has usually happened is that the farmer has failed to spray, with dramatic consequences. The same phenomenon is very familiar to the gardener, who knows that cultivation will often reveal stocks of common weeds even where the soil has not recently been dug over. We are as yet, however, very ignorant of the structure of wild plant populations, both in respect of their genetical make-up and also in terms of the importance of seed reservoirs for their survival. It is one of many areas where the enthusiastic ecologist can make a real contribution to botanical science by meticulous observation and quite simple experiments.

4

Hybridisation and Sterility

The sexuality of flowers

Although many accurate descriptions of plants were made by the early botanists, and careful comparisons of different kinds of flowers and fruits can be found abundantly in the botanical literature of the seventeenth century, it was not until after the time of Linnaeus that anything like the modern understanding of the function of flowers began to be expressed. The reason why interpretation lagged so far behind description seems to be, in part at any rate, the fact that sexuality in higher plants, unlike in the vast majority of animals, is obscured by the hermaphrodite condition of most flowers. Consider, for example, the date palm. It was widely known by the ancient civilisations around the Mediterranean that male date palms were essential to 'fertilise' the female to ensure a crop. If unisexual plants had been the rule rather than the exception, the elucidation of plant sexuality would have been made much earlier. It is easy to see this difficulty in the botanical writings of Theophrastus in the fourth century BC and, two thousand years later, the same problems were still largely unresolved. We can marvel, for example, that as late as the second half of the eighteenth century the then Professor of Botany in Cambridge, Thomas Martyn, could give lectures to his students on what we would call comparative morphology of the flower, using the Linnaean classification and all the scientific names we still use today, but apparently be in ignorance of the functions of the parts he was so carefully describing (Fig. 9).

Part of the difficulty undoubtedly lay in the fact that experimental investigation lagged behind description. Too many people were content to teach the names of plants and how they differed from each other, rather than to stimulate enquiry into the significance of the differences they had described. For all his genius, Linnaeus himself had a rather limited interest in experimental studies, and nowhere is this more obvious than in understanding the function of flowers. Nevertheless, in the less well-known writings of Linnaeus there is plenty of evidence that he was prepared to question the dogmatic view, expressed in his main works, about the fixity of species, and indeed to Linnaeus is usually given the credit of publishing the first account of an artificially-made species hybrid[1], which he produced by pollinating a plant of the salsify *Tragopogon porrifolius* with pollen from the common goat's beard *T. pratensis*, for which account he was awarded a prize by the Imperial Academy of Sciences in St. Petersburg in 1760. The hybrid seed supplied by Linnaeus to the Botanic Garden in St. Petersburg flowered in 1761, and was studied by the German botanist Koelreuter, who had been appointed custo-

---

[1]The nurseryman Thomas Fairchild of London crossed a carnation (*Dianthus caryophyllus*) with a sweet william (*D. barbatus*) in 1717, and there were probably many other examples of artificial hybridisation in the early eighteenth century.

(57)

PLATE XXIX. LETTER XXVI.

SYNGENESIA MONOGAMIA.

Viola odorata. *Sweet Violet.*

a   The calyx of five leaves.
b   The corolla of five irregular petals.
c   The horn-fhaped nectary.
d   A flower opened, to fhow the ftamens with the five connected anthers.
e   The ftamens within the calyx.
f   A fingle ftamen.
g   The piftil.
h h h   The heart-fhaped leaves.
i i   The young leaves, involuted, rolled inwards, or rather upwards.
k k k   The fcape, with the double bracte on the middle of it.
l   One of the ftolones, or runners, putting forth roots.

Fig. 9   Illustration of the Sweet Violet *Viola odorata* from T. Martyn's *Thirty-eight Plates...* 1788. From Walters 1981

dian of the natural history collections there in 1759. As a young medical student in Tübingen, Koelreuter had published a survey of all the known work on the sexuality of plants, and after his appointment in Russia devoted himself to a very careful, experimental investigation of plant hybridisation. There is a useful summary of Koelreuter's studies in Morton (1981).

Koelreuter established clearly what earlier authors (like our own Philip Miller at Chelsea) had only hinted at, namely that, in many flowers, insects play a very important part in the transfer of pollen from stamen to stigma. All the remarkable 'contrivances', as Darwin was later to call them, shown by so many flowers could be interpreted as mechanisms to attract insects in such a way that they would bring about pollination in a *different* flower. This important generalisation led to new studies of floral structure in terms of function, and culminated in the botanical writings of Darwin himself on the significance of cross-pollination and the mechanisms to promote it. Pollination biology is now a flourishing study of great significance for the understanding of flowering plant evolution. (See Proctor & Yeo 1973.)

Hybridisation

Koelreuter's careful hybridisation experiments used many different genera, well represented both in gardens and the wild, such as columbine *Aquilegia*, wallflower *Cheiranthus*, and mullein *Verbascum*, and he was moved to ask the question why, if so many species-hybrids involving two species of the same genus could be successfully made by artificial pollination, such hybrid plants seemed to be rare in nature. The answer he eventually gave was remarkably correct, as we would see it now. What he said was that closely similar species tend to be separated in nature, either by geographical barriers (as, for example, the Atlantic Ocean separates European from similar North American species) or by what we would now call ecological barriers (one species preferring shady woodland habitats, whilst an allied species grows in the open). But when we bring them all together in cultivation in our gardens, they have an opportunity to cross which is largely denied them in nature.

This promiscuous effect is even greater in botanic gardens than in ordinary gardens because it is the tradition in botanic gardens to grow, side by side, as many representatives as possible of related genera and species whether they have any horticultural value or not. Open pollination of plants arranged in systematic groups in the traditional 'order beds' inevitably leads to hybridisation, often on quite a grand scale. It should not therefore surprise us that many garden plants are of hybrid origin and prove to differ significantly from the wild plants from which we assume that they are derived. One of the most important ways in which hybrids often differ from either parent species is in their sterility. Koelreuter's first experimental hybrid, made in the St. Petersburg garden between two American species of the tobacco plant *Nicotiana*, showed complete sterility although the hybrid plants grew well, and he was able to establish that the pollen of the hybrid was defective and non-functional. The sterility of some hybrid animals was, of course, already well-known – the mule, produced as a cross between a female horse and a male donkey, was perhaps the best-known example – so that a demonstration of a parallel phenomenon in the plant kingdom was of special interest, confirming the essential similarities of sexual reproduction in all living organisms.

Partial or complete sterility is often used in practice as confirmatory evidence when wild plants intermediate between two related species are suspected of being hybrids. In his book entitled *Hybridisation and the Flora of the British Isles*, Stace (1975) collected together all the published evidence on hybrids wild in the British Isles: a glance at this volume of more than 600 pages is sufficient to convince anyone that wild plants with some claim to be hybrid in nature can hardly be said to be few in number. A closer look at Stace's book reveals, indeed, that most of the genera of British plants with more than a very few species are included, and indeed it is rather difficult to name any common British genus for which there is no evidence of species-hybridisation in the wild. (*Allium* and *Campanula* are two examples.) Nevertheless, it seems to be true in our experience, as Koelreuter found two centuries ago, that hybrids are not usually widespread in nature, and we must enquire more closely why this should be so.

We ought at the outset to look at one possible reason for the apparent rarity of hybrids in nature. In our recognition of any two species we generally require a degree of describable difference such that every individual specimen can unambiguously be classified as belonging to either one or the other species. If that is so, then we might conclude that species-hybrids are rare because of the way we play the game of naming and identifying. In other words, how we look at nature determines that we shall inevitably detect rather few cases of hybridisation. There is certainly some truth in this argument. A familiar case will illustrate the problem.

The common bladder campion *Silene vulgaris* is a very widespread and variable perennial of roadsides and rough ground throughout much of Britain except parts of north and west Scotland. This plant is not grown in our gardens except by accident as a weed. Closely related to it, however, is the sea campion, which has a much more attractive, creeping growth form and larger, more decorative flowers, and is common on rocks and cliffs around nearly all our coasts. Typical sea campion looks so obviously different from bladder campion (Plate 5) that the eighteenth century English botanists did not hesitate to call it a species, and we have generally continued to use for this plant the name *Silene maritima* given to it by William Withering in 1796, although the earliest name is *S. uniflora*, which we are obliged to use following the International Code.

Now it is easy to cross these two related campions, as Marsden-Jones and Turrill showed in a long and careful investigation, the results of which were published as a book in 1957. Moreover, the hybrid plants produced are fully fertile, and plants of the F_2 and later generations show the expected range of form according to Mendelian principles of segregation. In spite of this experimental result, Marsden-Jones and Turrill, finding that hybrid plants were 'relatively rare' in nature in the British Isles, continued to distinguish the two species, and it is certainly the experience of most British field botanists that they rarely have any difficulty in deciding which species they are looking at.

When we look outside the British Isles, however, we find a more complicated picture. In the European Alps, for example, there are low-growing prostrate plants with flowers somewhat intermediate between the typical lowland plant and our coastal sea campion, and Continental botanists generally call these subspecies or varieties of *S. vulgaris* (subsp. *glareosa* and subsp. *prostrata*). In the Continental sense, then, *S. maritima* is a strictly coastal plant from North Spain to North Scandinavia. For these reasons therefore Arthur Chater and I decided that in *Flora Europaea* (1964) we would treat all these variants including the sea campion as falling within the single species *S. vulgaris*, and call the variants subspecies.

This difficulty illustrates a general point, namely, that taxonomy is usually too parochial, and that when we look outside 'our own backyard' what we see is often a more complicated picture. Indeed, one of the great advantages of the *Flora Europaea* project was that it forced all the authors and editors to look at groups of plants on a Continental scale, often for the first time, and not surprisingly, when we do this, we find the picture looks rather different. Inevitably a great deal of parochial, even nationalistic, feeling has entered into taxonomic judgment, and plants do not respect national boundaries. This 'national bias' in taxonomy is worse in Europe than perhaps anywhere else because of the rapid rise in detailed studies of wild plants throughout the nineteenth century, a period which saw *pari passu* the rise of strong nationalistic feelings reflected in cultural and scientific work. It is ironical that we have to go back to pioneers like John Ray in the seventeenth century to find kindred spirits for the adventure of scholarship that *Flora Europaea* represents!

The case of the bladder campion leads us naturally to ask a question which lies at the root of much continuing argument about how plant species have evolved, and how they are continuing to evolve. If hybridisation is possible, and indeed widespread, when we bring species into our gardens, what exactly are the mechanisms keeping species apart in nature, and can we learn from such studies how evolution works?

What keeps species apart?

In the previous chapter we talked about the variation shown by wild populations, and how natural selection is assumed to operate. The picture we have
is of a randomly interbreeding group of individuals on which selection acts.
In an 'ideal' case there would be exchange of genetic material throughout
the whole population, and the population would be restricted to individuals
belonging to a single species. Our own species, *Homo sapiens*, is in this respect
'ideal', for all the different races of man are apparently interfertile. This sort
of picture seems to be true of higher animals in general, and is undoubtedly
responsible for the fact that most modern definitions of species stress the
interbreeding within the species and conversely the inability to cross with
other species.

Applying any such genetic species definition to the higher plants, however,
brings us up against formidable difficulties. We have already made the point
that many common perennial plant populations show clonal structure because of their power of vegetative spread, so that the model of many discrete
genetically different individuals is of very limited application. Whatever the
effect of natural selection on such populations, it can hardly operate in the
way of the ideal model. Even where sexual fusion and seed production are
necessary, however, as in annual weeds, the amount of self-fertilisation can
greatly affect the population structure. Let us, however, for the moment assume we are dealing with plant populations of discrete cross-pollinating individuals. What keeps them isolated from other populations?

The simplest case, as Koelreuter saw, is sheer distance. It really does not
matter whether, for example, the twin-flower *Linnaea borealis* growing in a
Scottish pine-forest will cross with the North American plant called by Reh-
der *L. borealis* var. *americana*, because they never get the opportunity to do so.
I have chosen this example because, so far as I am aware, no-one has ever
tried the experiment, so that the decision whether to call the American plant
a different species, *L. americana* Forbes, or to treat it as a variety of the Eurasiatic *L. borealis*, is made entirely on the taxonomist's judgment as to whether a
slight difference in flower size and shape is significant. Whether we like it or
not, this is true of the vast majority of such pairs of related taxa (and there
are very many) between North America and Europe.

The model we adopt to explain how such differences arise is that the ancestral population of *Linnaea*, wherever exactly it was, was continuous and interbreeding, but that, perhaps over long periods of geological time, what is now
the North American plant became totally isolated from the Eurasiatic one.
Once no interbreeding is possible, there will be genetical divergence accompanied by some morphological divergence, so that eventually it may be
possible, as in this case, to look at an individual and say 'this is var. *americana*'.
Such divergence can be thought of as being of two kinds. One the geneticists
would call 'drift' – genetic change due to isolation but not of selective importance – and the other would be the product of differential selection in the two
different regions. It is possible (though I am not aware of any information to
support this in the case of *Linnaea*) that the slight differences in flower size
and shape relate to differences between the insect pollinators in America and
Europe. If this could be established, we could think of the process of divergence as being to some extent fuelled by selection.

This process, by which we imagine pairs of related species arising in separated geographical regions, we call *allopatric speciation*. But many related species-pairs are *sympatric* – that is they grow in the same area and there is no obvious factor such as spatial separation to explain how they remain distinct. How then can we think of sympatric speciation? This is where the case of the bladder campion is helpful. Sea campion populations may not be geographically separated from those of the common bladder campion, but their adaptation to a very different habitat presumably means that the chances of cross-pollination are greatly reduced. Moreover, the differences between them, especially in growth form, are what we often now call ecotypic in nature, adapting each to its own environment, so that even if, for example, some cross-pollination were to produce in a sea-campion population individuals with a tendency to a tall, looser growth form, such individuals would be strongly discouraged and eventually eliminated by natural selection. So another important kind of isolation can be distinguished, namely ecological isolation, and there is no reason why some incipient species should not diverge under differential selection pressure in separated habitats. The ecotypes studied by Turesson may indeed be species in the making. Sympatric pairs of species, between which ecological isolation is operating, are not uncommon in our wild flora. The red and white campions, *Silene dioica* and *S. latifolia* (*S. alba*), illustrate the point beautifully. If we look at the maps of these two familiar wild flowers in the *Atlas of the British Flora* (Fig. 10), we see that over most of England both species occur. (Indeed, there is only one relatively small area, from the Wash southwards to the old county of Huntingdon, where white campion grows in the virtual absence of red campion.) But there is a marked ecological difference: the white campion is a weed of roadsides, gardens and arable land, whereas the red campion grows in woodland, and more or less shady hedgerows. So they often do not grow within pollinating

Fig. 10 Maps of red and white campion *Silene dioica* (left) and *S. latifolia* (right). From Perring & Walters 1982

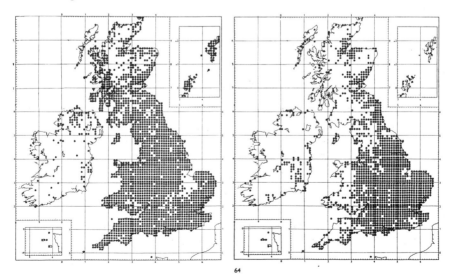

distance of each other. When, however, there is some drastic interference to this pattern, as, for example, when a new road is cut through woodland and strips of bare ground are temporarily created, pink-flowered hybrid plants, or even whole hybrid populations, can sometimes be seen. Such populations are often 'hybrid swarms', because the F_1 plants are interfertile and can produce a range of F_2 and later generations.

Something else is involved in the case of the two campions, however. Both campions are dioecious: that is, an individual plant is either male or female. This means that self-pollination is ruled out, and all female plants must, to achieve any seed set, have received pollen from some other plant. What is the pollinating agent? Red campion flowers open in the daytime, whilst white campions are evening flowers. In fact, like many pink, purple or blue flowers, the red campion is pollinated by bumble-bees or hover-flies, which visit the flowers in the daytime, whereas the white campion, whose flowers open in the evening and are slightly scented, attract night-flying moths to pollinate them. So not only is there a difference in habitat, but there is also a very important difference in the mode of pollination. Even where, exceptionally, many plants may be growing together, we must assume that pollen is rarely transferred between the two campions. A similar case, where there is quite effective separation between two sympatric species, is provided by the two native species of *Geum*, *G. urbanum* and *G. rivale* (see Briggs & Walters 1984, pp. 191-94 for a full description).

Whilst geographical or ecological isolation may be sufficient explanation for the distinctness of many related species-pairs, we find on investigation a whole range of other adaptations. For example, two sympatric species may have different flowering times, as in the case of the two closely-related wild violets *Viola riviniana* and *V. reichenbachiana*. In woods in lowland England, where these two violets commonly grow mixed together, *V. reichenbachiana* is normally in flower in early spring, some three weeks earlier than *V. riviniana*. The most obvious 'internal' barrier to crossing is, of course, sterility, which can express itself in different ways and to different degrees. The subject of sterility is of such general importance, especially with regard to its implication in our gardens, that we must treat it in a separate section.

Polyploidy and the abrupt origin of species

So far, most of what we have been saying is of a rather general nature and could apply (with some obvious reservations) to both plants and animals. We now come to the point where we must look at a phenomenon that is generally assumed to be nothing more than a rather odd and rare curiosity among animals, but which is very widespread among the flowering plants and has enormous implications – the phenomenon of polyploidy.

In our brief sketch of the rise of genetics in the early years of the present century, we mentioned that modern science took shape when it was discovered that the genes (or 'factors' as Mendel called them) were located on paired structures called chromosomes that can be seen after suitable staining techniques (the term 'chromosome' means 'coloured body' in Greek) in the nuclei of all ordinary cells of the plant or animal. All normal cellular organisms possess in each cell nucleus a fixed number of these paired structures, the number being characteristic of the species – the so-called 'diploid chromosome number' (2n). Examples range from $2n = 4$ in the Californian annual *Gilia*, through 2n = 46 in our own species *Homo sapiens* to the very exceptional 2n = c.1260 in one species of the adder's tongue fern *Ophioglossum*. This characteristic chromosome number is halved during a remarkable series of events called *meiosis* which takes place when the male and female gametes or reproductive cells mature, so that each gamete comes to contain only one member of each chromosome pair and therefore a number of chromosomes (the haploid number, *n*) that is half the diploid number. When two gametes fuse to form a zygote, each contributes one set of chromosomes and the diploid number is therefore restored in each new generation. The sorting or recombination of the genetic material, which we mentioned in Chapter 3, takes place in this process of meiosis.

To take this subject any further would be out of place in our book, but a more complete outline can be found in many reference books, including Briggs & Walters (1984). For our purposes we may note especially that the chromosome number is normally fixed for a particular species, and pairs or groups of related species often share the same chromosome number. An example from amongst the plants we have been discussing in this chapter would be the large genus *Silene*, the vast majority of whose species (including the red and white campions *S. dioica* and *S. latifolia*) share the diploid number of 24. Such species-pairs may prove to be interfertile, at least to some extent, when crossed. However, in many other cases, related species show a series of numbers which are simple multiples from some basic number. Such multiple chromosome numbers are called polyploid, and the species concerned are polyploids. The two related *Viola* species we used earlier to illustrate flowering-time isolation also illustrate the simplest diploid-polyploid relationship, *V. reichenbachiana* a diploid with 2n = 20 and *V. riviniana* a tetraploid with 2n = 40.

It is relatively easy to count the chromosome number of most flowering plants, and in modern Floras such as Clapham, Tutin & Moore (ed.3, 1988) and *Flora Europaea* the diploid chromosome number, where known with reasonable certainty, is given for every species. (The higher polyploid numbers are, however, understandably difficult to count with complete accuracy, so that, for example, the number for the limestone fern *Gymnocarpium robertianum* appears as 'c.160'.) A glance at a British Flora will soon show that polyploidy is a very widespread phenomenon indeed. It is not easy in fact to find, except amongst some tree genera, any cases of a reasonably large genus in our flora without any polyploidy numbers. The willow herbs, *Epilobium*, seem to be one of the very few, all of them having the same number, 2n = 36.

Polyploids, we now know, are of two different kinds, according to their mode of origin. The simplest kind, called autopolyploids, can in fact arise spontaneously as 'sports' on or from ordinary diploid plants, especially when the production of new shoots is stimulated by decapitation of young plants in vigorous growth. (Figure 11 shows this process diagrammatically in the experimental production of tetraploid tomatoes.) Such plants are autotetraploids, each cell nucleus possessing a set of 4 (not 2) representatives of each chromosome. More important, however, are the allopolyploids, which arise from doubling the chromosome number of a hybrid plant. In the most straightforward cases, two related diploid species produce a sterile hybrid, which is then converted into a fertile allopolyploid by chromosome doubling. What happens is that the diploid hybrid is sterile because the chromosomes

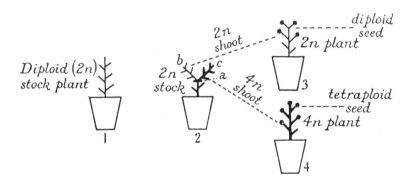

Fig. 11 The production of tetraploid tomatoes. 1, normal diploid tomato (2n=24); 2, diploid cut back at *a* giving rise to shoot *b* (diploid) and shoot *c* (tetraploid); 3, diploid plant raised vegetatively from shoot *b* of 2; 4, tetraploid plant raised vegetatively from shoot *c* of 2. (After Sansome and Zilva, from Crane & Lawrence 1934)

contributed by the two different parent species are too unlike to undergo regular pairing at meiosis, so that the whole mechanism of gamete production breaks down. However, a simple doubling of the chromosome number provides each unlike chromosome with an identical partner, so that the new polyploid 'species' can reproduce quite normally. So, quite abruptly, a sterile diploid F_1 individual can give rise to a fertile tetraploid which then breeds true. Moreover, it is reproductively isolated from both its parent species. One of the most famous cases of the origin of a new plant species in this way is that of the allotetraploid *Primula kewensis*, produced both spontaneously and experimentally from the sterile hybrid between *Primula floribunda* and *P. verticillata* (see Briggs & Walters 1984, p.221).

Polyploidy, then, provides a mechanism in higher plants for the sudden production of new species of hybrid origin and, as we have already seen, must have played a very important part indeed in the evolution of the flowering plants. (It seems to be very rare in the Gymnosperms – an interesting and as yet largely inexplicable fact.) Indeed, we have strong reason to suspect that the evolution of new species is still going on by this route, and two cases of new allopolyploid plants are often cited as evidence of this. One is the coastal grass *Spartina anglica* (*S. townsendii*), of hybrid origin from a native European and an introduced North American species, and the other a new species of groundsel, *Senecio cambrensis*, first detected in North Wales by Rosser (1955) as a fertile allopolyploid derived from the common groundsel, *Senecio vulgaris* and the Oxford ragwort *S. squalidus*. In both these cases it is probably significant that an introduced species is one of the parents: it emphasises the point already made that man, by bringing together widely-separated plants, provides new possibilities for hybridisation and therefore evolutionary change.

The significance of sterility

Outside my window, as I am writing this in early November, is a low bushy plant bearing many bright red flowers. It started to flower in late April, and has been flowering continuously ever since. Heavy frosts, just beginning now, will, I expect, soon bring the flowering to an end. The shrub is *Salvia micro-*

phylla (*S. grahamii*) in a rather large-leaved and large-flowered variant called variety *neurepia*, and its native home is Mexico. This continuous flowering shown by many garden plants is, of course, one of the features which gardeners appreciate, and which greatly increases the value of the plant. Over the years we have naturally selected such plants and grown them preferentially. Looking closely at the *Salvia*, I find that it shows no sign of setting seed; the whole flower, including the calyx, drops off after several days and new flower-buds open in succession. The plant is apparently sterile and, like most garden shrubs, it is always propagated by cuttings, which are easily rooted. But the flower shows well-developed stamens producing apparently normal pollen, and the long style has the two receptive stigmatic surfaces ready to receive pollen. What is wrong?

The answer may well be that there is no way to transfer pollen to stigma. This red-flowered *Salvia* from the New World is adapted to pollination by humming-birds, and there are no humming-birds in my garden – or indeed anywhere in Europe outside aviaries! It is easy to tell bird-pollinated flowers in our gardens. They are often red or orange, not purplish or blue, they have abundant nectar but no scent, and they have a conspicuous way in for the nectar-seeking bird but no landing-stage such as our familiar bee flowers usually provide. In fact, all these differences between bird and bee flowers can be seen if we compare this Mexican sage species with the culinary sage, *Salvia officinalis*, or with the blue-flowered meadow sage, *S. pratensis*. So one of the causes of sterility amongst our alien garden plants may be that we have introduced the plant, but not its natural pollinator, and by doing so, we have unwittingly encouraged a long flowering period. Actually, I now know that my *Salvia microphylla* can produce a little viable seed, and in later seasons I have observed hover-flies visiting the flowers. Gardeners are well aware that the practice of 'dead-heading' – removing the withered flowers and thereby preventing the ripening of seed – is more than a mere cosmetic exercise. There is a physiological balance mechanism in the growing plant by which shoots on which the flowers have been pollinated and are setting seed actually suppress the formation of more flowering shoots. Remove the flowering shoot and more flowers will develop to take their place. Another possible cause of sterility is the absence of any suitable partner for a plant that is self-sterile (self-incompatible). The slender speedwell *Veronica filiformis*, now such a familiar sight on our lawns with its pretty pale blue flowers in spring (Plate 37), was originally introduced from the Caucasus mountains as a desirable 'alpine' for our gardens, and was not in fact recorded outside gardens anywhere in Britain until 1927. Its spread throughout Britain seems to have been achieved entirely vegetatively, for ripe capsules with seed have been recorded very rarely indeed. The reason seems to be that the species is self-incompatible, and over very large areas all the plants are derived from a single genetically uniform clone which will remain sterile until it meets a different one.

A third, and very common, cause of sterility amongst garden plants is the 'doubling' of flowers. We are so familiar with 'double' flowers such as roses and carnations, in which some or all of the sexual parts of the flower (stamens and carpels) are replaced by petal-like structures, that we take them for granted; yet they represent an extraordinary development which requires explanation. In wild plants, 'doubling', in which petal-like or in some cases green leaf-like structures replace the inner, sexual parts, occurs sporadically and rather rarely. We assume that all such deleterious 'sports' or mutants remain rare because natural selection eliminates them. The advent of the gardener changed all that. 'Doubled' flowers were rare, interesting and often more decorative, and were therefore brought into cultivation and thereby removed from the influence of natural selection. Not only are many double flowers larger but, because they are usually sterile, the plants bearing them have a prolonged flowering season. As in the earlier examples, sterility, accompanied by longer flowering and vigorous vegetative growth, becomes a positive asset. This is surely the explanation of the well-known fact that many common European plants, such as the lesser celandine *Ranunculus ficaria* (Plate 4), were grown in 'double' variants (*'flore pleno'* is the Latin term) in our ancestors' cottage gardens. The soapwort *Saponaria officinalis* (Plates 6 & 7) provides a striking example. The wild plant is native over much of continental Europe, but in Britain and Scandinavia it behaves largely as an introduction and escape from cultivation, occurring commonly on roadsides and waste ground. British plants are sometimes double-flowered, but in Sweden they are very commonly so, and we assume that both the single and double-flowered plants were early cultivated for their 'soap' qualities. In addition, however, we have both double white-flowered and double red-flowered plants in cultivation. In the case of *Kerria japonica,* a commonly-grown shrub with double flowers, the wild type with single flowers is rarely seen in gardens (Plate 8).

Completely 'double' flowers, in which there are no functional stamens or ovary, can obviously only survive if they are perennials with the power of vegetative spread. This is presumably the reason why double-flowered annuals are rare. One such, still quite commonly grown, is the Mediterranean *Silene pendula*. Here the explanation is that the seeds obtained from the nurseryman will give a mixture of single and semi-double flowers on different plants, and some seed will be set to perpetuate the variant.

What general conclusions can we draw about sterility? Firstly, in our gardens as in the wild, failure to set seed can be due to many different causes, from failure of pollination to genetic irregularity indicating hybridisation. But in gardens, unlike the wild, sterility is often a sought-for quality because it is accompanied by long flowering and vigorous vegetative growth. Our gardens therefore tend to be full of genetic misfits which we have reason to think would not long survive in nature or, at best, might survive but remain rare and exceptional.

Apomixis

One of the success stories amongst garden plants is the lady's mantle *Alchemilla mollis* (Plate 33). There must be very few keen gardeners and flower arrangers who do not know this robust relative of the lady's mantles that grow wild in Britain, and are common on roadsides and in grassland in the north. If, as seems likely, your garden contains *Alchemilla mollis*, you will know that it not only holds its own in any herbaceous border, with robust growth and vigorous vegetative spread, but also reproduces quite effectively by seed. Each small flower from the massed yellow-green flowering stems will produce a single 'seed' (technically this is a one-seeded fruit that we call an achene). These 'seeds' germinate freely the following spring around the plant after some exposure to winter frosts. So far everything seems normal. If, however, we look closely at these tiny flowers, we might notice two things. Firstly, the four stamens look badly developed, and shed no pollen, and secondly, even before the flower-bud is fully open, the single ovary seems to be already ripening. In fact, what is happening is that seed is developing without any fertilisation at all, a condition that we call apomixis. Any apomictic plant will produce in the next generation from seed a set of identical offspring, just as if the single vegetative clump had been split up into a number of pieces and grown separately.

The events inside the embryo which lead to apomixis are both complicated and difficult to investigate, and need not concern us here. What is of general interest, however, is to know how widespread the phenomenon is. Although our knowledge is as yet very incomplete, and mainly derived from studies on European plants, we can at least say that in certain families, especially the rose family Rosaceae (to which *Alchemilla* belongs) and the dandelion family Compositae, several very familiar and important genera are partly or largely apomictic in their mode of reproduction. Further, we can point to a very interesting correlation between apomixis and what botanists have often called 'critical groups' of plants, in which the delimitation of species has been (and still is, in some cases) a matter for argument amongst the specialists. What seems to be the case is that apomictic groups like the lady's mantle *Alchemilla* consist of a relatively large number of 'micro-species' with small (though often remarkably constant) sets of distinguishing characteristics. Botanists who enjoy the taxonomic game can spend many happy hours learning to distinguish all these microspecies, whilst others – usually the vast majority! – are content to leave the game to the few specialists.

Apomictic species are, practically without exception, also polyploid, and often have high chromosome numbers. *Alchemilla* is a rather extreme case, with 2n ranging from 64 to c.220. The generally accepted view of how apomicts have evolved is that the onset of apomixis has followed the evolution of many polyploid derivatives of hybrid origin, but it is still quite uncertain whether we should view apomixis, as the plant geneticist Darlington did, merely as an 'escape from sterility' or, as seems more likely, that we should look upon it more positively as a device to reproduce quickly and accurately a plant well adapted to a rather specialised way of life. Nor is it yet clear whether the tendency towards high polyploidy and apomixis should be thought of as a one-way process leading ultimately to extinction. There is still much to learn about this remarkable phenomenon and its biological significance.

For the gardener there is one interesting feature about apomixis shown clearly by *Alchemilla*. Because seed production does not involve fertilisation, different *Alchemilla* species grown together cannot hybridise, so there is no problem of the original stock being insidiously replaced by other plants. Of course, it *is* still possible to find and propagate the occasional 'bud-sport' or mutant variant; but these remain rare curiosities. It is very remarkable that, in the century or so that we have grown *Alchemilla mollis* in our gardens, to my knowledge only one such variant has been detected and propagated – a form with variegated leaves. In the wild, the most significant genetic variation known in *Alchemilla* concerns dwarf varieties, such as the tiny var. *pumila* of the remarkable species *Alchemilla faeroensis*, endemic to East Iceland and the Faeroes. This mutant, which remains dwarf when propagated from seed, grows mixed with the normal plant in the sheep-grazed turf of the Fae-

Fig. 12 Dwarf variants of *Alchemilla*. Top row: *A. minima* from Ingleborough. Bottom row: *A. filicaulis* from Mickle Fell and Moorhouse Nature Reserve. All plants from upland grazed turf in the N. Pennine area, cultivated for 9 months. (Bradshaw, M. E., 1964, from Briggs & Walters 1984)

roes, where it has obviously been selected over centuries of grazing pressure. Detecting such genetic dwarfs in wild populations is not easy, and we need much more investigation to know how widespread the phenomenon is (Fig. 12). There is more information in papers of mine (Walters 1970, 1986b).

We return to consider in particular the impact of the science of cytogenetics on the practice of horticulture in modern times in the third part of this book, especially Chapter 9.

Plate 1 The honeysuckle and the rose illustrate how our gardens blend together wild and garden plants. This honeysuckle is the native *Lonicera periclymenum,* one of the wild flowers everyone is familiar with, and the rose is the rambler 'Paul's Scarlet', a garden plant of complex hybrid origin. Photo Martin Walters.

Above left Plate 2 Illustration of the bramble *Rubus fruticosus,* from a twelfth century herbal produced at Bury St. Edmunds and now in the Bodleian Library, Oxford. (See p. 29)

Above Plate 3 Mountain avens *Dryas octopetala,* in North Yorkshire. (See p. 46) Photo Andrew Gagg.

Above Plate 4 Variation in lesser celandine *Ranunculus ficaria.* (See p. 62). Photo R. G. Woods.

Right Plate 5 Sea campion *Silene uniflora* on shingle beach, Walney Island, Cumbria. (See p. 55). Photo Andrew Gagg.

Above Plate 6 Soapwort
Saponaria officinalis on waste
ground in garden. (See p. 62).
Photo Martin Walters.

Above Plate 7 Soapwort flowers. Centre, the
typical single pink: left, double red: right,
double white. Scale in cm.(See p. 62).
Photo Martin Walters.

Right Plate 8 *Kerria japonica*, commonly
grown in its double form. The single-
flowered typical plant (also shown here)
is rather rarely grown. (See p. 62).
Photo Andrew Gagg.

Left Plate 9 Evergreen ivy on deciduous oak: a wayside tree in Grantchester, Cambs., in early spring. (See p. 93). Photo Martin Walters.

Below Plate 10 Spurge laurel *Daphne laureola.* (See p. 90). Photo Andrew Gagg.

Part II

Life Forms and Adaptations

'...in a country that has been plentifully inhabited and diligently cultivated for centuries, there are numbers of plants and trees in a semiwild condition, which the young botanist cannot possibly distinguish from the aboriginal; and many of these introduced plants are much more attractive and of more frequent occurrence than is the case with hundreds of our truly native species. To be useful under all circumstances, a *Flora* should include both the introduced and the wild species, so long as care is taken to say which they are.'

Leo Grindon, Preface to British and Garden Botany, *1864.*

The term 'life form' may be unfamiliar to most readers, although the ideas conveniently brought together by the term are commonplace. We all make 'life form' distinctions when we speak of trees, shrubs and herbs. Indeed, this very obvious classification retained its pride of place as the primary division of all plants from the beginnings of scientific botany in ancient Greece through to the writings of John Ray in the seventeenth century. The life form of a plant, according to the Danish botanist Raunkiaer who first standardised the terms, is determined by the position of the dormant buds during the resting season; in trees and shrubs the buds are above the ground, in most perennial herbs they are at ground level, while in bulbs they are below ground. Raunkiaer's rather unwieldy technical terms for these life form categories need not trouble us here: they can be found in convenient summary form in any of the editions of Clapham, Tutin and Warburg's *Flora of the British Isles*.

The particular interest of the life form classification is that it groups plants quite differently from the systematic classification into family, genus and species, and that certain life forms are characteristic of certain climatic regions of the earth. A very obvious correlation is the absence of trees from the arctic regions, but there are, as we shall see, many others. The life form resemblances between plants are of adaptive significance and we shall use the term 'life form' to cover all such resemblances whether they have a special category in Raunkiaer's system or not. In the chapters that follow we consider wild and garden plants successively under the three broad categories of tree, shrub and herb, with a fourth chapter to deal with special life forms of interest to both botanists and gardeners.

5

Native and Exotic Trees

Trees and gardens

Very few English gardens are devoid of trees, even if, as was true in my early childhood, our single tree was a small, rather ill-favoured cherry in the middle of some rough grass we called 'the lawn'. Even the modern town patio can find a place for one or two suitably-shaped birches, willows or dwarf conifers. It is not surprising that we need trees in our environment: from pre-historic times man has had a dependent relationship to trees, which provide shade, shelter, fuel and food and were, indeed, venerated in many pre-Christian societies. Of course with the rise of civilisation came the gradual separation of the utilitarian role of trees into that area of activity we now call forestry, and our book is not concerned with trees as a source of timber or fuel. But it is worth noting that the great estates that flourished in the seventeenth and eighteenth centuries, many of which are now preserved and even restored for us by the National Trust and other conservation bodies, encouraged both in their fortunate owners and in their workers a love of trees for their own sake. The generous reaction of ordinary people to the wholesale destruction of woodland in the hurricane that devastated parts of southern England in October 1987 is clear evidence of the British love of trees.

The balance between woody and herbaceous plants in our gardens has varied greatly through the centuries. So far as the botanic gardens were concerned, which developed directly from mediaeval herb gardens, trees and even shrubs were of little importance, because the vast majority of medicinal plants were herbs. Why this should be so is not too clear. Of course in part it simply reflects the fact that the number of different trees and shrubs native in Europe north of the Alps is very small compared with the number of herbaceous plants, but it could be that the reason goes much deeper into the history of medicine and botany. After all, early botanists were often called 'rhizotomists' 'root-gatherers', and many herbal potions were prepared from the roots of wild plants rather than the aerial parts. Digging up an oak tree is a very different sort of operation from pulling up a groundsel! The fact that trees were not thought to have more than a limited medicinal importance might also explain why relatively few exotic trees were introduced into Britain before the seventeenth century, when John Evelyn's book *Sylva, or a discourse of forest trees* published in 1664, which looked at trees for their own sake and as elements in the landscape, began to have an enormous influence on fashion and design. (As for so many other questions of garden history and design, the reader is confidently referred for further information to Miles Hadfield's classic *History of British Gardening* (1960), happily still in print (1985).)

The fundamental change in the nature and purposes of the botanic garden began in the seventeenth century and was really effective in the later years of the eighteenth century. It was caused by the rise of botany as a science in its

GROUND PLAN OF THE BOTANICAL GARDEN, 1838.

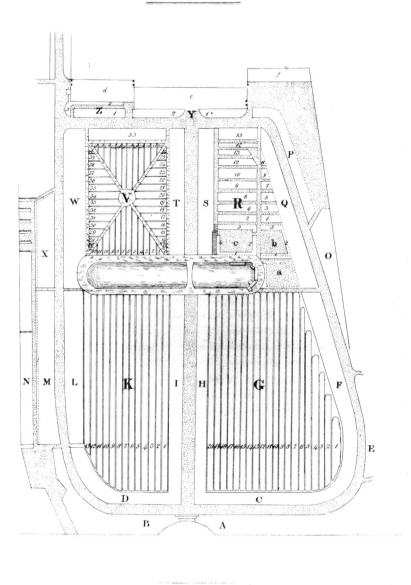

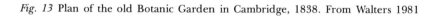

Fig. 13 Plan of the old Botanic Garden in Cambridge, 1838. From Walters 1981

own right, free from the restrictive requirements of medicine. In my own University, Cambridge, this change was delayed until 1825, when John Stevens Henslow was appointed to the Chair of Botany as a vigorous young man of 29. He found a moribund botanical museum in a small, traditional 'physic garden' growing mainly herbaceous plants in so-called 'order beds' (Fig. 13), and set about persuading the University authorities to replace this small, eighteenth century garden with an entirely new one on a much larger site because, as he put it, the existing garden was "utterly unsuited to the demands of modern science". Henslow was successful, and the present-day University Botanic Garden, covering nearly 40 acres in the south of the modern city of Cambridge, is a permanent tribute to this far-sighted teacher. In the same year (1846) in which, after a long delay, the University officially opened the new garden, Henslow published a pamphlet containing "a few observations to the members of our University, inviting attention to what may be considered requisite for a modern Botanic Garden". In this, he sets out with admirable clarity why he needs a much larger garden:

> "The reason why a modern Botanic Garden requires so much larger space than formerly, is chiefly owing to the vastly increased number of trees and shrubs that have been introduced within the last half century. The demands of modern science require as much attention to be paid to these, as to those herbaceous species which alone can form the staple of the collections in small establishments. The considerable portion of the ground which would be devoted to an Arboretum may be kept up at very much less expense than the rest, but would add very greatly to the ornamental as well as to the efficient character of the Garden."

If we visit the Botanic Garden in Cambridge today, we can still see and appreciate the fruits of Henslow's vision. In particular we can admire well-grown specimens of North American trees like the wellingtonia (as the Victorians wanted to call it), *Sequoiadendron giganteum* (Fig. 14), introduced into Britain in 1853. This extraordinary giant, confined as a native to isolated stands between 1500 and 2500 m on the western slopes of the Sierra Nevada in California, has made a great impact on the English countryside. Not only did the young trees grow moderately fast, but they continued their steady upward growth and still do to the present day, resisting high winds (even the 1987 hurricane) and towering above all other trees in the English landscape. In late Victorian times, almost every estate, large house, country vicarage or municipal park was planting its wellingtonias. The related coastal redwood *Sequoia sempervirens*, first planted in Britain in 1843, is not so spectacular a success in the English countryside; it is much more sensitive to hard winters and grows rather poorly in the more continental parts of England, though a Perthshire specimen reaching 40 m is recorded. In its native California it is claimed to be the tallest tree in the world, one specimen measuring 112 m.

By a curious coincidence, the approximate centenary of the introduction of the wellingtonia into Europe saw the arrival of an even more remarkable redwood relative, the deciduous *Metasequoia glyptostroboides*, which has been given the English name of dawn redwood. The story of this new Chinese tree is often told, but it is so interesting that I must repeat it here. In 1941 a

Fig. 14 Wellingtonia *Sequoiadendron giganteum* in University Botanic Garden, Cambridge. Photo Martin Walters

Japanese botanist published his discovery of fossil material of a new tree to which he gave the name *Metasequoia*. Late in the same year a Chinese botanist saw living trees, but no material was collected until 1944, and it was 1947 before seeds were obtained and sent to the Arnold Arboretum, who distributed them as the new species *Metasequoia glyptostroboides* to many botanic gardens throughout the world in 1948. This extraordinary tree proved to grow quickly and easily from seed, or (unusually for conifers) from cuttings, with the result that all the botanic gardens, and many private gardens, in

Europe had their young specimens by the 1970's. Indeed, during my time as Director of the Cambridge garden I soon ceased to say, when visiting an unfamiliar European garden, "Have you got a *Metasequoia*?" and substituted the question "How tall is your *Metasequoia*?" The friendly rivalry over who has the tallest and best *Metasequoia* continues to this day. Will the middle of the twenty-first century see yet another spectacular tree introduced into Europe? It seems unlikely, though by no means impossible!

Culturally, we could say that there were two powerful factors in the Victorian enthusiasm for an 'arboretum' of interesting and beautiful specimen trees grown for their own sake. One was clearly scientific, as stated by Henslow and many other teachers, but the other, perhaps equally powerful, was the Victorian romantic view of the 'pleasure garden' which harks back to the Paradise gardens of the ancient east. It is interesting to find that Henslow, at the end of the quoted passage, adduces this as an added bonus in the creation of a scientific collection of trees. Generations of students have cause to thank him for the happy combination of science and amenity in the Cambridge garden.

The Victorian taste for rarity

It is always dangerous to draw general conclusions from a limited experience, but I will risk a generalisation based partly on what I learned of trees in the Cambridge Botanic Garden. It is that any garden planted in the early Victorian period is likely to feature prominently two kinds of trees. The first, as we have seen, would be the impressive new introductions, especially, though by no means exclusively, from the New World. The other group will be odd variants of much more familiar native European trees. In the Cambridge garden it is indeed necessary to warn students, for example, that both the fine specimens of the common beech *Fagus sylvatica*, which are in their systematic position in the original planting from around 1850, are genetic variants rare in nature. (We have a fairly normal mature beech, but characteristically this is somewhat off the beaten track and not often visited.)

This Victorian taste for the new, the rare and the peculiar – even the grotesque – is of course easily exemplified from architecture, landscape and garden design, the contents of zoos and museums, and many other ways, and books have been written on the subject. As Lynn Barber puts it in her fascinating book on *The Heyday of Natural History* (1980), when talking of early Victorian England:

> "Almost every year produced a new sensation – new orchids, humming-birds, pitcher-plants, toucans, bird-eating spiders, giant tortoises, moon moths from Java, the *Victoria regia* water-lily which was so large it had to have its own conservatory built to house it – an endless list of ever bigger and better marvels to fire the public imagination."

The market for the rare, the sensational, the bizarre was constantly stimulated by the swift exploration of the hitherto little-known parts of the world, and the British role in this whole process was uniquely powerful.

37m

bark at 60cm

'Dawyck' 23m

'Pendula' 15m

'Copper' 25m

Fig. 15 Variants of beech *Fagus sylvatica*. From Mitchell 1974

To take first the common trees, and as an example the beech, *Fagus syl-vatica*. Many Victorian gardens have fine specimens of the cut-leaved beech, a particularly striking example of a familiar garden variant. This tree, together with the weeping beech, was introduced into our gardens from 1820 onwards. The even more familiar copper beech, in which the leaves are reddish-purple, was known as early as the seventeenth century, but was only widely planted in Victorian times. A later arrival, still popular for avenue planting today, is the narrow, fastigiate variant we call the Dawyck beech after the estate in South Scotland where it was first detected in 1860. This remarkable tree may well come to rival the Lombardy poplar, which made its debut in the English countryside around the middle of the eighteenth century, but which has declined in public taste in recent years, not least because it is rather fragile and can be dangerous in public places. All these beeches of our towns, parks and gardens greatly enlarge our idea of a beech tree, and illustrate the way in which gardening reveals a wide range of genetic variation presumably present, but largely undetected, in wild populations (Fig. 15). It would be possible to illustrate the same phenomenon in practically every other native British tree.

Sometimes, however, what is involved is not at the level of variation within the species, but within a familiar genus. The pines of our gardens illustrate this. We have only one native pine, the Scots pine, *Pinus sylvestris*, still present (though much reduced and now protected) in natural forests in the Scottish Highlands such as the Rothiemurchus Forest under the Cairngorm range. Although the Scots pine is sometimes planted, the commonly planted tree in mid-Victorian times (at least in Eastern England where climate and soil seem to suit it) was the so-called Austrian pine, *P. nigra* subsp. *nigra*. In many ways a larger version of our native tree, with longer needles and bigger cones, it is most easily told by the dark grey bark of the upper part of the trunk in contrast to the red-brown bark of the Scots pine. It is often a feature of the skyline in villages, together with the narrow towering wellingtonias: both were planted frequently in mid-Victorian vicarages and churchyards (Fig. 16). Although we have other European pines such as the maritime pine, *Pinus pinaster*, introduced before the seventeenth century and not uncommon in the south of England, the impressive burst of 'new' pines came from Asia and America in the nineteenth century. Two particularly successful introductions were the five-needled Bhutan pine, *P. wallichiana*, brought into cultivation in 1823, and the three-needled Monterey pine, *P. radiata*, from California in 1833, now remarkably successful in the mild climates of Southwest England and Ireland. The effect of all these introductions (Mitchell (1974) lists 35 species growing in the British Isles) is to make it possible to teach British students about the pine trees of the world on the basis of home-grown mature specimens. Had the Victorians not had this taste for novelty, we could not now reap this benefit.

Sometimes we might feel that the Victorians did take the whole fashion to absurd extremes. By the old Victorian rock garden, now the Terrace Garden where we grow our collection of dwarf conifers in the Cambridge Botanic Garden, is a dinosaur-like monstrosity planted some time after 1863 when it was first discovered. This pathetic, genetically-handicapped variant is a wellingtonia called 'Pendulum'; in our specimen the leading shoots cannot for long support themselves upright and bend over, making a long axis

Fig. 16 Austrian pine, *Pinus nigra* subsp. *nigra* at Manor Farm, Grantchester. A typical Victorian planting. Photo Martin Walters

Fig. 17 Sequoiadendron 'Pendulum' in University Botanic Garden, Cambridge. Photo Martin Walters

parallel to the ground, only a few feet high and clothed with pendulous side-branches (Fig. 17).

Trees in the landscape

Because of their size and longevity, trees have made a contribution to our appreciation of the landscape which is quite different from other cultivated plants. We are impressed by two qualities in particular: the relative permanence of individual specimens, especially if the tree has 'grown up' with us and we know it as an old friend and, in Britain, the beauty of the changing seasons in the case of deciduous trees, which constitute the great majority of our woody flora, both native and exotic. From the end of the eighteenth century onwards, what we call 'landscape gardening' – a term, incidentally, first used apparently by the great exponent of the art, Humphry Repton himself – has had an enormous effect on the British tradition of horticulture. Indeed, as Graham Thomas makes clear in his valuable book entitled *Trees in the Landscape* (1983), the way we look at the countryside has been shaped by the pioneers in landscape design who, following Repton's example nearly two centuries ago, used trees consciously to create pleasing views. Nowhere has the English genius had a more benign influence than in this particular area where art and science cooperate so effectively. What looks like 'unspoiled countryside' to us now is the product of a range of influences, not least of which was the power of the rich country landowners who could afford to employ a succession of gifted designers like Charles Bridgeman, 'Capability' Brown and Humphry Repton. In a later chapter we will look at how the English love of nature, inspired in part by the art of landscape design, has contributed to the modern interest in the conservation of nature: for the present we can think of the use of trees, native and exotic, in the British landscape.

Size, shape and colour are the three main attributes of a tree that are likely to determine its value in any view, whether it be in an 'open' landscape or in a more enclosed garden. It needs hardly stressing that size and shape have to fit the particular site, and that, for example, the widespread modern fashion to plant the handsome Atlantic cedar *Cedrus atlantica*, as a specimen tree in a small suburban garden is almost certain to cause trouble for the present or future owners of the property. This is, of course, one reason for the greatly increased interest in trees whose ultimate size and shape would comfortably fit the small modern garden, as evident, for example, in the appearance of the booklet *Trees for Small Gardens* (Rushforth 1987), one of the excellent 'Wisley Handbooks' of the Royal Horticultural Society. But, on a larger scale, the function of specimen trees or groups of trees in the composition of landscape has obviously attracted the attention of all landscape gardeners since the days of Repton.

One of the remarkable aspects of the work of the pioneers responsible for the great estates, arboreta and botanic gardens in which we can now enjoy the fruits of their labours in the form of mature trees is that they were able to envisage the scene as they themselves could not possibly have expected to live to see it. But there is one important point to remember here. Not even the genius of a Repton or a Henslow could get it right all the time. In particular, there was a great difference between the confident use of familiar native trees such as oak and ash or the early introductions such as sycamore, horse-chestnut and cedar of Lebanon, and the new exotics from North America or the Far East. In the one case, silvicultural study and experience has already built up a knowledge of the familiar trees in cultivation, from the raising of seedlings to the successful growth of the adult tree whereas, for newcomers like the wellingtonia, all the keen growers, professional and amateur, had to go on were reported observations by the early plant collectors about the conditions in their native habitats in another continent. Fundamental questions about hardiness, for example, were answerable only by long, expensive trial and error, and the exotics were understandably likely to be used as specimen trees or avenues in the immediate vicinity of the great house, or in special 'arboreta' where their progress could be noted. As Graham Thomas puts it:

"The main difference in the nineteenth and twentieth centuries in what we may now call the garden landscape, as opposed to wild forest and natural countryside, was the introduction of tall-growing conifers from North America and the Far East. The whereabouts of a great Victorian mansion can often be determined from afar today by the spires of wellingtonias and other conical tree-tops piercing the skyline of native trees."

It may in fact take many years before we know enough about an exotic tree to predict its success in the very varying soils and climates of the British Isles.

How long, for example, did it take to establish the fact we have already mentioned, that wellingtonia would thrive almost anywhere in Britain, whilst the related coastal redwood of California is somewhat damaged by hard winters in the more continental parts of England, and only really successful in the west and north? And, in the case of the dawn redwood, *Metasequoia*, we have still to learn, since no tree anywhere in Europe can yet be more than 50 years old. All we can tentatively say is that, over a large part of lowland Britain, *Metasequoia* can grow healthily, but in dry soils its growth is, after the first few years, significantly slower than in wetter places. Will it ever effectively set viable seed? We do not yet know, but our children and grandchildren should do.

As we all know, the contribution made by trees to the colour of the garden or landscape is in large part a seasonal phenomenon. No-one who has had the opportunity to travel in North America in late September or October and see a New England 'fall' would ever need reminding of the glories of autumn colour, nor would they be surprised to learn that most trees we grow especially for the brilliance of their autumn foliage turn out to be natives of North America. It is, of course, true that native trees can make a more muted colour display, but in one case after another we find that exotic hardy North American and Asiatic trees colour much more brilliantly in our gardens than do our more restrained species. We have oaks, but the Americans have *red* oaks (*Quercus rubra*, more correctly known as *Q. borealis*); we have a single native maple, the field maple *Acer campestre*, but in our gardens we can grow the North American red maple *A. rubrum*, which contributes brilliant deep red colours to the wooded New England landscape in September. Much has been written about the glory of the autumn landscape in North America, and there is really no satisfactory general theory to explain why European deciduous trees put on a much more subdued autumn show. One point worth remembering is that by no means all North American oaks, maples, etc colour spectacularly, and that the rich variety of 'fall' colour reflects in part at any rate the undoubted fact that the North American (and East Asiatic) woody flora is vastly richer in species than is the European one – a point to which we return in Chapter 6. Another relevant difference between, say, England and New England is that we have an Atlantic climate, profoundly affected by the Gulf Stream, whereas the New England climate is a continental one, and it is undoubtedly true that hot summers and cold winters accentuate spectacular autumn colour displays: from which we might conclude that the complex chemical reactions accompanying leaf fall have some selective value in more continental climates that they do not have in our mild Atlantic air. But, whatever the reason, as our Victorian forebears discovered we can grow successfully in Britain exotic trees, often related to our own native ones, that provide us with this impressive extra show of autumn colour.

Of course, the gardener's art does not finish here. We have already mentioned the purple-leaved variants of common British trees, such as the familiar copper beeches of Victorian gardens. New colour variants of wild and garden trees are constantly being made available, and may be strongly promoted by commercial nurseries for their beauty, or at least their novelty. In recent years the cultivar 'Frisia' of the North American false acacia *Robinia pseudoacacia* has been very widely planted in Britain; first grown in Holland in 1935, this tree has golden-yellow leaves from June to October, when it colours to a deeper orange-yellow tint before falling. The use of such 'golden' varieties of trees – and, even more, variegated forms in which the leaves are splashed with pale, sometimes whitish patches – is very much a matter of taste: Graham Thomas is very fierce in his denunciation of their use outside a suburban garden, for example, and many would agree with him.

Dwarf trees

The difference between a tree and a shrub is, like so many other ordinary distinctions we make, clear enough in most cases, but, as with the term 'flower' that we talked about in Chapter 3, a 'tree' may well be somewhat differently defined for different purposes. Alan Mitchell, in the introduction to his popular *Field Guide* (1974) attempts a definition: a tree, he says, "may be defined as a woody, perennial plant which can attain a stature of 6 m or more on a single stem. The stem may divide low down, but it must do so above ground level." So two criteria are involved, namely height and the possession of a single trunk. Having made his definition, he proceeds to discuss the border-line cases. Hawthorns *Crataegus*, he says, qualify because there are tall specimens with a single trunk, although he admits that the common hawthorn we see in hedges is "only a shrub with many stems". The elderberry *Sambucus nigra* and the dogwood *Cornus sanguinea*, he says, are shrubs and "do not qualify for inclusion." We could follow Alan Mitchell's lead and exclude here all reference to plants which do not manage to grow more than 6 m, but if we did this we would be diverting attention from one of the most remarkable phenomena linking wild and garden plants, the question of dwarf varieties of trees.

We have already made the point in Chapter 3 that much variation in wild plants is adaptive. It does not surprise us when we see a gradual change in the average height of the trees as we climb a mountain. Our own mountains have been largely denuded of their natural tree cover, so we have to go to the Alps or Scandinavia to see the zonation of woodland and scrub communities in a more natural state, and appreciate the idea of a 'tree line', above which only low-growing shrub communities are found. To a large extent, as we explained in Chapter 3, the dwarf woody plants on our mountains (like the mountain avens *Dryas octopetala*) are distinct species with no tree relatives. On the other hand, we can find dwarf examples of what seem to be the same species as taller-growing trees in more favourable and sheltered positions lower down the mountain. The downy birch *Betula pubescens* illustrates this very well. In this variable species we can distinguish a northern and mountain subspecies, subsp. *tortuosa*, with low, twisted growth (Fig. 18). Such trees grade into more typical trees with straight trunks in less exposed sites, and we can be reasonably sure that part of this difference in habit is genetically fixed.

We also know, however, that by suitable manipulation almost any tree can be forced to grow in dwarf form, as the Far Eastern garden art of bonsai shows. Whilst bonsai cultivation of dwarf trees may appeal to the few, there is a far greater demand for genetically dwarf variants of trees suitable for the modern small garden with its formal patio area and rock garden. Sensibly, we mostly take and use what nature has already provided for us in a suitable growth form. Nowhere is this more obvious than amongst the conifers, and we should now look at the dwarf conifer fashion a little more closely.

The enthusiasm for 'greens' – what we would now call 'evergreens' – can be traced back to seventeenth century writers. At this time, that most majestic of

Fig. 18 Birch *Betula pubescens* subsp. *tortuosa* on a Norwegian mountain. Photo Martin Walters

all our garden conifers, the cedar of Lebanon *Cedrus libani*, was just coming into cultivation in England, and Sir Thomas Harmer, who wrote his *Garden Book* in 1659, is enthusiastic about this marvellous new arrival, and predicts that it will "without question prosper with us". In this he has been abundantly proved right. The successful introduction of the cedar must have done much to stimulate landowners to plant new, exotic conifers as they became available but, as we have already noted, we had to wait until the nineteenth century before the really big developments took place. It was the Victorians who really grew conifers as never before, and great Victorian nurseries like Knight's of Chelsea prided themselves on offering hundreds of named conifer species and varieties. From this rapidly developed the dwarf conifer fashion, and early rock gardens in Victorian times used these low or prostrate variants in their increasingly 'natural' arrangements of stones. Our own 'terrace garden' in Cambridge, with its collections of dwarf conifers, is a direct descendant of one such Victorian rock garden, and contains a number of venerable dwarf specimens, some of them rare variants like *Pinus sylvestris* 'Moseri' (Fig. 19).

It is by no means obvious why the conifers should produce such a range of variants. Perhaps the stimulus of Victorian demand produced a generation of sharp-eyed nurserymen who spotted the odd 'sport' and propagated it assiduously, and it is certainly true that similar dwarf variants are known of familiar broad-leaved trees, though our gardens show very few of these. One remarkable example which is rapidly becoming fashionable is the dwarf elm tree *Ulmus × elegantissima* 'Jacqueline Hillier'. This neat conical little tree not exceeding 3 m is ideal as a specimen for a small garden and, apparently because it *is* small, it escapes the attention of the bark beetle responsible for the

Fig. 19 Pinus sylvestris 'Moseri'. Photo Martin Walters

spread of the devastating elm disease. It will be odd if the 'Jacqueline Hillier' of our gardens becomes the only elm tree that the next generation of gardeners is likely to see in England!

Naturalised trees

The cedar of Lebanon has been in Britain for some 350 years – time for a whole generation to mature and die of old age (Fig. 20) – but it remains an introduction, apparently unable to establish itself from seed outside our gardens, though ripe seed is abundantly produced. Some exotic trees, on the other hand, have been spectacularly successful, and behave in every way like true natives. The most impressive example is undoubtedly the tree we call sycamore *Acer pseudoplatanus* but which John Ray called, with more justification, "The Great Maple, falsely called 'Sycomore'."[1] Authorities differ about when this familiar tree was brought to Britain: Mitchell (1974) attributes the introduction 'probably' to the Romans, but most other writers look to Elizabethan times. Since it occurs naturally in Europe as far north as the Paris region, it did not have far to come! Its great success seems to be due in part to its abundant production every year of the familiar paired winged 'seeds' which germinate freely on any waste ground. Over much of Britain, from the continental east to the oceanic west, it is *par excellence* the 'weed' tree of neglected shrubberies and woodland, and it is quite surprisingly hardy in cold, upland moorland-edge sites in Scotland and the North of England.

The cedar and the sycamore are two extreme examples of non-native trees. We speak of *Acer pseudoplatanus* as a naturalised tree, establishing itself effec-

[1]This incorrect use of the Biblical name – which refers to a kind of fig tree, *Ficus sycomorus* – serves as a warning against the use of common names in scientific works.

Fig. 20 The famous Cedars of Lebanon in the Chelsea Physic Garden in 1795.
(Engraving in Lysons, 1795)

tively from seed in the wild without direct human aid. What other examples
are there in Britain? The sweet chestnut *Castanea sativa*, whose introduction
from South Europe is usually attributed to the Romans, is certainly a naturalised tree over a good deal of lowland England on light, acid soils. The
unrelated horse-chestnut *Aesculus hippocastanum*, one of our most beautiful
introduced trees, is less effectively naturalised. Clapham, Tutin and Moore's
Flora (ed.3, 1987) states that it is "commonly planted and often self-sown",
and it is not uncommon for young saplings to establish themselves on waste
ground, but they often fail to come to maturity. For a long time after its introduction into Northern Europe in the sixteenth century the native home of
the horse-chestnut was uncertain: it is now known to be a Balkan mountain
endemic. Another example of a partly naturalised tree is the evergreen or
holm oak *Quercus ilex*, the finest of all introduced evergreen broad-leaved
trees, known in Britain since the sixteenth century, and much planted in the
south and west of England.

   These examples illustrate an important feature of the practice of growing
exotic trees. It is relatively easy, in many cases, to grow in a garden a specimen tree of a rare, exotic species. It may even prove to be both hardy and
fertile in our climate, like the cedar of Lebanon, so that we can perpetuate it
with a new generation of seedlings planted out from our nurseries. It is, however, much rarer for the exotic to succeed, like the sycamore tree, in being
totally independent of man in the British countryside. We do not know
exactly why one exotic succeeds where many others fail. What is, however,
very clear is that the establishment of seedlings against competition from na-

tive plants and animals is one of the 'bottlenecks' in the way of effective naturalisation. The sycamore succeeds in getting through, perhaps by sheer numbers of seedlings, but to define the exact conditions for success and failure
would be beyond our present knowledge.

This process of introduction and occasional naturalisation is, of course, still
going on, and it is interesting to speculate whether future generations might
know some rare exotic as a common wild tree in Britain. One possible candidate, to judge by its present performance, is the Italian alder *Alnus cordata*.
Introduced in this country as early as 1820, it remained a relatively unknown
tree until recent years – so much so that Alan Mitchell's 'Guide' can say as
recently as 1974 "uncommon; in some parks and large gardens, also beside
main roads in a few places." Unusually, it was a tree I knew as a student in
Cambridge because, thanks to contacts between keen, informed tree specialists and the City Council,[1] we had a row of *Alnus cordata* planted on public
land in the early 1930's.

These trees are now mature, handsome specimens more than half a century old. The Italian alder has proved to share several qualities with the sycamore: it is totally hardy, and grows very quickly from seed, which it seems
to produce abundantly in most years. Moreover, cones and apparently ripe
seeds are produced on trees as young as five years from planting out. What
is not yet known is how effective the seed will be in competition with native
plants. I can as yet trace no record of self-sown *Alnus cordata* in the wild, but,
having admired its performance as a planted tree in wet, acid soils in the
West of Ireland and relatively dry, chalky soils in Cambridgeshire, I am prepared for anything. It certainly 'puts in the shade' both our native alder *A.
glutinosa*, and the grey alder *A. incana*, neither of which, in my experience, is
so handsome or so vigorous.

The Italian alder illustrates the unpredictability of successful introductions.
Why a tree whose native distribution is confined to such a very small area in the
world (Fig. 21) should prove so easy and adaptable in cultivation remains a mystery. There is a further point about this tree. Corsican plants, now commercially
available in Britain, differ significantly in leaf shape from the more familiar Italian ones, emphasising the genetic variation available in the wild even when the
native range is so restricted. If our present cultivated stock is so successful, what
might we achieve with a wider range of material from different wild origins? And
what of the possibilities of hybridisation, as yet almost unexplored? The hybrid
with our native *A. glutinosa* is known in the wild and may indeed have originated
also in cultivation. Wild-pollinated trees like alder and birch are especially prone
to hybridisation when grown together, and the wide recent planting of the Italian alder in Britain must have increased enormously the likelihood of hybrids
in the generations to come.

New trees

A mention of the possibility of hybrid alders leads us naturally to the question
whether hybridisation has played a significant part in producing new garden
trees as it most certainly has in the smaller garden plants. On the whole it

---

[1] The botanist responsible for this enlightened choice of avenue tree was Dr W. Balfour
Gourlay, a great friend of the then Director of the Botanic Garden, Humphrey Gilbert-Carter.
Dr Gourlay also popularised in Cambridge the fastigiate 'Dawyck' beech that had originated on
his family estate in Dawyck, Scotland.

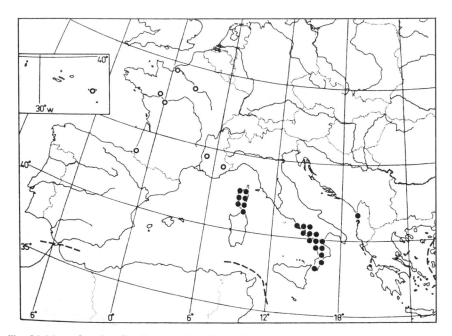

Fig. 21 Map of native distribution of Italian alder *Alnus cordata*. Solid dots: native, hollow circles: naturalised. From Jalas & Suominen 1988

seems we have to answer negatively. One reason may be that the generation time of a forest tree is enormously greater than that of a herb. Having said this, however, we should say something about the few cases that are known and assess their importance.

Outstanding amongst the cultivated trees generally thought to be of hybrid origin is the magnificent London plane tree *Platanus acerifolia*[1]. Although this origin cannot be said to have been conclusively proved, the London plane seems to have arisen as a cross between the Old World *Platanus orientalis*, native from the eastern Mediterranean through much of South Asia to India, and the New World buttonwood *Platanus occidentalis*, soon after the introduction of the latter into South-west Europe in the sixteenth century. Of all our introduced trees, surely the London plane is the most familiar, resisting to a very remarkable degree the atmospheric pollution of the capital and becoming its commonest street tree. Outside London one of the most famous historic specimens grows in the grounds of the Bishop's Palace at Ely: according to Mitchell it measured 35 m in 1969. It is our tallest broad-leaved tree over much of lowland England, and seems to be with us to stay. But no *Platanus* is naturalised in Britain, and we must go to Greece, Crete or Asia Minor to see a really wild plane-tree (Fig. 22).

[1] I have followed Clarke in Bean (ed.8, 1976) in using the name *P. acerifolia*. Other names are *hybrida* and *hispanica*. The choice of name is a complex story, of little interest to the general reader, but Clarke gives all the relevant facts.

Fig. 22 Oriental Plane *Platanus orientalis* native in mountain woodland, Kalavrita, Greece. Photo Martin Walters

Another exotic tree of some scientific interest is quite a familiar street and garden tree in present-day England. This is the red-flowered horse chestnut *Aesculus carnea* whose origin, though not recorded, is almost certainly from a chance garden hybrid between the European horse-chestnut and the North American red buckeye *Aesculus pavia*. The tree is a fertile allopolyploid (see Chapter 4, pp. 59-60), the chromosome doubling having probably arisen on a branch of the original hybrid tree, and its seeds produce good *carnea* plants, showing no segregation as ordinary hybrids would.

So far as the wide gardening public is concerned, however, one tree hybrid has surely beaten all the others in popularity – the fast-growing conifer universally called 'Leylandii'. This remarkable tree, which is now known in several different cultivars, is the hybrid between the Monterey cypress *Cupressus macrocarpa* and the Nootka cypress *Chamaecyparis nootkatensis*. The Monterey cypress, though making a fine tree in South-west England, is not very hardy, but the Nootka cypress, from North-west America including Alaska, is very hardy indeed, and 'Leylandii' has inherited the hardiness of this northern tree. What is enormously impressive is the vigour of the hybrid. Hybrid vigour is well known to plant breeders, and is indeed one of the main reasons for the spread of the use of F_1 hybrid seeds in horticulture: in 'Leylandii' the speed of growth is quite exceptional. For this reason, and because of the ease with which it can be propagated from cuttings, it is now the best-selling conifer in the nursery trade. Since some trees not yet a century old already exceed 30 m, this tree could well be rivalling the wellingtonias in the twenty-first century – although, of course, the vast majority of Leylandiis are planted in rows to be clipped as neat, efficient hedges screening the windows of suburban houses.

So much for the exceptional, famous cases, which are rather few in number. There is, however, a much wider question about hybrid trees that we should consider. As we saw in Chapter 4, many related species pairs are kept apart in nature by effective barriers to cross-pollination, and the general effect of man's interference with nature is increasingly to break down these natural barriers. So far as European trees are concerned, this drastic interference began many centuries ago, when man began the permanent destruction of the continuous forest. The trees we find today in the British countryside are remnants with a complicated history, and part of that history could have involved hybridisation. It is no accident that, although we can easily distinguish, for example, birch trees *Betula* from oak trees *Quercus* or lime trees *Tilia*, when we are confronted with a particular specimen and asked to say exactly which species of birch, oak or lime we have, we may find it very difficult to say. In each of these very familiar cases there has been in Britain widespread hybridisation between species which we can reasonably assume were much more distinct before forest clearance interfered with natural patterns. The case of the birch trees can be used to illustrate this general point.

We have three species of birch *Betula*, in the British Isles.One of these, the dwarf birch *B. nana*, is a small arctic-alpine shrub, but the other two are often of tree stature. We have already mentioned the downy birch *B. pubescens*, which has low-growing arctic and mountain variants, but which can easily reach 20 m in the lowlands. The other species, the true silver birch *B. pendula*, is well named, with its silvery-white bark and slender, pendulous twigs; it is obvious why this tree is preferred to *B. pubescens* in parks and gardens.

Much wild birch woodland in Britain, however, shows a rather bewildering range of trees with varying combinations of intermediate characters. The reason seems to be that the general ecological separation between the two tree birches, which can still be seen in Scandinavia or Finland where the natural forest is less destroyed, has very largely disappeared in Britain. Much of our birch woodland arises secondarily after forest clearance or as trees colonise waste ground, and the genetic make-up of the new colonising trees is obviously quite mixed.

If this is true in the wild of our two native tree birches, how much more true it will be in our gardens, where we grow several exotic birches together with the native ones. Of course, in a small garden, when we want a specimen birch tree, we would expect to buy the kind of birch we need (often a grafted clone), rather than promote a casual seedling; but in the larger gardens and arboreta, much genetic mixing takes place, and hybrid birches of very doubtful parentage are commonly found. So far as I am aware, no-one has yet assessed how far the range of Asiatic and North American birches now increasingly grown in parks and gardens is having a genetic effect on wild populations. Perhaps this effect will be too insidious to come to our notice for some time to come, but one feels that it must already be happening.

We can finish this section on new trees with a word about some extraordinary garden trees called graft-hybrids or (a preferred technical term) chimeras. The first of these mysterious plants arose in a French nursery belonging to one Jean Louis Adam in 1825. Adam tells us that he had grafted the dwarf purple broom *Cytisus purpureus* on to a stock tree of the common yellow-flowered laburnum *Laburnum anagyroides*, and that on this successfully-grafted plant appeared a branch of purplish-yellow flowers intermediate in colour between the scion and the stock. This is the plant we still grow and call +*Laburnocytisus adami*. The '+' sign before the scientific name signifies that it is a chimera (Greek word for a monster), a genetically composite plant, with a core of the tissue of one species and a skin of the other. Such chimeras are unstable, and a tree can produce shoots of pure laburnum, pure broom and the chimera all on the same plant.

The other famous chimera is between the hawthorn *Crataegus* and the medlar *Mespilus*. In this case, both the true sexual hybrid (× *Crataegomespilus grandiflora*) and some chimeras are known. Again, these plants are unstable, and branches of pure hawthorn or pure medlar can be produced. Chimeras are, not surprisingly, totally unknown in nature, since they arise only from grafted plants in which the art of the gardener has caused a shoot of one species to grow on a rootstock of an allied one. So they are the most extreme 'new' plants we can grow in our gardens and, though they are bizarre and full of interest for the geneticist, they will remain, at least among the trees, rare curiosities.

Whole books are written about cultivated trees, even if we limit ourselves to those lacking any particular interest for the forester, and I am aware that my selection of topics in this chapter is inevitably a personal one that may disappoint some readers. If, however, it serves to impart some enthusiasm I shall be well contented.

6

Shrubs and shrubberies

The rise and fall of the Victorian shrubbery

The appreciation of the beauty and, indeed, the architectural importance of individual trees came to English gardeners, as we have seen, as early as the seventeenth century. With shrubs it was a somewhat later change of fashion, if only for the obvious reason that an individual shrub generally makes a less dramatic impression than a tree. But there is, perhaps, something else involved, to do with fashion and style. There is, apparently, no word in the English language for a *planted* collection of shrubs until the middle of the eighteenth century: the earliest use of our collective term 'shrubbery' is in fact, according to the Oxford Dictionary, 1748. Why should this be? Surely, what is involved is art copying nature. The eighteenth-century garden designers, working mainly for the landed gentry, and the 'nouveau riche' middle-class who were increasingly building fine country houses, saw 'nature' as a landscape of tended fields and defined woodlands. Scrub communities in lowland Britain were (and still are, in the eyes of many farmers) so much unproductive waste ground waiting to be cleared and ploughed or planted with trees.

The recognition of the garden value of shrubs, unlike the trees or the 'flowers', depended upon the introduction of almost wholly unfamiliar kinds of plants. Broadly there are two groups of popular garden shrubs that are hardly represented in our native flora: the evergreen, broad-leaved species such as those we collectively call 'laurels', and the winter-flowering, often deciduous, shrubs such as winter jasmine. A few individual examples of both these groups were, of course, known to English botanists and gardeners from early times, but their use did not become fashionable until the eighteenth century. Hadfield (1960, p.180) quotes from a letter written by Horace Walpole in 1781, in which he is commenting on Sir William Stanhope's 'improvement' of the garden originally made by the poet Alexander Pope at Twickenham:

> "The poet had valued himself on the disposition of it, and with reason. Though containing but five acres, enclosed by three lanes, he had managed it with such art and deception that it seemed a wood, and its boundaries were nowhere discoverable ... Refined taste went to work: the vocal groves were thinned, *modish shrubs replaced them* and light and three lanes broke in; and if the Muses wanted to tie up their garters, there is not a nook to do it without being seen."

What were these 'modish shrubs'? In this particular case we are not told, but plants becoming popular at the time included laurustinus *Viburnum tinus* (of which more later), and the strawberry tree *Arbutus*, both prized for their winter-flowering and evergreen habit, and both native in the Mediterranean area.

By the turn of the century, and especially in the great expansion of smaller, private gardens during the Victorian period, 'laurels' and similar evergreen flowering shrubs became ubiquitous in English parks and gardens. Indeed, the dense Victorian laurel shrubbery became almost a symbol of dull, private gentility, and an inevitable reaction began to set in. William Robinson, whose writings (1870, 1883, and later editions) played a great part in determining late Victorian and Edwardian taste in gardening, castigates the Victorian 'laurel' shrubbery, and in particular the swamping effect of *Rhododendron ponticum*, already by the turn of the century an aggressive, naturalised shrub in many parts of the British Isles. The story of laurels and rhododendrons is so remarkable that we must give it a separate section below.

Shrubs in the world's flora

We have already made the point that what we often call 'scrub' in the countryside is generally seen, with some justification, as a temporary vegetation of waste ground, and the native shrubs found there are for the most part plants that would not naturally find a place in our gardens except in the rougher, unkempt corners. Indeed, we tend to think of several of our commoner native shrubs such as hawthorn *Crataegus monogyna*, blackthorn *Prunus spinosa* and dogwood *Cornus sanguinea* as the seasonally interesting constituents of the hedgerows that, until recently, were taken for granted in the countryside. Faced with the rapid changes brought about by mechanised agriculture, we are now for the first time realising that hedges are artefacts whose preservation is justifiable on scientific, aesthetic and historical grounds and must be a conscious act of conservation. What is the natural habitat of our familiar hedgerow shrubs? Broadly there seem to be two possibilities. Some low-growing woody plants are at least locally dominant above the tree-line on mountains or in exposed coastal habitats where erect trees cannot grow. These will be shrubs like the wild juniper *Juniperus communis*, adapted to high exposure and high light intensity in the growing period, yet quite intolerant of competition from forest trees. Another set of shrubs, such as the hazel *Corylus avellana*, are much more shade-tolerant, and can therefore grow as an understorey in broad-leaved woodland. As we saw in Chapter 1, the hey-day of shrubs in Britain must have been the period we call 'late glacial', after the final retreat of the ice, and before the forest closed over the land. But the number of different kinds of shrub that were able to re-invade what is now Britain after the ice was only a very small fraction of a rich and diverse woody flora we know to have existed in Europe before the Ice Ages. This rich 'Tertiary flora' survived much better in North America and in East Asia than in Europe, with the result that very many of our familiar hardy garden shrubs come from temperate America and Asia, not from anywhere in Europe.

We can illustrate this imbalance by giving some facts and figures about a familiar genus of garden shrubs – *Viburnum*. About 150 species of *Viburnum* have been described, mostly in the North Temperate regions, though there are a few in South America. Sixty of these are included in 'Bean' (Clarke, ed. 1970), which mentions all hardy woody plants cultivated anywhere in the British Isles. The native European flora contains only *three* species: the two familiar deciduous British native shrubs, the guelder rose *V. opulus*, and the wayfaring tree *V. lantana*, and the gardener's evergreen laurustinus *V. tinus*. Twelve other species given in Bean are North American, and no fewer than 43 are East Asiatic, mainly Chinese. Similar patterns are found in many other hardy shrub genera. Sometimes they are even more extreme: in the genus *Magnolia*, which contains about 125 temperate and tropical trees and shrubs, Bean lists 8 North American species and 19 East Asiatic ones. There is not a single European *Magnolia*, though we know from fossils that the genus was widespread in Europe in Tertiary times, and several American and Asiatic species and hybrids are quite hardy in English gardens.

The extraordinary richness of the woody floras of Eastern North America and East Asia in contrast to the European flora is a phenomenon that asks for some general explanation. From the fossil record it seems to be clear that the diverse Tertiary floras of Europe suffered much greater extinction through successive ice-ages than those of North America or East Asia. Why should this be? An elegant explanation draws attention to the difference between the main mountain ranges of Europe, which run in an almost unbroken chain from the Pyrenees in the west to the Balkans in the east, and the Rocky Mountains of North America, which run north to south like a backbone to the Continent. The hypothesis is that in Europe the east-west chain of mountains blocked the gradual retreat of the Tertiary floras as the ice came down from the north, so that they were unable, except in a most fragmentary form, to retreat south of the ice and wait for warmer times. In Eastern North America, on the other hand, there was a wide lowland corridor down which from north to south the Tertiary floras could retreat, to march north again when the ice retreated. Similar considerations apply to Asia where there is no significant mountain chain east of the Himalayas to block the way into China. This seems a very plausible general explanation, although it is obviously unprovable. What is strikingly true is that many of these old Tertiary trees and shrubs grow perfectly well in present-day Britain when man re-introduces them, and a few of them, indeed, succeed only too well, becoming aggressive competitors with our native vegetation, a point we made in Chapter 1.

Two kinds of exotic shrubs, then, both rather unfamiliar in our native flora, have made a great impact in British gardens: the evergreens and the winter-flowering kinds. Sometimes, as in laurustinus, both qualities are combined in one plant but, on the whole, our best-loved winter-flowering shrubs bear their flowers on leafless twigs, and our gardens would be immeasurably poorer without them. These two groups deserve a more detailed account, and we can conveniently begin with the evergreens, since they *are* represented in the British flora, though rather sparsely.

Laurels and other broad-leaved evergreens

The majority of our native woody plants are deciduous, and almost the only familiar evergreens are the conifers like pine, spruce and cedar. We tend, therefore, to think that a tree or shrub that sheds its leaves in the autumn is the norm, and those that keep their leaves through the winter are the exceptions. But this is really a rather parochial view. On a world scale, we get a very different picture. Starting from the wet tropics and working outwards, we find that a synchronous leaf fall in plants, resulting in bare twigs for part of the year, is to be looked on as a positive adaptation to a seasonal climate in which good growing weather alternates with difficult weather. All over the north temperate zone, which includes Britain, the winter with its frost and snow is the unfavourable season, and plant growth is adapted to this regular and dependable seasonal cycle. The outstanding exception to this is provided, in the northern hemisphere, by the belt of coniferous forest, and we understandably, therefore, tend to associate the needle-leaved evergreen habit of our common conifers with extreme hardiness and resistance to cold. Whilst this is true for some few conifers such as the Norway spruce *Picea abies*, our familiar Christmas tree, we should remember that the majority of conifers in the world's flora are not in fact especially winter-hardy, and, indeed, most exotic conifers grow better in the milder west of Britain than the more continental east.

Because of its association in our mind with Christmas, the most familiar broad-leaved evergreen shrub or small tree native in Britain, the holly *Ilex aquifolium*, is probably thought by many English gardeners to be unusually hardy. This is emphatically not the case, as we find if we look at its distribution as a native tree in Europe. *Flora Europaea* says it is native to "S. and W. Europe, extending north-eastwards to N. Germany and Austria." Although holly has been widely cultivated and planted outside its native limits in the British Isles, we can see the same tendency if we compare, for example, its absence from the semi-natural oak-ashwoods of Cambridgeshire with its abundance and importance in, say, oak-woods in the west of England and Ireland (Fig. 23).

Holly is in fact a representative of a whole group of evergreen trees and shrubs that we may naturally associate together as 'laurels'. They have quite large, simple, often shiny, evergreen leaves, and are characteristic of damp, mild climates of the western fringe of our continent, including the Atlantic

Fig. 23 Holly *Ilex aquifolium* under sessile oak *Quercus petraea*. Yarner's Wood, Devon. Photo Martin Walters

islands of the Azores. Holly could indeed be thought of as the hardiest and most successful representative of the group; most 'laurels' are much more restricted in their native distribution. Just as we do not expect that all deciduous shrubs will be closely related, so we should not be surprised if different 'laurels' belong to quite different families of plants, and this is what we find. Within the same genus *Viburnum* some species have evergreen laurel-like leaves: and the gardener's name for *Viburnum tinus* – 'laurustinus' – goes right back to the sixteenth century, when all laurel-like shrubs could be called 'laurels', the classical Latin name for the true laurel or sweet bay *Laurus nobilis*.

Laurus nobilis the bay tree is one of the most famous trees of classical Europe, with a unique place in Greek and Roman mythology, and much prized today for the fragrance of its foliage. As a shrub or small tree it occurs throughout the Mediterranean region, but its exact original native distribution is very uncertain, because it was grown in gardens from ancient times. No-one knows when it first came to Britain: it was certainly familiar to the English botanist William Turner as long ago as the middle of the sixteenth century, who said it was commonly grown in gardens in the south of England. By John Evelyn's time a century later there was apparently already quite a trade in imported Dutch bay-trees, and English growers were discovering that the tree was reasonably hardy over a good deal of lowland England. Today it is rather uncommon as a free-planted shrub or small tree, and most gardeners know it only as a culinary 'herb' to be conveniently grown as a tub-plant near the house and easily protected from the occasional hard winter.

Is there any native British shrub that really looks and behaves like the true laurel? (We have to admit that most people would not readily call holly a 'laurel', if only because its leaves are often spiny-toothed.) One small British shrub, however, does qualify – the spurge laurel *Daphne laureola* (Plate 10). This plant looks oddly out of place in an English oak-ash wood – and indeed one's immediate reaction to it is to think it must be some bird-sown Mediterranean alien, with its thick, shining 'laurel' leaves and its yellow-green heads of flowers, often out already in February. Yet such is the benign effect of the Gulf Stream in our islands that spurge laurel is not uncommon in woodlands throughout much of lowland England. Like several English woodland plants, it is unknown in Ireland as a native, though it occurs throughout northern and western France. In their monograph on *Daphne*, Brickell and Mathew (1976) say: "our native spurge laurel *D. laureola* has long been cultivated, although it is seldom given much attention in gardens", and refer to Turner and Gerard writing in the sixteenth century. They assign it a modest garden role, particularly as a shade-tolerant shrub preferring alkaline soils. But, of course, many other *Daphne* species are rightly prized as beautiful in flower and fruit, not least our only other native one, the rare, deciduous mezereon *D. mezereum*, of which Brickell and Mathew say: "it is scarcely necessary to extol the virtues of this superb, early-flowering shrub which has been a favourite for many centuries."

The first 'laurel' to become really common in English gardens was, as we have already noted, the winter-flowering evergreen *Viburnum tinus*, and this plant has rightly never been supplanted from popular esteem. It is astonishingly hardy, and seems to survive, undamaged and in full flower, through all but the really continuous hard winters at least in Southern Eng-

land. William Marshall, writing in 1785, comments on this: "the boldness of
its buds, at a time when other flowers and trees shrink under oppressive cold,
is a matter of wonder and pleasure", and two hundred years later, gardeners
can emphatically endorse this tribute. Like nearly all plants that have been
cultivated over a long period, laurustinus is represented by a number of different variants, some of which are obviously hardier than others.

The 'laurel' that everyone knows, the cherry laurel *Prunus laurocerasus*,
achieved its garden dominance gradually through the late seventeenth and
early eighteenth centuries. Its origin, as an exotic from Asia Minor, is very
well recorded: it apparently came to France via Italy in the middle of the
sixteenth century, and to England by the early seventeenth – in time for
Johnson to include it in his edition of Gerard's *Herball* (1633). It was at first
assumed to be tender, and treated like an orange or other *Citrus*, to be grown
in tubs and brought in to the orangery for the winter. Gradually it was
allowed out and began to show that it was reasonably hardy, until the late
eighteenth century fashion gave it its real chance. Curiously enough, its
relative, the Portugal laurel *P. lusitanica*, which is a good deal hardier and in
the opinion of most people a more attractive shrub, has always been much
less popular, though apparently a fine specimen grew in the Oxford Botanic
Garden from 1648 to its removal in 1826. Perhaps our mistake with both
these Victorian 'laurels' is to cut them about: as single, spreading shrubs or
even trees they can make impressive subjects in a wooded area.

The latest of the gardeners' 'laurels' to achieve success was the Japanese
plant usually called the variegated laurel *Aucuba japonica*. This curious shrub,
which is so familiar in our city gardens, is totally unrelated to any other garden laurel, and in its common form with the familiar yellow-spotted leaves is
quite unmistakable. There *is* a normal, unspotted *Aucuba japonica* – which I
personally much prefer – so it is as well not to rely on the spots for identification. (A very easy character by which you can recognise a twig of this 'laurel'
is that it is the only common 'laurel' with *opposite* pairs of leaves.)

There was great interest in this odd Japanese shrub after it was first introduced into Britain in 1783. The original, variegated stock was female, and in
the absence of male plants none of the handsome red fruits were produced.
It was not until the middle of the last century that new Japanese stock was
introduced and both male and female normal and variegated plants became
available. Male plants became very valuable – one was said to be priced at
"over a guinea a leaf" in the 1860's – and in the period between 1860 and
1890 many named varieties were raised. A great point in favour of *Aucuba*
was its tolerance of city smoke and this, combined with its ability to thrive
under quite dense tree shade, endeared it to Victorian and Edwardian park
superintendents. In recent years tastes have changed again, and no doubt
the passing of the Clean Air Act has meant that city smog tolerance is no
longer quite so important an attribute in an evergreen shrub, so that *Aucuba*
is out of fashion. But remember its remarkable tolerance of shade and root
competition: as Bean puts it: "even under a beech, lime or horse chestnut,
where grass will not grow, it maintains a cheerful aspect."

We come now, at the end of our survey of laurels, to the rhododendron,
one of the really great horticultural success stories. In respect of their large,
simple, often shiny, evergreen leaves most rhododendrons are obviously 'laurels', though their showy flower-heads are very different; their native homes

are mainly in mountainous regions with relatively high seasonal rainfall and, often, snow-cover in winter. The first rhododendrons grown in Britain were a few North American species such as *R. catawbiense* and *R. maximum* from the Eastern United States, together with *R. ponticum* from forests of the Black Sea area and Western Caucasus. These shrubs were in commercial production in English nurseries before the end of the eighteenth century, and selected cultivars, some of hybrid origin, soon became widely available. But the great rhododendron break-through came with the botanical exploration of the Himalayas which began in the middle of the nineteenth century. As Clarke points out in his introduction to the treatment of *Rhododendron* in Bean (8th ed., 1970), some 50 species only were described before 1849, when Hooker's *Rhododendrons of the Sikkim Himalaya* was published: now there are about 800 species known, more than 500 of which are or have been cultivated in Britain.

There is, of course, one fundamental difference between the rhododendrons and the other 'laurels' of our gardens. As every gardener knows, rhododendrons grow badly on limy soils, so the great banks of flowering rhododendrons – the very name means, in Greek, 'rose tree' – are to be seen only in gardens off the chalk or limestone, particularly on well-drained sandy soils. The worst possible soils are the calcareous clays: in such soils it is best to accept defeat, and concentrate on growing roses! This pattern is even more obvious when 'wild' *Rhododendron ponticum* is mapped (Fig. 24): this aggressive shrub is now well able to hold its own on acid soils throughout the British Isles, and the only two large lowland areas virtually free from the

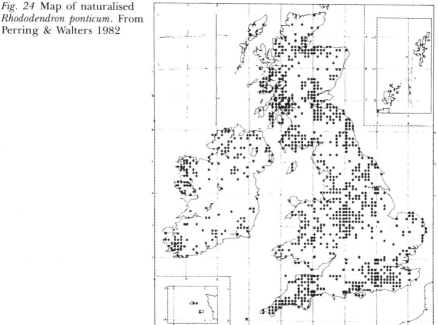

Fig. 24 Map of naturalised *Rhododendron ponticum*. From Perring & Walters 1982

invasion are the strip of chalk and limestone running from the Cotswolds to Cambridgeshire in England, and the limestone Central Plain of Ireland. The success of *Rhododendron ponticum* is a striking example of the phenomenon we discussed earlier, namely that many plants we know to have been in the European flora in Tertiary times and rendered extinct in the Ice Age can be very successful when re-introduced. Actually, it seems that this rhododendron was never totally wiped out in Europe: an interesting relict group of populations has survived in southern Spain and Portugal, and there is, indeed, some evidence that an early introduction into English gardens came from Gibraltar and might therefore be of Atlantic, not Black Sea, origin. The differences between the typical plant from Asia and the European plant are very slight and quite inadequate as a basis for specific distinction, though the latter is often distinguished as subsp. *baeticum*. One important feature of the rhododendron story is the widespread use of *R. ponticum* by the nursery trade as the stock for grafting the choice Himalayan species and, even more, their hybrids. Given the social history of most large Victorian and Edwardian estates, it is not surprising that these banks of grafted 'new' rhododendrons, established in the days of abundant, cheap labour, were often later relatively neglected and reverted to ordinary *R. ponticum* as the vigorous, freely-suckering stocks gradually and inexorably replaced the choice grafted scions. The problem of controlling the resultant *ponticum* thickets is of course still with us. There are, occasionally, advantages in gardening on chalk!

Ivy

One native evergreen woody plant is neither a tree nor a shrub, and really needs a special category. The common ivy *Hedera helix* is a woody climber, or liane (Plate 9). Because it is so abundant, we take this extraordinary plant for granted, and indeed to many people it is an aggressive 'weed' which needs control if it is not to smother trees and buildings. The life form, a woody climbing plant with evergreen leaves, adapted to flower and fruit at the top of the forest canopy, is common in tropical and sub-tropical vegetation, but very poorly represented in temperate regions. In fact, ivy is unique in the British flora, which contains only three native woody climbers, the other two of which are deciduous, and totally unrelated to each other or to the ivy – the honeysuckle *Lonicera periclymenum*, and the handsome wild *Clematis* we call old man's beard or travellers' joy, *C. vitalba*. Both native deciduous lianes are weaklings when compared with the introduced Russian vine *Polygonum baldschuanicum*, which can reach 10 m. and is capable of more than 4 m. growth in a single season (Fig. 25).

Like the holly, ivy has been used in Europe from Classical times as a conveniently available evergreen decoration, especially for mid-winter religious festivals. Thus, in a *Survey of London* published in 1598, Stowe says that "every man's house, the parish churches, the corners of the streets, conduits, market crosses, etc. were decorated with holme (holly), ivy and bayes (sweet bay or laurel) at Christmas." Together with mistletoe *Viscum album*, they still constitute the most familiar evergreens used for Christmas decoration about the house. We can add one more evergreen to this trio: the box tree *Buxus sempervirens*, though here the Christian symbolism has been much more associated with Lent, especially the use of box as a 'palm' for Palm Sunday preceding Easter. Box and mistletoe are both rare as wild plants in Britain,

Fig. 25 Russian vine *Polygonum baldschuanicum* covering garden shrubs and poles, with the author and grandchildren for scale. Photographed in August in Grantchester. Photo Martin Walters

however, and our use of them may be partly due to Roman influence, but with the holly and the ivy we are using common evergreens available practically throughout the land. Is it, perhaps, precisely because holly and ivy are so common that the horticultural use of both is comparatively restricted? Does familiarity breed contempt? In the case of holly, it is the Americans rather than the British who have taken to growing different cultivars, using both native American species such as *Ilex opaca* and the British holly *I. aquifolium* (see, for example, Hume 1953). With ivy, modern taste is turning back to the neglected Victorian tradition and there is a newly-revived interest in growing decorative ivies, an interest growing on both sides of the Atlantic, although no species of *Hedera* is native to the New World.

Ivy is unique, not only in its being our only native evergreen liane, but also as the only European representative of a very large and important tropical and sub-tropical family of flowering plants, the Araliaceae. A very few of these are known to gardeners: the most familiar is *Fatsia japonica*, an erect small shrub with large, glossy, palmately-lobed leaves hardy in the South of England. This pattern, whereby we have in the British flora a single, outlying representative of an important tropical family, occurs in several different groups. Among the non-woody British climbing plants we have two examples, both called bryony, though they are quite unrelated – the white bryony *Bryonia*, our only native member of the cucumber family Cucurbitaceae, and the black bryony *Tamus*, sole representative of the important tropical family Dioscoreaceae to which the edible yams belong. These odd members of important world families of flowering plants serve to open the door a little, as it were, on the rich diversity of tropical floras, reminding us yet again of how poor a truly native flora we have.

Ivy occurs as a wild plant throughout the British Isles, with the exception of parts of the higher Scottish mountains, and can be found throughout Europe except the north and east (Fig. 26). It tolerates deep shade, and is perhaps most obviously at home in open woodland on well-drained but not very

Fig. 26 European distribution of ivy *Hedera helix*. From Hegi 1926

dry soils, where it can carpet the ground and climb individual trees. It spreads freely by rooting from the creeping stems, and it is widely distributed by birds eating the black berries. It flowers on the climbing shoots when they reach the light, and flowering is accompanied by a change in leaf form and habit of growth. The flowering heads, which open in October and November, are terminal on stocky branches bearing simple, not ivy-shaped, leaves which arise all round the erect stems. Gardeners have long known that, if you propagate ivy from the ordinary ivy-leaved, flattened, climbing or scrambling shoots, you will get the expected climbing plant, but if you strike cuttings taken from the flowering branches you get a so-called 'tree ivy', which makes a small, erect bush with simple leaves. Such 'tree ivies' can, in fact, be used as individual shrubs in a shrub border and remain quite stable without reversion to the more familiar 'ivy' form.

This behaviour is an extreme case of a phenomenon for which as yet there is no agreed expert explanation. We expect that a developmentally-induced change in the appearance of a shoot borne on an individual plant will not prove persistent if we propagate from that shoot by vegetative means. But the ivy breaks this rule. So much so, indeed, that many different 'tree ivies' were regularly grown in Victorian times as potted shrubs for their neat 'laurel' appearance and their handsome heads of berries. In his monograph on cultivated ivies, Rose (1980) abandons any special cultivar names for these 'tree ivies', which in Victorian times were generally distinguished by the additional epithet *arborea* or *arborescens*. His discussion of the yellow-berried plant called *chrysocarpa* by Hibberd (*Hedera helix* subsp. *poetarum* according to *Flora Europaea*) makes one wonder why this extraordinary plant is not yet back in favour. Hibberd wrote a marvellous 'gothic' monograph on ivies in 1872. Listen to him singing its praises:

> "*Chrysocarpa*, Yellow-berried ivy (syn. *Baccifera lutea*). – The most beautiful plant in this section, and one of the most valuable hardy evergreen shrubs to grow in pots for plunging in the outdoor winter garden. The growth is dwarf and compact, forming a dense, close, round bush; the leaves are ovate and entire, the colour, a fine, rich, full green; the berries, which are produced in great abundance, are a dull deep orange colour, affording a quite unique and novel feature when the plant is used (as it is at Stoke Newington) with Skimmia japonica, Crataegus pyracantha, Pernettya mucronata, Cotoneaster microphylla, the female form of Aucuba japonica viridis, and the small-leaved Hollies, in the plunging system. The plant figured at page 44 represents one of our best specimens, when covered with berries. It measures two feet across, and is only twenty inches high from the rim of the pot. The clusters of berries on the plant selected numbered forty-two. This is probably the true 'poet's ivy', if the poets lay claim to any one in particular, because it occurs frequently in Italy and Greece."

A final word about ivy. Unlike the lily and the rose, or even the holly, the character of ivy in Christian Europe is not unblemished. From classical times the plant was associated with Bacchus: as Hibberd puts it "we have but to read the Greek dramatists to make abundant acquaintance with the Baccha-

Plate 11 Winter jasmine in flower in Cambridgeshire garden in January. (See p. 97)
Photo Martin Walters.

Above left Plate 12 Chives *Allium schoenoprasum* in flower in June on the Lizard peninsula, Cornwall. (See p. 102). Photo Andrew Gagg.

Above right Plate 13 Borage *Borago officinalis.* (See p. 103). Photo Andrew Gagg.

Left Plate 14 Feverfew *Tanacetum parthenium.* (See p. 103). Photo Andrew Gagg.

Above Plate 15 Arable 'set-aside'
field on chalk, Gog-Magog hills,
Cambridgeshire, with weed flora.
(See p. 109). Photo Martin Walters.

Right Plate 16 Poppies *Papaver
rhoeas* and wild mignonette *Reseda
lutea* in same field. (See p. 109).
Photo Martin Walters.

Plate 17 Oxford ragwort *Senecio squalidus* on waste ground by railway, Cauldon Low, Staffordshire, 1985. (See p. 111). Photo Andrew Gagg.

Plate 18 White campion *Silene latifolia*, a 'weed' promoted into the herbaceous border, with *Delphinium*, *Hemerocallis* and other perennials. (See p. 112). Photo Martin Walters.

Plate 19 Self-sown dog violet *Viola riviniana*, in garden border with *Spiraea*. (See p. 113). Photo Martin Walters.

nalian orgies and the relation of the plant to them." So the association with wine and drunken behaviour is very ancient, and similarly the use of a 'bush' of ivy as the sign of an ale-house, from which comes the proverb 'Good wine needs no bush'. It is, presumably, because of these ancient associations not entirely acceptable to the Christian Church that the custom arose, still remarkably widely observed, that holly could be used for internal decoration but ivy should be kept outside. The ancient carol 'The Holly and the Ivy' makes this distinction well, and draws Christian symbolism from the contrast between, for example, the red berries of holly and the black of ivy. Allied to this ancient suspicion is the age-long argument, still an open question in the minds of most people, about whether ivy damages the trees it grows on directly by 'feeding' on them or only by sheer weight and shading effect. What scientific evidence there is exonerates ivy from all charges of parasitism, but the doubt persists in the public mind.

Winter-flowering shrubs

If one were to choose a single shrub to illustrate the value of Chinese plants in English gardens, it would be difficult to think of a better example than the winter jasmine *Jasminum nudiflorum* (Plate 11). Every winter, during the darkest days, we are guaranteed a cheerful display of bright yellow flowers on the slender, trailing leafless green twigs of this remarkably hardy shrub. As Bean says: "No plant does so much to lighten up in midwinter dull suburban streets of London, and the fact that it will thrive in such places adds much to its worth." Yet this plant was unknown in Britain before 1844, when the plant-collector Robert Fortune brought it from the gardens of Shanghai. Coats (1963) tells us that "like most new introductions it was treated here as a greenhouse plant before being tried in the open ground; but it soon proved its hardiness by surviving a series of hard winters, including that of 1879-80 which culminated in a twelve-day fog in February." Now few well-established English gardens are without it, and most Christmas table decorations contain a sprig of the cheerful yellow flowers.

Although it is perhaps the most spectacular winter-flowering garden shrub, jasmine is of course by no means the only one. The winter-flowering *Viburnum farreri* (*V. fragrans*) (and its hybrid *V.* × *bodnantense*) are almost as familiar. One of the most popular garden shrubs of Northern China, it is very surprising indeed that its effective introduction into English gardens dates from as late as the early years of the present century. A third group of garden shrubs flowering in mid-winter on leafless twigs are the witch-hazels *Hamamelis*. Here the story goes back to 1736 when Collinson introduced the autumn-flowering American plant called *H. virginiana*, but the important, more decorative Far Eastern species, *H. japonica* and *H. mollis*, were Victorian introductions. Nowadays *H. virginiana* survives in our gardens almost only as a stock plant for the choicer Asiatic species grafted on to it.

All these shrubs seem to be entirely hardy in our climate. Why do they combine what seems to us a mutually incompatible pair of qualities: losing their leaves in winter, and mid-winter flowering? It is true that some few of our native shrubs flower on bare twigs in winter or early spring, but nearly all the most familiar examples are wind-pollinated 'catkin-bearing' plants such as hazel (*Corylus*) and alder (*Alnus*), quite different from these showy Far Eastern shrubs with flowers apparently constructed for insect pollination. We

Fig. 27 Blackthorn *Prunus spinosa* in flower in early spring on a sea-cliff in Devon. Photo Martin Walters

do, however, have one common native shrub that regularly opens its showy white flowers on leafless twigs – the blackthorn or sloe *Prunus spinosa* (Fig. 27). Admittedly, the flowering of blackthorn is not in mid-winter, but in March or early April, and we rightly think of it as a harbinger of spring; but biologically what the blackthorn, the winter jasmine and other shrubs are doing is presumably similar. They are utilising early insect-pollinators ahead of the main seasonal rush. Of course we are very familiar with this in the case of the decorative cherries, other members of the genus *Prunus*, again of Far Eastern origin, that we grow for their winter flowering. We might ask, there-fore, are there special ecological circumstances in the Far East that provide more niches for these, to us, winter-flowering shrubs? Perhaps there is a clue in Fortune's own description of how the winter jasmine behaves in its native country. He says: "it is deciduous, the leaves falling off ... early in autumn, and leaving a number of prominent flower-buds which expand in early spring, often when the snow is on the ground, and look like little primroses." What the winter jasmine expects (if we can risk a little teleology) is a regular snow-cover each winter. The English climate does not provide this, so there is no natural suppression of the opening of the flower-buds in winter when we grow it in our gardens. The same effect is visible in the case of many familiar winter-flowering 'bulbs', which we discuss in Chapter 7.

But regular winter snow-cover is a feature of the climate of much of Con-tinental Europe, yet it is from the Far East that our choicest winter-flowering shrubs come. Is there some other factor involved? Probably not: we have already seen that the Far Eastern woody flora is in any case enormously richer and more varied than the European one, and this provision of a few outstanding winter-flowering shrubs is just another reflection of this extraor-dinary richness.

Before we leave the topic, one other familiar woody genus deserves a mention here – the willows (*Salix*). Like the evergreen box, the early-flowering deciduous willow has been used traditionally over much of northern Europe as a 'palm' associated with the Christian festival of Palm Sunday. The flowers of willows are unique, combining 'catkin' qualities (massed inflorescences of small individual flowers) unusually with insect-pollination (Fig. 28). The closely-related poplars *Populus* are indeed wind-pollinated, and show it by having long loose dangling male catkins freely shedding pollen when ripe. Otherwise very respectable reference books make the mistake of calling willows wind-pollinated without qualification; although some pollen may be shed and transferred by the wind, observation of a flowering willow on a mild day in March or April will soon convince any sceptic of the role of early bees and flies as the main pollinators. Each flower, indeed, is supplied with a nectary, a structure that is entirely absent from the wholly wind-pollinated flowers of poplars. The genus *Salix* is, incidentally, unique amongst our woody plants in another way: there seem to be very few genetic barriers to hybridisation between the species, which range from tall trees to very dwarf mountain shrubs, and many willows both in gardens and in the countryside are of hybrid origin.

Berries and their biological significance

Why do we associate berries with shrubs? At one level we can answer quite simply: because they are most conspicuous and decorative on shrubby plants, and the attractive appearance of hedgerow and garden alike in autumn is due in no small measure to the colour of the fruits. There is, however, more to it than that. If we take our native flora, and analyse the different life-forms according to their type of fruit, we soon find that the vast majority of plants with succulent fruits (some, but not all, of which we would call 'berries') are shrubs or small trees. Indeed the British flora contains one large family with many woody representatives, the Rosaceae, which supplies many of our most familiar edible fruits, from strawberries to plums and apples. The main forest trees do not have succulent fruits, nor do the vast majority of herbs, and this correlation is as evident in our gardens as it is in the wild.

The reason seems to be that the shrub is the ideal plant for bird dispersal. It can offer conspicuously in the autumn a large number of small, hard-seeded, succulent fruits at a time when wild birds are actively seeking food. In the nature reserve of Wicken Fen, for example, the phenomenal spread of the very local shrub alder buckthorn *Frangula alnus* at the end of the last century was largely brought about by two factors: the decline of the traditional patterns of harvesting fen crops (reed, sedge and peat), and the extremely efficient dispersal of the small berries of *Frangula* by visiting flocks of birds such as fieldfare and redwing (*Turdus* species) in the onset of winter (Fig. 29). Nor is it the case that scrub and hedgerow 'berries' are only borne by woody plants: both bryonies for example, *Bryonia* and *Tamus*, are herbaceous climbers benefiting from the support of shrubs (and, of course, fences and other artefacts) to offer their berries to the birds. Although we have in Europe no role for wild birds as pollinators, they have an extremely important relationship to our native plants as dispersal agents.

The attitude of the average gardener to the natural role of birds as dispersal agents tends to be somewhat equivocal. Do we forgive the blackbirds for

Fig. 28 Male and female catkins and twigs of sallow *Salix caprea*. From Hickey &
King, 1988

Fig. 29 Edge of scrub cover, largely of alder buckthorn *Frangula alnus*, Wicken Fen, August 1977. Photo Martin Walters

stripping our sweet cherry of all its fruit before it has a chance to ripen properly? Do we mind very much if, as sometimes happens in an early hard winter, the birds take most of our berried holly before Christmas? Of course, it is different for those involved in commercial fruit-growing, and the depredations of the bullfinch *Pyrrhula pyrrhula* on the flower-buds of fruit orchards is an important topic outside the scope of this book. (There is much interesting information on this and other examples in Murton's book in this series entitled *Man and Birds* (1971).) What most gardeners hope to achieve, to some extent by trial and error, is a reasonable balance whereby they tolerate some natural bird activity while tending to grow some decorative shrubs whose fruit has proved to be relatively unpalatable to birds. Some of the familiar Rosaceae seem to be in this category – species of *Sorbus* and *Cotoneaster* for example – and certain exotics, like the white-fruited snowberry (*Symphoricarpus*) from North America, lack any attraction for birds.

One final point: what is a berry? To the man in the street, and to the gardener, it is any small succulent fruit containing seeds ... and it is, of course, in this sense that we have been using the term. The botanist, however, faced with the necessity of classifying fruits on the basis of their structure, has made a narrower, stricter definition. Unfortunately, under that definition, many common fruits we call 'berries' are excluded. This explains why, for example, Floras do not use the term 'berry' for either *Frangula* or *Cotoneaster*. The difficulty is just like the use of 'flower' that we discussed in Chapter 3: it does not matter, provided we remember the context – the company – in which we are using the term.

7

Herbs, 'Flowers' and 'Grasses'

Herbs and the herb garden

Botanically speaking, all non-woody plants are herbs, and this is how the word is used in Floras. The adjective 'herbaceous' then simply means 'non-woody', and 'herbaceous' is used in this sense by gardener and botanist alike. But gardeners, like the general public, tend to use 'herb' only in the traditional sense of a plant that has culinary, medicinal or other domestic importance, with the result that a certain number of woody plants are classified as herbs. Good examples are sage *Salvia officinalis* and rosemary *Rosmarinus officinalis*. The specific epithet *officinalis* tells us that these are anciently-cultivated plants available to man as a source of flavouring, scent or medicine, and many familiar 'herbs' were so designated by Linnaeus. (Even trees can be 'herbs' in this sense – for example, the New World tree *Guaiacum officinale*, source of the heaviest of all commercial timbers, and yielding a medicinal resin).

Given the early history of botany as a European activity, it is not surprising to find that most of our culinary and medicinal herbs are wild European plants, very many from the Mediterranean area. Sage, rosemary and many other examples come readily to mind and, because of their Mediterranean origin, we need to grow them in rather sheltered conditions if we are not to lose the plants over winter. Moreover, these purely Mediterranean 'herbs' have quite failed to find a permanent place in the British flora, in spite of centuries of cultivation in Britain. This absence emphasises a general point about garden plants: for every one successful 'garden escape', like *Rhododendron ponticum*, there are dozens of familiar half-hardy garden plants which never become wild. Hardiness of the adult plant, however we measure it, is only one of a large number of qualities that may determine whether a garden plant escapes and becomes naturalised.

In addition to these classical Mediterranean herbs we have, of course, our own indigenous products. Sometimes, as in the case of marjoram *Origanum*, the really hardy plant native in Britain, *O. vulgare*, is a different species from the tenderer, choicer sweet marjoram of the Mediterranean, which is *O. majorana*. In other cases the whole genus may be more at home in Europe north of the Alps than in the Mediterranean area. A good example is mint, the genus *Mentha*: the British love for mint sauce with roast lamb may reflect the indigenous origin of some at least of our garden mints, though the exact hybrid origin of culinary mints is a complex story we can only partly elucidate. There is an excellent account of garden mints in the Wisley Handbook entitled *Culinary Herbs* (Page & Stearn, ed.2 1985).

Have we, indeed, any straightforward cases of an undoubtedly native British plant commonly grown in our herb gardens? One of the very few is chives *Allium schoenoprasum* (Plate 12), which can be found growing, usually in rocky limestone pastures, in a number of places mainly in the west of Britain. The native plant differs very little from the cultivated chives we commonly grow. A much commoner situation is that where we have admitted to the British flora a herb which is almost certainly not originally native in Britain but whose exact history we cannot now expect to trace – such as the beautiful bright blue annual borage *Borago officinalis*, for which Gerard (1597) makes extravagant claims: "used everywhere for the comfort of the hart, for the driving away of sorrowe, and increasing the joie of the mind" (Plate 13). Until recently, when whole fields of borage have appeared as a commercial crop, I had never seen a borage plant outside a garden anywhere in Britain, and I have a sneaking suspicion that we 'bend the rules' a little to let in to our Floras such a beautiful and historically interesting plant.

Chives and borage, then, illustrate two extreme cases of British plants that are familiar herbs. Most cases fall somewhere between the two extremes of certain natives and certain introductions. One of the most familiar of traditional medicinal plants, feverfew *Tanacetum parthenium* (Plate 14), is a good example. *Flora of the British Isles* (Clapham et al. 1987) tells us that feverfew is "probably introduced" into the British Isles, and is "a frequent plant of walls, waste places, waysides throughout Great Britain" and "formerly cultivated as a medicinal herb". Further, the *Flora* states that it is "probably native in S. E. Europe, Asia Minor and the Caucasus, but now established throughout Europe and in North and South America". Incidentally, there is a revived interest in feverfew as a medicinal herb, and its use to alleviate the pain of migraine and arthritis seems to be accepted increasingly as a real phenomenon by the medical profession – so much so that the biochemical composition of different feverfew stocks is under active study at several medical research centres, including the Chelsea Department of Pharmacy on material specially grown at the Chelsea Physic Garden (Heptinstall 1988).

As we saw in Chapter 1, our only direct evidence for the native status of plants comes from the identification of what are called sub-fossil remains, usually pollen-grains, seeds or fragments of leaves. Unfortunately such evidence is not available in many cases for herbaceous plants, depending as it does on both the chance preservation and the unequivocal identification of the preserved part. At least we now have for the British flora an excellent compilation of all the evidence in Godwin's book (ed.2 1975), so that we can assess what evidence there is. Neither feverfew nor borage appear in this sub-fossil plant record. A more 'border-line' case, however, on which Godwin reports, is vervain *Verbena officinalis*. This medicinal plant of roadsides and waste places, mainly in Southern England, is accorded unquestioned native status in modern British Floras, yet, according to Godwin, although three separate finds of its fruits are recorded from an interglacial period in Britain, the only post-glacial record is from a Roman site. How do we assess such evidence? Perhaps vervain is a plant like *Rhododendron ponticum* that was here before the last Ice Age, but eliminated by the ice and eventually re-introduced by man. Can we ever hope to know what actually happened? We must be content with partial knowledge: in science, as in ordinary life, half a loaf is better than no bread.

Herbaceous perennials

It is a great pity that we have in English no simple word to describe the life-form of ordinary, more or less herbaceous, perennial plants. In German botanical and horticultural works such plants are often called 'Stauden'. They are the 'hardy plants' of our gardens, familiar in the herbaceous border. A glance at a British Flora would soon confirm that the vast majority of our wild plants also fall into this category, and indeed many familiar genera contain numerous species of both botanical and horticultural interest (not necessarily the same species, of course). Good examples of such hardy plant favourites are *Geranium* and *Veronica*, and we can illustrate some general themes connecting the wild with the garden flora by using these familiar cases.

The speedwells *Veronica* illustrate admirably an important point about the classification of plants, namely that species are usually defined on a whole range of differences including leaf shape, hairiness and other so-called 'vegetative' characters, whilst the genera tend to be defined on a basic similarity of flower and fruit structure only. This means that it is quite easy to answer the question "is this plant a *Veronica*?" given a single complete flower, because the floral structure is precise (Fig. 30). This works without much difficulty for all native British speedwells, though with some small annual species a complete flower may not be too easy to find because the tiny corolla drops off early. In gardens, however, there is an interesting complication. 'Speedwell-type' flowers can be found on some garden shrubs – the closely-allied genus *Hebe*, which is native in the Southern Hemisphere. Most of our garden hebes come from New Zealand, and several species and hybrids are now sufficiently naturalised in Ireland, South Wales and Southern England to be included in modern British Floras.

Speedwell in fact illustrates beautifully the two-way process of exchange between wild and garden. Initially, if we go back to mediaeval times, common speedwells such as *V. officinalis* and *V. chamaedrys* were no doubt brought in from the wild and used as garden plants. The handsome spiked speedwell *V. spicata*, so rare in Britain, was very familiar on the European Continent, and was known early in cultivation. The herbaceous beds in modern gardens are more likely nowadays to contain the taller, allied, European *Veronica longifolia* (or plants that are probably hybrids of this species) than *V. spicata* itself, thereby illustrating a

Fig. 30 Speedwell *Veronica persica*. Whole plant and close-up of flower. From Hickey & King 1988

general pattern, that an original native is often ousted in the history of gardening by a related more handsome foreigner.

One recent success story amongst the speedwells that outshines all others is the delicate, trailing slender speedwell *Veronica filiformis* from the mountains of Turkey and the Caucasus, which was originally introduced into Europe as a new plant for rock gardens (Plate 37). It proved to be remarkably adapted to the European countryside, and spread rapidly in grazed pastures and garden lawns. In Britain it was first recorded outside gardens in 1927; sixty years later it is now one of the commonest speedwells both inside and outside gardens over a good deal of England, especially the South.

This charming plant, which often produces pale blue 'pools' of colour on our lawns in late April, has succeeded in spreading in spite of the fact that it very rarely sets any seed. As most gardeners know, any small piece of its trailing stem will easily root and grow away, on bare ground as in closed, mown turf, to produce a healthy patch. The inability to set seed seems to be due to the fact that the species is strictly self-incompatible: that is, two genetically different clones must be involved in cross-pollination before seed can be set. Many plants are self-incompatible, but the effect is rarely so absolute as is apparently the case with *Veronica filiformis*.

Another reason why the slender speedwell does so well is that, like other members of the genus, it is relatively resistant to common kinds of selective herbicides. Those who are misguided enough to feel it necessary to try to eliminate all plants other than fine-leaved grasses from their lawns by using chemical methods will probably already know this. Add to this resistance to herbicides its extraordinary facility to root from any small piece, and its spread from one suburban lawn to another, via human boots or borrowed lawn-mowers, is very easy to explain.

Actually, our story of successful alien speedwells is not fully told, though the remaining case, an annual weed, is strictly out of place here. The early nineteenth century had seen the arrival in Britain (the date of the first record is 1825) of the annual that the British *Flora* actually now calls common speedwell – *Veronica persica* (Fig. 30). This pretty, trailing weed, whose relatively large bright blue flowers can be found at almost any season of the year, is now in cultivated ground throughout the whole of the British Isles. As its name suggests, its native home is South-west Asia, but not in the mountains like its perennial cousin. Every British gardener must know it as a persistent annual weed, along with our native chickweed *Stellaria media* and groundsel *Senecio vulgaris*.

On a world scale, *Veronica* is a large genus with about 300 species, mostly in the North temperate regions. The cranesbills *Geranium*, with a rather similar world distribution, are somewhat more numerous, at about 400 species, and in this case we are very fortunate in having an up-to-date account (1985) by an acknowledged international expert, Dr Peter Yeo, who is taxonomist in the University Botanic Garden at Cambridge. The pattern of this familiar genus is quite similar to *Veronica*: our native British species are herbaceous and contain both perennials and annual 'weeds', and familiar wild species like herb robert *G. robertianum* and the meadow cranesbill *G. pratense* must have been in cultivation for centuries. Indeed, herb robert has one of the longest recorded histories of any cranesbill because of its medicinal use. As a wild plant, herb robert is found throughout the British Isles. It is best described as an 'over-wintering annual' (see p. 109), though individual plants seem to be able to persist for several seasons in cultivation. Yeo describes it as "essentially a species for the wild garden". A neat, dwarf, rather compact white-flowered variant, often called '*celticum*' in gardens but best called 'Celtic White', seems to be an albino lacking the reddish-brown pigment that suffuses the whole of an ordinary herb robert plant.

Interest in cranesbills has undoubtedly been greatly stimulated by Peter Yeo's book, and many nurserymen now stock a range of species to cater for the growing demand. It seems an admirable example of how a professional botanist who is also a keen gardener can bring his expert knowledge before a much wider public. We need more of such studies of familiar genera that bridge the gap between wild and garden plants.

We can hardly omit from any discussion of *Geranium* the group of exotic garden plants that most people understand by this name. To the botanist these showy 'garden geraniums' all belong to a different genus, *Pelargonium*, within the family Geraniaceae. So the gardeners' 'Geranium' is the botanists' *Pelargonium*! This is not mere perversity: there is an interesting historical reason behind the confusion, which is clearly explained in detail by Yeo in the first chapter of his book. Broadly what happened was that Linnaeus in the eighteenth century did not accept that these showy plants of South African origin, the earliest of which were called '*Geranium africanum*' (Fig. 31), were sufficiently different from our wild European cranesbills to merit separation as a distinct genus. As Yeo says: "in view of Linnaeus' reputation and the importance of his publications" it is not surprising that gardeners continued to call them geraniums. By the end of the eighteenth century, however, botanists generally were following the French school and using the name *Pelargonium*, but gardeners, who often do not much care for 'new-fangled scientific names' anyway, remained traditional, and the more popular kinds of *Pelargonium* are still known as geraniums.

Most perennial herbs in the British flora have a tufted or creeping habit with the over-wintering buds at ground level and, as we discussed in Chapter 3, they usually spread quite freely by vegetative growth. Gardeners grow such plants in the traditional herbaceous border and propagate many of them exclusively by dividing up the rootstock and re-planting portions during the winter. Many hardy plants of our gardens are indeed sterile, and can only be propagated vegetatively if their particular genetic constitution is to be perpetuated. Although we are familiar with this in gardens, it may come as a surprise to learn that many truly wild plants also reproduce largely if not entirely by vegetative means. Sometimes we can easily see that wild populations are behaving in this way. For example, the common spring-flowering woodland herb dog's mercury *Mercurialis perennis* usually occurs in quite large patches, within which all the individual shoots are either male or female (they can easily be told apart in flower or fruit). Within any one patch, conveniently defined by its sex, we can reasonably infer that all the individuals present originated by vegetative spread from a single original plant. This is called clonal reproduction, and the individual plants are ramets of a single, genetically uniform clone. In extreme cases, as with the slender speedwell already mentioned, seed reproduction hardly ever takes place. We do not know how old many wild or garden clones of various species may be, but there are good grounds to believe that they can be centuries old. They may, indeed, be older than the individual trees that tower above them. In the

Geranium. Africanum, arborescens Ribes folio, angulofo, floribus amplis purpureis.

Fig. 31 '*Geranium africanum*', an early *Pelargonium*, depicted by John Martyn in 1728. From Walters 1981

Cambridge Botanic Garden, where we know in some detail the history of planting, no mature tree, not even the fine cedar of Lebanon standing in the middle, can be more than 150 years old, but some clumps of perennial herbs growing in the order beds, and brought directly from the small eighteenth century garden when the new Garden was laid out in 1846, could be the original clones and therefore much older than the cedar. An example of this is a stand of orris root *Iris florentina*, a famous mediaeval herb recorded as growing in the old Garden and transplanted to the new one.

This raises the further question of senility in the plant kingdom. Individual oak trees, on the one hand, and groundsel plants on the other, age, bear seeds and eventually die. But does the daisy on the lawn or, for that matter, the grasses of which the lawn is made up, ever die of old age? We have no evidence that they do. Perhaps we should look at senility, death and reproduction via a fertilised egg as only one way of securing the continuity of life, which is potentially immortal – a fact that is much more obvious amongst plants than it is in the animal kingdom.

Annuals and biennials

Plants that do not survive more than one season except in the form of seed are known to botanists and gardeners alike as annuals, and are common in both the native and the cultivated flora. By far the most familiar group of annuals, indeed, makes a special link between the two worlds: these are the common weeds such as groundsel *Senecio vulgaris*, and shepherd's purse *Capsella bursa-pastoris*, some of which may easily run through more than one generation in an average year and therefore might more strictly be called ephemeral than annual. The short life-cycle of such plants is obviously an adaptation to growing in temporary open habitats, where their quick germination, flowering and setting seed enable them to succeed. Since neolithic man first introduced the agricultural practice of sowing cereal and other crops on tilled ground, annual plants have greatly benefited, and specialised weeds have evolved to suit farming methods. In modern times, of course, the farmers' war against weeds of arable land in particular has been greatly intensified, and some conspicuous, even beautiful, weeds have become quite rare in the British countryside.

Weeds can only be defined as plants growing in the wrong place, and this definition implies that there must always be a human being to decide what is the wrong place. Any plant can under this definition be declared a weed, though of course we restrict the definition in practice by using suitable qualifying words or phrases like 'arable weeds' or 'weeds of tree nursery plantations'. Any detailed consideration of the complex relationship between Man and the weed flora is obviously outside the scope of this book, but there are a few aspects of such general interest that we must examine them.

The first concerns the relationship between the annual life-form and the general systematic classification of plants. It is evident that only seed plants can be strictly annual under our definition; but all Gymnosperms are woody plants, so that annuals are confined to the Angiosperms, where we find that there are examples in most of the familiar large families of Dicotyledons and Monocotyledons alike. Indeed, in many herbaceous genera, such as *Geranium* and *Veronica* that we have already discussed, both annual and perennial species occur, and the distinction is normally (though not always, as we shall see) reasonably clear-cut. Further, we have reason to think that annuals are, in general, descended from related perennial species that are usually much larger individual plants with larger, more showy flowers. Reduction in size and quick, efficient seed production often look like recent adaptations to unstable open habitats, and we might ask where such habitats occur in nature. There are two very obvious places: the sea-shore, where the sea itself is the cause of instability, and mountains, where extremes of temperature and wind velocity may produce unstable scree and rock communities. In between the sea-coast and the mountains naturally open habitats are very limited in extent and largely confined to river gravels affected by sporadic floods. These are the places from which we might expect our annual weed flora to have been recruited in the early days of agriculture, and it is certainly the case that a good many coastal plants are also weeds. The mountain flora, however, contains remarkably few annual plants (the beautiful alpine gentian *Gentiana nivalis* is one of the rare examples in our flora) and none of these behave like weeds. As we saw in Chapter 1, not very long ago all of the land we now call Britain was emerging from ice, and plenty of open ground was becoming available. But on the whole, annual weedy species did not colonise it: rather the success stories were dwarf shrubs and perennial herbs, rapidly succeeded by forest trees, against which small annual species could not compete.

If our weed flora came only in small part from open native habitats, especially the coastal ones, where then did most of it come from? All lines of evidence point to the fact that many annual weeds came from further south in Europe, brought, no doubt unwittingly, by early Man and primitive agriculture. Indeed, some of our best-known wild flowers are annual weeds – if we can stand back and look at them with a cold, scientific eye. Poppies, *Papaver*, are the most striking example (Plates 15 & 16). Bright red is not a 'natural' colour for a northern flower: it is much more characteristic of Mediterranean climates where there is a rich ephemeral flora associated with seasonal rain. In other words, familiar weeds such as poppies are originally adapted, not to survive through a hard, cold winter, but rather the opposite, a long, hot, dry summer. This introduces us to the idea of the 'winter annual', a short-lived plant whose seeds germinate in the autumn or winter to produce seedlings which survive to flower and set seed early in the following spring, dying as the summer begins.

It may come as a surprise to many readers to learn that the British flora does contain some true winter annuals. They can be found easily in that remarkable country called Breckland in East Anglia, where there are still quite large areas of open, sandy soil in a region which has the lowest annual rainfall in the British Isles (of the order of 550 mm). These tiny plants are a special study of their own, and a patch of Breckland heath in early spring can produce up to a dozen of them, very diverse in systematic relationship but similar in life form. Here is a short list of eight, with the families to which they belong:

Aira praecox	Gramineae
Aphanes microcarpa	Rosaceae
Cerastium semidecandum	Caryophyllaceae
Crassula tillaea	Crassulaceae
Myosotis ramosissima	Boraginaceae
Teesdalia nudicaulis	Cruciferae
Veronica verna	Scrophulariaceae
Vicia lathyroides	Leguminosae

Fig. 32 Breckland scene: the home of winter annuals. Photo P. D. Sell

The tiny *Crassula*, incidentally, makes a good claim to be the smallest land flowering plant in Britain. The bright red patches on paths and cart-tracks in the sandy Breckland in spring betray its presence: it then needs very careful inspection with a strong hand-lens to convince oneself that it *is* a diminutive stonecrop, not a moss (Fig. 32).

The familiar ephemeral weeds, as also these small winter annuals, are never able to grow again for a second season, and must rely entirely on seed to persist. Many plants, however, can perennate or not, according to the conditions, and the distinction between annual and perennial plants, though useful, is by no means always clear. Of course, gardeners know this, because the half-hardy 'annuals' they regularly grow as summer bedding plants are often in full and vigorous growth when they are dug up in the autumn to be replaced by spring bedding. Bedding dahlias and petunias are very good examples. We know that the first heavy frosts will spoil the show of flowers, and that the plants themselves will soon be dead in all but the very mildest of English winters. The original *Dahlia* and *Petunia* species come from South America, and are perennial in their native home in sub-tropical or at least very largely frost-free climates. So the same plant can easily be annual or perennial according to where you grow it.

A very familiar example of this is the Oxford ragwort *Senecio squalidus*, described by Linnaeus in the eighteenth century from plants he grew from seed obtained from plants growing on old walls in and around the Oxford Botanic Garden. Linnaeus describes this species accurately enough as he grew it in the Botanic Garden in Uppsala, in Central Sweden, and says it is annual, without qualification. The hard Swedish winters were too much for it! Nineteenth-century British botanists generally followed Linnaeus' description, though J.D.Hooker in his *Student's Flora* (1870) is moving in the right direction when he writes 'annual or biennial'. Hooker and other contemporary writers had some excuse, for the Oxford ragwort remained a rather rare plant "naturalised on old walls, etc., Oxford, Bideford, Warwick, Cork", as Hooker says. Since the Second World War, however, the plant has spread very rapidly, and there are probably now no English towns where it is not a reasonably common weed. Since it is likely to be in flower on and off throughout most of the year it is often a very conspicuous plant of waste ground, especially railway sidings (Plate 17), and we really have no excuse to continue to call it annual as most books still do. The British *Flora* still says "an annual herb, rarely biennial or perennial", and we have to turn to *Flora Europaea* to find the order of these descriptions reversed, as they should be, to read "short-lived perennial, biennial or annual". Another example of the authority of early writers persisting in an unquestioned manner right to the present day!

It might be expected that the term 'biennial' – a plant lasting only two years – would be subject to the same kind of difficulty in application. However, when we look at some familiar culinary biennials like carrot *Daucus* and parsnip *Pastinaca*, we find that there is a clear cycle of development. In the first year the seedling plants make vegetative growth and lay down in their swollen tap-roots a food store which persists in the ground and is available to the plant to draw on to flower, fruit and die in the following season. Of course, we treat these as annual crops in the vegetable garden, and harvest the roots; but we know that only plants left in the ground over winter will flower next season. Many wild members of the carrot family Umbelliferae, including wild ancestors of carrot and parsnip, are more or less strict biennials. To distinguish between these strict biennials, which die after flowering in their second year, and other plants which are relatively short-lived but not strictly biennials, we can use the term 'monocarpic biennial', meaning one which sets only one crop of seed, in its second year. Other 'biennials', such as wallflowers *Cheiranthus*, sown in early summer, planted out in the autumn, and flowering in spring, are not monocarpic, as old wallflower plants growing wild on walls and flowering year after year will testify. The wallflower, in fact, is a short-lived perennial, with essentially the same life-form as the Oxford ragwort: and old walls in many of our towns can often boast displays of both plants in showy flower in spring.

Wild flowers and weeds

Gardeners make a distinction between wild flowers which they do not cultivate, and garden flowers which they do. This is on the whole a very workable distinction but, since the ancestors of all our garden plants must have been wild at some time, it cannot be pressed too far. As we have seen already, the distinction between a wild and a garden flower becomes clearer with the passage of time as more and more attractive plants of exotic origin are brought into cultivation, and more and more different hybrids and cultivars derived from wild ancestors come into being. The obvious contrast between the wild flower and its improved garden derivatives seen in many familiar genera leads to a tendency among gardeners to refer to 'species' (and even to employ a spurious singular form 'specie'!) when they want to distinguish unimproved wild plants grown in gardens. Some 'geranium' growers, for example, specialise in wild-type *Pelargonium* species, amongst which are the ancestors of our modern *Pelargonium* cultivars.

Occasionally we find a wild flower jumping the fence, as it were, and being promoted to a place in the herbaceous border in its unimproved state. The familiar red and white campions *Silene dioica* and *S. pratensis* provide interesting examples. Over a good deal of lowland Britain the white campion occurs quite commonly, as a weed of waste and cultivated ground, on disturbed roadsides and in similar places. It is rarely specially grown, though it makes a very attractive herbaceous border plant if allowed to take its place (Plate 18). Not least among its attractions is that the large white flowers open in the evening and are sweetly scented to attract pollinating moths. Gardening books make little or no reference to it, although it must have been in cultivation in former times, as there are references to a double form (a plant I have never seen). I suspect that one reason why the white campion has never really been accepted is that it is uncomfortably uncertain whether to be perennial or not, and for their herbaceous borders gardeners like dependable perennials that can be propagated by division of the rootstock. No such doubt, however, attaches to the closely-related red campion, a very familiar wild flower of hedgerows and wood-margins in late spring. Why is this attractive flower also neglected in our gardens? It is, as I can testify, as easy to grow as any garden plant, and positively prefers those rather damp, shady corners not easily filled with 'flowers'. Moreover, it is very variable in the wild, and attractive variants with condensed heads of large deep red flowers could easily be selected from wild stocks. Is it possible that familiarity has bred contempt yet again, and that gardeners take it for granted *outside* the garden but discourage or at best ignore it inside? Even that is not the end of the story, because pink-flowered 'hybrid swarm' populations not infrequently occur in the wild where red and white campions grow close together, and these can be quite spectacular. Indeed, I suspect that any proud possessor of woodland in a red campion area can almost produce these hybrid swarms to order by felling a strip of woodland or scrub against field margins where the white campion grows, and waiting a year or two for nature to perform the hybrid trick. Curiously, in spite of all this wealth of variation, until recently almost the only garden red campion ever available was an interesting old double variety, certainly worth growing as a curiosity, but not so attractive as the wild single type. Here is an opportunity for garden selection and 'improvement' of a common wild flower.

A second example where the gardener's distinction between wild flowers, garden plants and weeds is marvellously blurred is the ground elder *Aegopodium podagraria*, a notorious perennial weed for both flower beds and vegetable plots. In recent years a variegated form of this plant has come into gardens, and is even achieving some popularity among the growing company of enthusiasts for variegated and other coloured foliage plants. Actually, as I have proved, the wild type ground elder, which produces quite a hand-some white head of flowers, can be quite effective if cultivated in a semi-shady border, and a surprising number of visitors admire it and ask what this white flower is. An extreme example of the problem of defining a weed!

One group of popular garden plants that has its origin from very familiar wild flowers and weeds includes the pansies and violas in the genus *Viola*. Unlike the sweet violet *Viola odorata* and its many cultivars, which has ob-viously had a long and complex history of cultivation in Western Europe since classical times, our garden pansies and violas are of surprisingly recent origin. Moreover, we in Britain have played much the most important part in their development – and that in spite of the fact that we adopted the French name 'pensée' rather than the English name 'heart's-ease' for a wild flower familiar to us all. The most important ancestors of our garden sweet violets on the one hand, and pansies (including violas) on the other, are in fact two very different native species of *Viola: V. odorata* and *V. tricolor*, which conveniently represent the two main groups into which the genus *Viola* is naturally divided: Section *Nominium* and Section *Melanium*. The obvious dif-ference in the flower is one of several ways in which the two sections differ: another, that can easily be seen by comparing a wild or garden pansy with a violet plant, is the cut or lobed stipules of the former (Fig. 33), and a third difference is that cleistogamous flowers (pollinated in the bud) are never pro-duced in Sect. *Melanium*, but are characteristic of Sect. *Nominium*. No hybrid has ever been made across this Sectional boundary, but hybrids are very fre-quent within each Section. A final point worth noting is that our commonest wild violet by far, occurring in different forms from lowland English woods to the tops of Scottish mountains, *Viola riviniana*, rarely gets any mention in hor-ticultural works, lacking as it does the fragrance of the sweet violet and the extraordinary bright colours of the pansies and violas (Plate 19).

The story of pansies and violas is worth telling in outline, partly because it is unusually complete and well documented. Although Parkinson, in his fa-mous book that makes a good claim to be the first English horticultural work,

Fig. 33 Pansy *Viola arvensis* (left) and violet *V. reichenbachiana* (right): flower and stipule. Drawn by M. Hickey

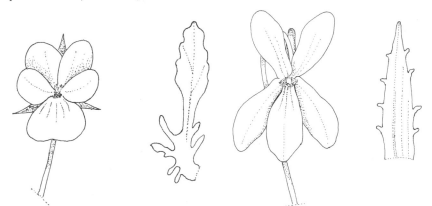

published in 1629, refers to both the ordinary wild pansy *Viola tricolor* and the 'great yellow pansie' – which must be the mountain pansy *V. lutea* – as being in cultivation in English gardens, there is good evidence that, for the next 150 years, little or no 'improvement' took place. We have to wait till the early years of the nineteenth century for pioneers, especially Lord Gambier's gardener, Thomson, on his estate in Iver, Buckinghamshire, to begin the large-scale growing and selection of many different variants of the wild *V. tricolor*. This and similar work brought a fashionable explosion of pansy-growing throughout the country. Charles Darwin, who was very interested in the role of domestication in producing new variation in both plants and animals, tells us that by 1835 there were already more than 400 named varieties of pansies on sale in England. These English 'Show Pansies' were used as a basis for the so-called 'Fancy Pansies' largely raised in France and Holland, which returned to Britain, particularly Scotland and the North of England, in the 1850s and 1860s.

Like the ancestral weed *Viola tricolor*, these garden pansies were, and indeed still are, essentially annuals or short-lived perennials, propagated readily from seed. It is true that the perennial mountain pansy *V. lutea*, which is closely related, was almost certainly involved from an early stage, but the big advance in incorporating hardy, tufted perennial stock came from the gradual introduction of other, non-British species into the breeding programmes. James Grieve, a Scottish nurseryman whose name is perpetuated in an apple variety, was one of the pioneers who used other wild *Viola* species such as *V. altaica* and *V. cornuta* in addition to the native Scottish *V. lutea* in breeding programmes. Presumably because other *Viola* species entered into their ancestry, these new, hardy, 'tufted pansies' became known as 'violas', and the distinction persists to the present day, thereby providing another case where the gardeners' use of a Latin name in a rather different sense from the botanical one can only be explained if the history is known.

Undoubtedly, some of the impetus in using *V. cornuta* as a parent came from the hope that it would impart into its progeny something of its sweet scent, a character unique to this species within the whole Section *Melanium*. In the event, scented flowers seem to be restricted to the group of cultivars called 'violettas', whose precise origin is very accurately recorded for us by the originator Dr Charles Stuart (see Cuthbertson, 1922). By the time the violetta had been accepted as a new race of violas in 1894, the perfume of the flowers was written into the rules pertaining to these new 'show' plants. It is a pity that these charming, hardy plants are not more widely grown: Crane, clearly an enthusiast, wrote (1951): "a few blossoms arranged in tiny vases are pleasing to look upon and their fragrance pervades the room."

Geophytes

In introducing the life-form classification of Raunkiaer, I said that the technical terms were rather cumbersome, and implied that we could largely do without them, using 'tree', 'shrub', 'herbaceous perennial' and 'annual' to cover roughly the same meanings. One term, however, we cannot ignore, for there is really no convenient equivalent term in English (or for that matter in German) – the term geophyte. A geophyte is a special kind of perennial herb, one in which the organ of perennation (through a cold winter or a hot summer) is a structure buried in the ground. In many cases this structure is a bulb, as in hyacinths and tulips, but in other cases it may be a bulb-like corm, as in crocus, a rhizome, as in some irises, or a tuber, as in dahlias or oxalis. Technically all these structures differ, but biologically speaking they all perform a similar function. They are swollen underground parts containing stored food, from which new growth can begin after a resting period.

One of the interesting generalisations that the life-form classification enables us to make concerns the proportion of different life-forms in different wild floras. Some results, such as the complete absence of trees from arctic and mountain floras, are rather obvious: but the one concerning geophytes is perhaps much less/expected. Because 'bulbs' are so familiar to us amongst common garden plants, we may not realise that geophytes constitute only a very small percentage of our wild British flora. Indeed, we have surprisingly few bulbous plants as really common native species. One springs to mind immediately – the English bluebell *Hyacinthoides non-scripta* – but there are not many others. Most of the familiar garden 'bulb' genera such as *Crocus* and *Tulipa* only scrape into the British Flora because single species are naturalised as early garden introductions. In fact the geophyte is really at home in warmer, drier climates than our own, as rock garden enthusiasts know. Many of them are adapted to grow and flower during a rainy season and to wither above ground during a hot, dry summer. The English bluebell shows something of this tendency, for its splendid show of flowers in late spring is succeeded by dead fruiting stalks in the height of summer. One might expect that the geophytic life form would be well adapted to really cold climates, for the storage organ could be protected in the ground, but this is emphatically not the case. Arctic and really high mountain floras are almost exclusively composed of dwarf shrubs and ordinary perennial herbs, and geophytes (like annuals) are practically absent. The reason seems to be that in arctic soils there is a 'permafrost' layer not far below the surface which never thaws, so that winter buds must be at or near ground level to enable quick growth during the short arctic summer.

The British flora, in fact, contains just one arctic-alpine geophyte which could be said to be "the exception that proves the rule" ... the famous Snowdon lily *Lloydia serotina*, called after its discoverer, the seventeenth-century Welsh naturalist, Edward Lhuyd (Lloyd). This delicate bulbous plant with white, purplish-veined, usually solitary flowers grows only on a few mountain rock-ledges in Snowdonia in the whole of the British Isles. We really have no idea why other British mountains should be scorned by *Lloydia*, especially as it occurs in Arctic Russia and much of Siberia, the Urals, Caucasus, and some of the main European mountain-ranges in the Old World, and from Alaska to the mountains of New Mexico in the New World. Nor do we know how *Lloydia* manages to be so successful over such a wide range in mountain and arctic territory where few or no other bulbous plants succeed.

Sensibly, gardeners tend to use 'bulbs' or 'bulbous plant' to cover all geophytes that they cultivate, especially if they are monocotyledons. In their excellent, richly-illustrated standard work on the bulbous plants of Europe and their allies, the Kew botanists Christopher Grey-Wilson and Brian Mathew (1981) decided to restrict themselves to the monocotyledons, but perhaps rather oddly then included all the aquatic and marsh plants with petaloid (coloured) flowers. Since frog-bit, water-plantain and the like only occupy six out of more than 250 pages of text they can perhaps be forgiven.

Why, in view of what we have said about arctic-alpine floras being so poor in geophytes, do we find the richest 'bulb' floras in the main European mountain ranges from the Pyrenees to the Balkans? The answer lies in the detailed structure of mountain vegetation. The rich alpine meadows traditionally used for hay and pasture are not natural communities, any more than our traditional meadows and pastures are. If human beings had not cleared by felling, burning and grazing much of the mountain slopes, the alps – a term meaning mountain *grassland* – would not exist as we know them. In their place would be a dense, largely coniferous forest with none of the rich beauty of flowering that the alps provide. Indeed, once grazing and cutting ceases in the European mountains, the forest returns with remarkable speed, as we now know from the history of strict mountain reserves or depopulated mountain areas. Cutting and grazing, alternating with a regular winter snow cover, provide ideal habitats for early-flowering geophytes like *Crocus*, *Muscari*, *Narcissus* and *Scilla*, whose above-ground growth is over by the time of hay harvest or summer grazing (Fig. 34). The truly native habitat of such plants we can only guess at, but it seems very likely that they were restricted to open rocky slopes where the tree cover is naturally sparse

Fig. 34 Wild grape hyacinth *Muscari neglectum* in a Cambrigeshire hedgerow, April 1977. Photo Martin Walters

and the rather shallow soils dry out quickly in the hot summer sun. Such plants in the British flora are not mountain plants, but occur in lowland meadows and open woods. This explains why British botanists are surprised to find our meadow saffron *Colchicum autumnale* (and the similar but smaller *C. alpinum* which we do not have) as a plant of alpine meadows when they botanise in Continental Europe.

Grasses, sedges and rushes

By far the most important family of plants, without which our civilisation could hardly have come into being, are the grasses (Gramineae), which have such great agricultural importance. From my study window as I write this chapter in mid-winter, the view is of green, largely treeless fields beyond the garden that are devoted to crops of winter wheat, an annual grass, *Triticum*. This and other main cereal genera – barley *Hordeum*, rye *Secale* and oats *Avena* – are the important grain-providers of temperate Eurasia and North America. In every case, except wheat itself, we have closely-related wild British grasses, but the modern cereal crops are very specialised cultivars evolved over thousands of years from ancestors that were almost certainly growing in the cradle of civilisation in the Near East. Man brought into north-west Europe these already specialised crop plants and with them, as we discussed earlier, must have come a number of weeds, some, like poppies, still familiar to us. The contrast between the arable agriculture outside the garden fence, with its monocultures of mainly cereal crops, and the diverse flora of the garden, where we pack into a very small area a variety of plants from many parts of the earth representing a range of life-forms, could hardly be greater. Our lawns, however, represent a subtler contrast – that between two different life forms of the grass family – so perhaps we can look a little more closely at the composition of the average lawn to lead into other interesting subjects.

Cultivated cereals are strictly annual, even though related wild grasses may be perennial. So within the grass family, and indeed within many individual genera, the difference between annual and perennial herbs is not a very fundamental one. This point is brought home to us by one of the most successful grass weeds in the world, the little meadow-grass we call, following Linnaeus, *Poa annua*. Growing on dry, stony ground, a plant of *Poa annua* may well wither and die in the hot summer sun. But that is much less likely to happen in our mild, moist Atlantic climate than in other warmer countries. Outside the hotel where I stayed for some days in Delhi during a visit in March some years ago, I collected the weeds from the flower-beds (full of *Canna* and similar, quite familiar, garden bedding plants), and amongst them was *Poa annua*, already yellowing and setting seed. Even if the weeding were not very efficient, it seemed certain that such plants would not survive a hot, dry summer except as seed. *Poa annua* may well be annual, or ephemeral, in Delhi, but very often it behaves as a short-lived perennial in Britain. Interestingly enough, we do have a more strictly annual relative in the British flora. If you go to the Lizard peninsula in Cornwall in winter or early spring, you may well see a little *Poa* looking rather yellowish and setting seed in trodden areas and tracks. This is *Poa infirma*, best told from *P. annua* by the lower branches of the inflorescence being held upwardly-spreading in seed, whereas those of the common species spread at right-angles or are deflexed. There is, indeed, good evidence that the common weed, which has a tetraploid complement of chromosomes, actually originated from a cross between the small annual diploid plant *P. infirma* and another, perennial, northern diploid *P. supina*, which grows in Scandinavia but not (so far as we yet know) in Scotland.

Although we are right in pointing out that *Poa annua* is often a short-lived perennial, its life form is really rather different from the obviously perennial meadow-grasses, especially *Poa pratensis*, which has a rhizomatous habit of growth, and can survive well in closed grassland in competition with other perennial grasses. Our lawns are not fundamentally different from other grassland communities cut or grazed for agriculture, in that the grass species they contain are all perennials that do not depend on setting seed to survive. Quite large grass clones can be identified in grassland, all originating from a single colonist by vegetative spread. Before we leave *Poa annua*, we might note that it is not a very 'safe' grass in lawns or other grassland, because of its low competitive power. Indeed, it is often seen marking the edge of a trampled path through grassland, where the turf has been broken and the competition from other grasses is at least temporarily reduced.

What are the other grasses in our lawns? Botanically, this seems to be an oddly neglected area, partly because it is quite laborious to survey even a small patch of grass to find exactly which grass species are there. (The non-grass species that the gardener often calls 'lawn weeds' are much easier to tell – daisies, plantains, speedwells, etc. – because they are nearly all dicotyledons with very different leaves from grasses.) Of course, if you have sown a new lawn and used fine fescue lawn-seed, you may have a monoculture of uniform pure green: but most gardeners do not have this, and an increasing number, I am happy to say, do not want to have it. Given that you have an ordinary 'old' lawn, how can you decide its composition? Basically, there are two ways: either you can sample the lawn grasses and identify them by their leaf and basal characters, or you can leave uncut several patches of your lawn in spring, so that the grasses have an opportunity to flower for you and then you can use the combined vegetative and floral characters for identification. If you have an extensive lawn, this latter method is quite attractive and indeed might make an interesting talking-point when your gardening friends visit. If you do adopt the second method, and can use both flowering and vegetative characters, a recent semi-popular book that can be recommended to use for identification of grasses is Hayward (1987). The standard work on the native grasses of Britain (and all our lawn-grasses are included) is Hubbard (ed.3 1984), an excellent detailed study with clear black and white illustrations.

Old grassland, rich in species, contrasts with carefully-weeded and tended lawns. But gardeners increasingly like to experiment with grassy areas that are somewhere in between the formal, manicured lawn and, say, a hay-meadow community. In the final chapter of the book we take up some of these questions and look at a range of new ideas. There is another quite separate area where the botanist interested in grass species for their own sake, and the gardener interested in the decorative quality of grasses, can find some common ground – the increasing use of cut grasses for floral decoration. Most of the grasses grown by gardeners for this purpose are exotic species. The familiar stately pampas grass *Cortaderia selloana* exists in our gardens in several cultivars: as its common name suggests, its native home is South America. A generally similar, robust, clump-forming grass from the Far East, *Miscanthus sinensis*, has become quite popular in recent years and can be used like *Cortaderia* as a specimen plant in a formal layout. Quite different are the rather delicate annual species of *Setaria*, the bristle-grasses: these and several other grasses common in South Europe and Asia are included as aliens in the British flora, principally because they frequently appear where bird-seed is scattered. *Setaria* and related genera belong to a group of grasses called 'panicoid' after the genus *Panicum*, which are common in tropical and sub-tropical countries and very poorly represented in Europe. Finally, a word about the feather-grasses *Stipa*, surely among the most attractive of all the ornamentals we can grow. These mainly perennial grasses are characteristic of warm, dry grassland, particularly what we call 'steppe', in Europe and Asia; the most impressive ones carry in their inflorescence florets with feathery twisted points or awns that can reach up to 30 cm long!

There is one group of grasses which are so obviously different from the rest of the family that we do not easily think of them as grasses at all, and indeed have a special name for them – the woody, largely tropical bamboos. The bamboos are not native anywhere in Europe and, although several are familiar garden plants, until very recently the authors of the British Floras apparently did not consider any of them sufficiently well established outside gardens to be worthy of even a brief mention.

In spite of this, no fewer than six different bamboos in the account in *Flora Europaea* (Tutin et al., vol 5, 1980) are explicitly stated to be naturalised in Britain, and two relatively short broad-leaved Japanese species, *Sasa palmata* which spreads very rapidly by long, far-creeping rhizomes, and *Pseudosasa japonica* (Fig. 35) are said to be "widely naturalised in Britain, Ireland and the Channel Isles". It looks as if we British botanists are very unwilling to take any bamboos on board as naturalised aliens, even though some have as good a claim to be 'wild' as, say, the invasive species in the dock family Polygonaceae such as *Polygonum sachalinense* and *P. cuspidatum*[1], which, like *Sasa*, come from the Far East via our gardens. It may be that one reason for our unwillingness to 'register' that there are bamboos about the countryside, especially in damp corners of formerly cultivated gardens, arises from the undoubted fact that although we can all recognise a bamboo – it is simply a large grass with a persistent woody stem and evergreen leaves – it is quite another matter saying which bamboo is which. Partly this difficulty arises from the very irregular flowering, at least when cultivated in Europe. The flowering of bamboos is a very complicated subject, but at least one thing can be said with certainty. Quoting David McClintock, a British expert on the growing of bamboos: "most of the earlier tropical botanists said that all the plants of a bamboo species flowered and seeded at the same time and then all died. This article of faith is still widely believed, but the facts in this country (and I believe elsewhere too) deny it, with rare exceptions." McClintock's paper (1981) is well worth reading: it provides an excellent example of how careful observation by a keen plantsman can really open our eyes to how erroneous some statements, copied from one book to another, may actually be.

[1] I have elected to retain the name *Polygonum cuspidatum* for this plant, partly because there is as yet no consensus among modern Floras and reference works about what generic name to use if the large genus *Polygonum* is divided.

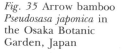

Fig. 35 Arrow bamboo
Pseudosasa japonica in
the Osaka Botanic
Garden, Japan

Because they have little or no agricultural importance, the other two groups of monocotyledons with inconspicuous, wind-pollinated flowers usually grouped together with the grasses, the sedges (Cyperaceae) and the rushes (Juncaceae), are relatively neglected. To the enthusiastic field-botanist, however, sedges in particular, mostly species of the large genus *Carex*, have a very special fascination, and a knowledge of the common sedges (and rushes) is very useful to understand the ecology of wetland vegetation (Plate 20). Indeed, there is a very important generalisation valid for grassland communities, not just in the British Isles but throughout the north temperate regions of the earth, namely, that the grasses are usually the dominant and most numerous species in relatively dry situations, whilst the sedges and rushes become much more important in the wetlands. Of course, this fact is generally familiar to the farmer, who tends to use the tufted rushes in particular, like *Juncus effusus* and *J. inflexus*, as indications of waterlogged grassland needing drainage if it is to be improved for grazing. Only one native sedge makes much of a contribution to our gardens – the very handsome pendulous sedge *Carex pendula*, which grows in many parts of Britain in wet woodland, but can be cultivated surprisingly easily in gardens, tolerating much drier conditions than one might expect. You could hardly do better, if you are just beginning a study of British sedges, than to take flowering *Carex pendula* as your first practical example, for its robust habit and large inflorescence enable you to see and interpret all the vegetative and reproductive characters needed for identification. There is an excellent, cheap and well-illustrated handbook (Jermy et al., ed.2, 1982) available to help you.

8

Some Special Life Forms

Water plants

Within the broad spectrum of perennial herbs, certain life forms stand out as exceptional. Amongst the most important of these, both in botany and horticulture, are the specialised water plants and, at the other extreme, succulent plants including the cactus family, characteristic of arid regions of the earth where water shortage is one of the most obvious problems set by the environment. We begin with an account of aquatic plants, adapted to growing either totally submerged or floating on the surface of rivers, lakes and ponds.

In the course of evolution of the higher plants, botanists envisage that the dry land was gradually colonised by primitive plants that had evolved in the sea. Indeed, recognisable flowering plants appear relatively late in the fossil record, and are preceded on land, for example, by the ferns and fern-allies whose massive remains we burn as coal. This means that all flowering plants growing in water today are assumed to be secondarily adapted to a floating or submerged existence, and that somewhere in their ancestry were plants growing on the land. There are many lines of evidence for this: we must be content with mentioning two only. Many aquatic flowering plants continue to flower above the water surface, where pollination takes place mainly through the agency of insects or wind, just as we find with ordinary land plants. A second line of evidence is that there are aquatic representatives in a wide range of different families of flowering plants, a fact that would be very difficult to interpret in the context of evolution unless we are prepared to imagine some specialised offshoots of each family adopting independently an aquatic life. In fact, an aquatic life form is just like any other ecological adaptation: it can be present in systematically very diverse families of plants whose basic relationship is revealed by the form of the flower and the fruit. Let us look at a few examples.

Water violet *Hottonia palustris* (Plate 21), is a widely-distributed submerged water plant whose underwater stems and leaves would tell us little about its systematic relationships. When the pretty lilac flowers appear on racemes above the surface of the water in May and June, however, we can easily satisfy ourselves that it is a member of the Primulaceae, the family which contains not only the familiar primroses and cowslips and many garden primulas, but also *Cyclamen* and *Lysimachia*. Not only does the flower of *Hottonia* resemble a *Primula* in several features such as the regular, five-lobed corolla and the single style, but it also shares with *Primula* the property known as heterostyly, familiar to us in the wild primrose, which exists in so-called pin and thrum forms (Fig. 36). The leaves of *Hottonia*, however, grouped in whorls of 2 or 3 spaced along the flexible, submerged stems, could hardly be more different from an ordinary primrose leaf: they are very finely-divided, offering minimum resistance to water flow and maximum surface for photosynthesis. It is

Fig. 36 Heterostyly
in cowslip *Primula
veris*. Left, pin-eyed:
right, thrum-eyed.
From Proctor & Yeo
1973

this feature in particular that the submerged parts of many water plants share, a feature that is an obvious adaptation to aquatic life. This character, of submerged stems with whorls of narrow or finely-dissected leaves, has been called "the *Hippuris* syndrome" by Professor Christopher Cook, an expert on aquatic flowering plants. In his paper (1978), Cook distinguishes between plants strictly resembling the common mare's tail *Hippuris*, in which the submerged stems have whorls of simple, linear leaves, and '*Hippuris* mimics' in which the whorls of leaves consist of finely-divided leaf segments. Figure 37, taken from Cook's paper, shows diagrammatically a range of possibilities, which can be easily demonstrated, for example, in a peaty dyke on Wicken Fen nature reserve, where types (b), (c) and (e) – *Ceratophyllum*, *Myriophyllum* and *Ranunculus circinatus*, can be found growing together, sometimes with both *Hottonia* and *Hippuris*. Until they flower, these five totally unrelated plants look remarkably similar, and constitute a very striking example of adaptive convergence. Any small garden pond can grow some of these fine-leaved aquatics: *Hottonia* is a special favourite.

Two other, quite different, life-form adaptations of water plants are perhaps even more familiar to gardeners than the *Hottonia* type: these are the floating duckweed type and the water-lily type. Duckweed, a familiar sight on farm and garden pond alike, looks so unlike an ordinary Angiosperm that it may come as a surprise to learn that all duckweeds are, botanically speaking,

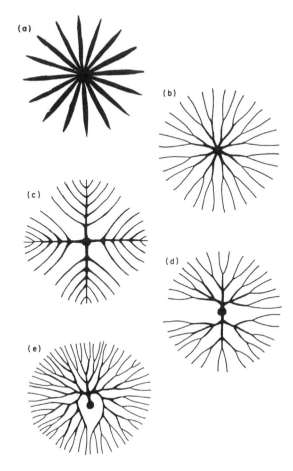

Fig. 37 The 'Hippuris syndrome': diagrams of five types of whorled submerged leaves ((a) is *Hippuris*). From Cook 1978

flowering plants. Indeed, the very diminutive *Wolffia arrhiza*, a rare plant in Britain and not often grown except by botanic gardens as a curiosity, makes a strong claim to be the smallest flowering plant in the world. Each complete plant is usually less than one millimetre across, a tiny, green, ovoid body of cells with no roots, and reproduces like all duckweeds by budding off daughter plants. No flower – which is in any case microscopically small – has ever been seen in Britain. Our commonest duckweed *Lemna minor*, in which the tiny round plants, each with a short root, are usually about 3 mm across, flowers not uncommonly in England, though even botanists rarely record the fact because the flower is so minute. But flowering plants are not the only possible 'duckweeds' to be seen on the surface of still fresh water. In addition we may find a remarkable water-fern *Azolla*, and a liverwort *Ricciocarpus*, both able to spread freely by vegetative means on the water surface with essentially the same life form as duckweed itself. *Azolla* (Plate 22), in particular, is well worth growing in your garden pond: a native of sub-tropical America, it is not entirely at home in Britain, but persists, and indeed shows signs of extending its range out of the warmer southern English counties into York-

Fig. 38 Water-lilies *Nymphaea* and *Nuphar* at Wicken Fen, Cambridgeshire. Photo Martin Walters

shire and even the Isle of Man. Like many introduced plants adapted to warmer climates than ours, *Azolla* tends to have good years when it flourishes, and bad years when it is hardly seen. In good years, perhaps a long, hot summer followed by a mild winter, it can cover a pond or ditch with a very characteristic reddish layer in autumn.

Finally, the water-lilies, familiar to botanist and gardener alike. The water-lily family, *Nymphaeaceae*, is unique among the Dicotyledons as the only family of water plants with large, insect-pollinated flowers. Our native water-lilies, the white and yellow, belong to the two principal genera, *Nymphaea* and *Nuphar* respectively (Fig. 38). Although we classify water-lilies as Dicotyledons, no single character by which we usually distinguish Dicotyledons from Monocotyledons holds for all the water-lilies, in which, for example, some species have one and others two cotyledons. This and other evidence encourages many botanists to see in the water-lilies a very remarkable primitive stock going back in evolution to a time before Monocotyledons as we now know them were distinct from Dicotyledons. Our two wild water-lilies, happily still common through much of the British Isles, can easily be distinguished from each other, even when not in flower, by the leaves. In the white water-lily *Nymphaea alba* the floating leaves are more or less circular in outline, in contrast to the oblong-ovate leaf of the yellow water-lily *Nuphar lutea*. Submerged leaves, thin and lettuce-like in texture, are produced by *Nuphar* but not by *Nymphaea*. The flowers are very different, not only in colour but in structure, and the English name commonly used for *Nuphar* – brandy-bottle – refers to the characteristic flask-shaped fruit and the alcoholic smell given off by the flower. Although gardeners grow *Nuphar* (there is indeed some evidence that it is a little more shade-tolerant than *Nymphaea*), the cultivated water-lilies are nearly all derived from the species of *Nymphaea* which have been hybridised and selected. In particular, the North American sweet-scented *N. odorata*, the yellow *N. mexicana*, and the Asiatic blue lotus *N. stellata*, have introduced both colour and scent into numerous cultivars. The British flora also contains a remarkable water-lily mimic in *Nymphoides peltatum* the fringed water-lily, which can be seen wild in the river-systems of the Fenland and the Thames Valley. It is sometimes recorded elsewhere, but seems to be an introduction outside the two main areas, and is indeed not uncommonly cultivated in garden ponds. The shining green floating leaves look very like those of a true water-lily, *Nymphaea*, but are rather smaller. The yellow flower, borne just above the surface in July and August is, however, fundamentally different: it is in fact quite closely related to the bog-bean *Menyanthes*, and both are related to the gentians.

Succulents

The hobby of growing succulent plants in England goes right back to Richard Bradley, at the beginning of the eighteenth century, who published in a series of parts between 1716 and 1727 his remarkable work *Historia Plantarum Succulentarum*. Fifty succulents are beautifully illustrated here, all in cultivation in the hothouses of gardens on the Continent if not in Britain, and of the plants, Gordon Rowley (1954) says: "the majority are at once recognisable from the plates alone, and there can be no doubt that they were drawn by someone acquainted with living plants". As Rowley points out, Bradley has a marvellously practical definition of a succulent as a plant "not capable of an *hortus siccus*" – that is, one cannot press it and put it in a herbarium – and he undoubtedly laid the foundation of the hobby as we know it today. Bradley became the first Cambridge Professor of Botany in 1724: he was a controversial and enigmatic figure, a prolific and gifted writer on agricultural and horticultural topics whose influence in Britain and adjacent Continental countries was very considerable. My own book, *The Shaping of Cambridge Botany* (1981), gives some account of his achievements and difficulties.

The cacti which Bradley knew and saw in cultivation in the great gardens of England, France and Holland were the few forerunners in Europe of that extraordinary New World family of plants we nowadays call Cactaceae. But Bradley also knew in cultivation some of the 'cactus mimics' from Africa which belong to a totally different group of plants, the genus *Euphorbia*, and even tells us how they differ from the cacti. He says, in his book *A Philosophical Account of the Works of Nature* (1721: Fig. 39): "they [the Euphorbias] differ from the foregoing plants [Cacti] in having a milky juice, and flowers and fruits of small regard" – a very adequate distinction! In this clear recognition of the fundamental difference between the New World and the Old World groups, Bradley was pointing to one of the most remarkable examples in the whole plant kingdom of that phenomenon of life-form similarity in unrelated plants that we saw in the case of the gardeners' 'laurels' in Chapter 6. Both the true cacti, almost entirely restricted as native plants to the Americas, and the cactus-like succulent euphorbias of Africa, inhabit desert regions, and have produced a parallel range of succulent forms independently during the course of evolution. Such parallel but independent variation is well known in the animal kingdom, as in the range of marsupial

Fig. 39 Illustration of cacti from Bradley's *Philosophical Account* ..., 1721. From Walters 1981

mammals in Australia which parallels the more advanced placental mammals of the rest of the world.

Cacti and succulent Euphorbias are mostly stem-succulents, in which the leaves are absent or greatly reduced, and the fleshy stems are often protected from grazing animals by spines. Succulents represented in the British flora are, in contrast, nearly all leaf-succulents, in which the leaves are well developed, but thick and fleshy. Stem-succulents are characteristic of desert floras in regions where the sparse rainfall is irregular, and survival through long hot dry periods is difficult. Interestingly, though the popular image of a desert flora is of scattered columnar or obese cacti, in the extreme deserts of the world such as the Gobi desert in Asia, where there is virtually no rainfall, the life form which persists is not a succulent plant, but a very stunted, often intricately branched shrub showing little above ground but possessing a very large, deep root system. Such extreme desert plants, of course, have no attraction for the gardener. The two life-forms have clearly different strategies to cope with water shortage: the succulent has a reservoir of water in specially adapted fleshy tissue, whilst the extreme desert shrub taps deep underground reserves and reduces its aerial shoots to a minimum.

None of the large groups of stem-succulents has any representatives in Europe, though species of *Opuntia*, the prickly pear, are nowadays widely naturalised around the Mediterranean. But an important group of leaf succulents, the family Aizoaceae, is represented in the modern British flora by a few plants originally grown in our gardens. The best known of these, with very large, handsome purple or yellow flowers, is *Carpobrotus edulis* the hottentot fig (Plate 23), native of South Africa. In parts of Devon and Cornwall this robust trailing succulent covers sheltered sea-cliffs in a thick evergreen carpet. Other 'ice-plants', to use the popular gardening name, occur as garden escapes, but none is so completely naturalised as the hottentot fig. If the promised global warming proceeds, we may expect more of these frost-sensitive succulents to add themselves to the naturalised flora in the warmer parts of the British Isles.

So far we have not mentioned any truly native succulents. There is, however, one family of succulent plants well represented in the British flora, the stonecrop family, Crassulaceae. Stonecrops – the botanical genus *Sedum* and its relatives – occur throughout the north temperate zone, usually in dry, stony or rocky places, and in Britain several of the most familiar species are common on walls. The little wall pepper or biting stonecrop *Sedum acre*, with bright yellow flowers, occurs throughout the British Isles, and is happily tolerated on rockeries and patios in gardens. Other species are white or pink flowered, and some, originally garden plants, are now effectively naturalised. Not all stonecrops are plants of dry ground, however, in spite of their fleshy leaves. One species, *Sedum villosum*, with pink flowers, occurs on streamsides and wet stony ground in the upland areas of North England and Scotland, and another, *S. rosea* the rose-root, is a mountain plant often cultivated in rock gardens. The houseleek *Sempervivum tectorum*, a familiar succulent on old roofs and walls, is not a native plant, but has a long association with man in Europe.

As one would expect, there are individual succulent species in several of the larger flowering plant families whose members are typically not fleshy. Thus in the carrot family Umbelliferae the rock samphire *Crithmum maritimum* has thick, fleshy leaves, as does the sea rocket *Cakile maritima* in the cabbage family Cruciferae, and the sea purslane *Honckenya peploides* in the pink family Caryophyllaceae. All these plants grow only around our sea coasts, and it is there that we find the succulent life form very well developed.

This association between sea-coast habitat and succulent habit is clearly to

Plate 20 The sedge *Carex elata* in flower in mid-April, Wicken Fen, Cambridgeshire. (See p. 120). Photo Martin Walters.

Plate 21 Water-violet *Hottonia palustris* in flower in early June at Wicken Fen. Notice the finely-dissected submerged leaves. (See p. 122). Photo Andrew Gagg.

Plate 22 The floating water fern *Azolla filiculoides* photographed in the Shropshire Union Canal. (See p. 124). Photo Andrew Gagg.

Plate 23 Hottentot fig *Carpobrotus edulis* on coastal cliff, Lizard peninsula, Cornwall. (See p. 128). Photo C. D. Preston.

Plate 24 Greater dodder *Cuscuta europaea* on nettle *Urtica dioica*, Hasfield, Gloucestershire. (See p. 135). Photo Andrew Gagg.

Plate 25 Bird's nest orchid *Neottia nidus-avis* under beech trees, Whitcomb Wood, Gloucestershire. (See p. 136). Photo Andrew Gagg.

Plate 26 Purple toothwort
Lathraea clandestina in early
April, parasitic on willow in
the Cambridge University
Botanic Garden. (See p. 136).
Photo Andrew Gagg.

Plate 27 Lesser broomrape
Orobanche minor in July,
parasitic on lovage *Levisticum
officinale* in vegetable garden.
(See p. 136). Photo Andrew
Gagg.

Above Plate 28 Forsythia trained against a north-facing wall: left, *F.* x *spectabilis*, right, *F.* 'Karl Sax'. Photo Martin Walters.

Below Plate 29 Close-up of the flowers (as above). Note capsule fruit of previous year on 'Karl Sax'. Natural size. (See p. 147). Photo Martin Walters.

do with salt-tolerance, though its scientific explanation is still by no means clear. Gardeners know that plants vary greatly in their tolerance of salt. Garden asparagus, for example, can be very effectively weeded in spring by applying a strong solution of common salt, which kills many ordinary seedling weeds but does not harm the crop, and this reminds us of the fact that truly wild *Asparagus officinalis*, from which our garden cultivars have arisen, grows on coastal rocks and sand in South-west England, as elsewhere in Europe. Salt-tolerance is also important in selecting shrubs for gardens exposed to salt-laden winds near the sea, though here other factors than just sea-salt concentration are involved.

One pair of native plants illustrates very well the relationship between leaf succulence and salt tolerance. The common bladder campion *Silene vulgaris* occurs throughout much of lowland Britain in hedgerows, roadsides and grassland. It is an erect, branched herb with little appeal to gardeners, and hardly deserves a place in the herbaceous border. The closely-related sea campion *S. uniflora* (*S. maritima*), by contrast, is largely restricted to our coasts, and rarely grows together with *S. vulgaris*; it is a very attractive, mat-forming rock garden plant, and is indeed often grown in the form of the double-flowered cultivar 'Robin Whitebreast' (Fig. 40). Part of the attraction of the sea campion in rock gardens is its neat, blue-green, fleshy leaves which persist on the matted stems throughout the winter. In contrast, the leaves of the tall inland bladder campion are of normal texture, and do not persist. Thanks to the research of Marsden-Jones and Turrill (1957) we know that these two species are totally interfertile when tested in cultivation, so we cannot escape the conclusion that they have relatively recently diverged from some common stock. The succulent salt-resistant habit, therefore, is apparently easily acquired or lost in evolution, and it is not surprising to find individual succulent variants in otherwise normal non-succulent groups.

Fig. 40 Distribution of bladder campion *Silene vulgaris* and sea campion *S. uniflora* (*S. maritima*). From Perring & Walters 1982

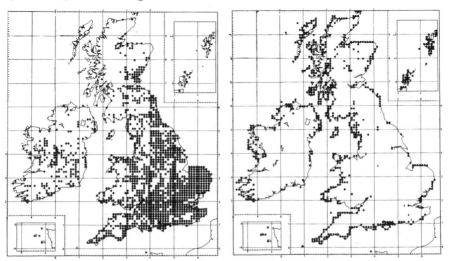

This leaves us with a final, very significant, generalisation about succulent plants. We do not in Britain think of coastal salt-laden habitats as 'deserts'. As we go south and east in Europe, however, we begin to realise that the distinction between what we think of as a salt-resistant coastally-distributed flora and a desert flora becomes more and more blurred. Inland saline habitats in south-east Europe, for example, which are often very dry in summer, can look remarkably like our coastal salt-marshes, not only in general appearance but even in terms of the individual species. In fact there is a specialised halophytic (salt-plant) flora in Europe and Asia, of which we can think of British coastal communities as outlying examples. As is so often the case, we begin to realise that if we look outwards from the British Isles into the European Continent as a whole, we are 'reading the book from the wrong end'. The whole family Chenopodiaceae illustrates this well. In Britain most members of this family are either coastal plants (like the beetroot *Beta*) or agricultural weeds (like the goosefoots *Chenopodium*). In the steppes of European Russia and Asia, however, the family constitutes one of the most important elements. There is even one British coastal plant, the shrubby sea-blite *Suaeda vera,* which is found all the way from its northernmost station in the world on the Lincolnshire coast, right down the Atlantic side of Europe, round the Mediterranean and as far as Afghanistan and India. The explanation of this remarkable pattern seems to be that in many semi-desert and desert conditions high concentrations of salt accumulate in the upper layers of sand because the intense evaporation during the hot season greatly exceeds any downward movement of water during the rainy periods. Succulence, in these circumstances, is an adaptation to enable the plant to resist the normally harmful effects of high salt concentrations in the soil, however these may come about.

After all this is said, there remain many features of the succulent adaptation that are very mysterious. One of the very recent successful invaders of ponds in England is in fact a leaf succulent, *Crassula helmsii,* a native of Australia and New Zealand. Originally introduced as an aquatic for garden ponds about 1927, it has been spreading rapidly in England in recent years and is now recorded in Scotland. Some botanists have become concerned that its spread could endanger certain rare native species that easily succumb to the aggressive competition of this mat-forming little alien. Some pond-margin habitats in the New Forest for example have long been famous for rare plants such as *Elatine hexandra* and *Illecebrum verticillatum,* both very small species with low competitive power. We do not know why an antipodean plant should suddenly spread so aggressively in this very special aquatic habitat. There are other species of *Crassula* in Europe that are more or less aquatic, specialising in winter-wet habitats such as pool margins where they behave as annuals: the best-known of these is the diminutive *C. tillaea,* described in Chapter 7, and we can see that succulence may be important in the later stages of the plant's life-cycle when the temporary pool dries up. But *C. helmsii* grows vigorously with its feet – or even the main plant – permanently submerged, and is moreover a perennial with freely-rooting stems. We watch its inexorable spread in Britain with interest and some concern, and have to confess we do not know how it can be so successful.

Epiphytes

A native English woodland provides a range of habitats for herbaceous plants in addition to the obvious ground layer. One of these, which we are apt to miss, is provided by the trees themselves, and plants adapted to grow on other plants, and particularly on the branches of trees, constitute a special life-form group which we call epiphytes. Many of these are lower plants, especially mosses and lichens, which can festoon the trees of old woodland, at least in the damper, milder parts of the British Isles; but ferns in particular among the higher plants are also important epiphytes, and the polypody *Polypodium* (Fig. 41), is one of the most frequent of these. Since an epiphyte is using its host tree only as a base and is in no sense parasitic on it, the same species will often be found growing on totally artificial supports such as walls and buildings or, of course, on the ground. No doubt it was through noticing such plants that our ancestors began to cultivate a range of attractive 'house plants' which will tolerate the relatively low light intensity of an ordinary living room.

English woodland has rather few true epiphytes amongst the vascular plants and, as is so often the case, we have to go abroad to find rich epiphyte floras. In the tropics and sub-tropics two families of flowering plants in particular specialise in the epiphytic habit, both of them monocotyledons. One of these, the orchids, Orchidaceae, is among the largest families in the world, with, according to recent estimates, nearly 800 genera and some 17,500 species. The extraordinary and often quite bizarre form and colour of tropical orchids has long attracted the attention of gardeners, and an enormous industry has grown up around their cultivation, and particularly their hybri-

Fig. 41 Epiphytic *Polypodium* with ivy in a wood in Anglesey in March. From Page 1988

disation to produce ever more new cultivars for the orchid fancier. Peter Hunt, orchid expert at Kew, has recently stated that new commercial hybrid orchids enter the trade at the rate of some 150 per month! Compared with these exotic marvels, most of our own native orchids seem unremarkable; they are distinguished by orchid fanciers as 'ground orchids' and not much cultivated, but are full of interest for the field botanist. The New Naturalist library contains an excellent book on the wild orchids of Britain (Summerhayes, ed.2 1968).

Orchids fascinated Charles Darwin, who devoted a whole book to the subject of their pollination mechanisms (1862). Some of these are almost incredibly precise and complex. A good general account can be found in Michael Proctor and Peter Yeo's New Naturalist book *The Pollination of Flowers* (1973). One general question arises from these studies. Why are orchids so freely inter-fertile when many other groups of plants are not? The answer seems to lie in their exclusive use of specialised insect pollinators, which itself may be correlated with their exploitation of the epiphytic habit. The cathedral-like interior of a species-rich tropical forest is an extraordinarily complex habitat, in which wind pollination would be useless in the sheltered, humid air. Cross-pollination limited precisely to transfer between two widely-separated plants of a particular epiphyte can be effected by a particular kind of animal (usually, but not always, an insect) which is actively seeking the particular flower. All this precise, marvellously-timed mechanism is short-circuited by man's planned artificial cross-pollination. It appears that, in general, internal sterility barriers between different species (arising from genetic factors) do not operate where precise pollination mechanisms have evolved to ensure that pollen is accurately transferred in nature.

The other remarkable group of tropical epiphytes, unlike the world-wide orchids, is almost entirely confined to Central and South America. These are the bromeliads, which constitute a separate family, Bromeliaceae. The best-known member of the family, the pineapple *Ananas*, is a terrestrial plant, but many bromeliads are epiphytic, and the group contains what by any standards must be the most specialised epiphytic flowering plant in the world. This is the plant called Spanish moss in America: it is common on trees in the South-east United States, particularly Florida and Georgia, and looks exactly like a pale greyish, tangled mass of lichen hanging from the branches. Its scientific name is *Tillandsia usneoides* ('Usnea' is the name of a lichen genus). Spanish moss is not difficult to grow, provided you keep it reasonably warm and damp: all you have to do is to hang a piece up in a warm conservatory and wait! It is more difficult to persuade it to flower – and even if you do, the flowers are small and inconspicuous. Other species of *Tillandsia*, a large genus of over 400 species, are more rewarding if it is flowers you require. Bromeliads manage to survive with inadequate or, in the case of *T. usneoides*, non-existent roots by absorbing atmospheric moisture directly through their leaf surface. This they do by means of a very specialised covering of stalked, flattened scale-hairs which can easily be seen with a hand-lens on most tillandsias. Many also accumulate water in a central 'tank' made by the overlapping leaf-bases. Although many Bromeliads are now in cultivation, only one has escaped and begun to qualify for a place in the British flora. This is the Chilean terrestrial species *Fascicularia pitcairniifolia*, now quite naturalised on parts of the coasts of the Scilly Isles (and in Guernsey).

Epiphytes are by their habit ideally suited to culture in pots and hanging baskets, and some of our most familiar and decorative conservatory plants have the epiphytic life form. Among these are the extraordinary group of true cacti which gardeners generally call Christmas or Easter cacti, related to the large *Epiphyllum* species often called 'Phyllocactus'. The scientific names of these plants are confused, and different works of reference unfortunately settle for different names. In such a situation the nurseryman can be forgiven for distinguishing only between 'Christmas cacti' flowering around Christmas, and 'Easter cacti' flowering somewhat later.

Carnivorous plants

Of all the extraordinary adaptations shown by flowering plants, none is more remarkable than the carnivorous habit. The ability to trap and eat small animals, often but not exclusively insects, exists in a number of different genera, which fall into two main groups from the point of view of their systematic classification. One group, with regular, polypetalous flowers, is classified near the saxifrage family; the other group, with two-lipped, gamopetalous flowers, is near specialised families like the mint family, Labiatae. Both these groups are represented in the British flora, the sundews *Drosera* belonging to the first group, and the butterworts *Pinguicula* and bladderworts *Utricularia* to the second group. Gardeners grow species of *Drosera* and *Pinguicula*, often in raised bog gardens, together with several exotic genera, of which the North America pitcher plants *Sarracenia* and the famous venus fly-trap *Dionaea* are especially popular.

Most carnivorous plants grow in peaty or boggy ground, where the soil is likely to be deficient at least in certain mineral nutrients, and it is tempting to see the carnivorous habit as evolving as an accessory nutritional device to cope with such shortages. It has to be stressed, however, that all carnivorous plants contain chlorophyll and are therefore feeding themselves normally, and many do not seem to require supplementary animal diet, as you can see by the ease with which some commercially available species can be grown in the home or in the greenhouse without feeding them insects or any sort of meat. The precise devices to catch the animal prey are remarkably diverse in different genera, but can be roughly grouped into two kinds: the sticky fly-trap, where the unwary visitor is lured on to a sticky surface and held and eventually digested there, as in the sundews and butterworts, and the trap mechanisms where the prey are caught in a specially-shaped container, as in the pitcher-plants and bladderworts. Venus fly-trap, in many ways the most spectacular carnivore, combines attraction to a surface with a rapid closure of the 'jaws' of the trap. It is relatively large and easy to grow, and has therefore become popular as a house plant. As a native plant, it is restricted to a coastal region of North and South Carolina in the United States, from where it was early described and brought into cultivation in Europe. There is a single species, *Dionaea muscipula*, which seems to be very closely and precisely adapted to a very peculiar belt of 'pine barren' country near the coast, where it grows in quantity in wet, acid soil together with species of pitcher plants *Sarracenia*. It is now strictly protected inside one or two large nature reserves, and its commercial cultivation is undertaken on a large scale to protect the wild plant from the depredations of traders who have in earlier times dug up and sold large quantities.

Of the three British native genera, the aquatic bladderwort *Utricularia* has the most specialised trap device (Fig. 42). The under-water parts of the plant bear small bladders, each provided with a trapdoor and a group of trigger hairs. In the resting position, the door is closed and the interior of the bladder is under tension. Any small water-flea or other animal that brushes against the hairs stimulates the door to open, when the prey is sucked in to the bladder and the door closes again. The prey is digested by the juices secreted by the cells lining the bladder cavity. Though the bladders are small, and apparently each only lasts for one 'feed', it has recently been shown that a healthy population of the common bladderwort *Utricularia vulgaris* can have a very marked effect on the population of small water animals inhabiting its pool (Friday, 1991, 1992).

Although the main groups of carnivorous plants are well known, there is much evidence that the habit is present to some degree in plants not normally thought of as carnivorous. A good example is the family Bromeliaceae which we discussed earlier. In this family, one terrestrial member with 'tanks' accumulating water in the leaf-base rosette has now been conclusively proved to feed to some degree on small animals trapped in their tanks. This is

Fig. 42 Bladderwort *Utricularia vulgaris*: leaf with bladders (x 4/3). From Friday 1991

Brocchinia reducta, which grows together with *Heliamphora*, a carnivorous 'pitcher plant', in the remarkable vegetation of the Guyana Highlands (Givnish et al. 1984). Plants with glandular hairs in which insects are often caught and held are also potential carnivores, though there is no evidence that the familiar glandular-hairy 'catch-fly' adaptation in some British members of the Caryophyllaceae has any carnivorous significance. This adaptation is usually interpreted as a defence mechanism against small insects such as beetles seeking to rob the flowers of their nectar by entering from behind and below. On the other hand, there are many examples where structures performing one function come to perform quite a different one in the course of evolution, and the range of flowering plants with sticky glandular secretions on leaves and stems is very large. It seems we can expect more carnivory to be detected in such plants as their ecology is studied.

Carnivorous plants are a study in themselves, and there is a useful literature, including Charles Darwin's own work (1862). The recent books by Slack (1986) and Juniper (1989) are strongly recommended.

Parasitic and saprophytic plants

Totally parasitic flowering plants, which lack all traces of chlorophyll in their tissues, are, like the carnivorous plants, found in several different Angiosperm groups. Some of them, because they are capable of causing damage to agricultural crops, have been recognised from early times. A good example is the dodder *Cuscuta*, an annual twining plant whose thin, often reddish stems attach themselves to their host plant with specialised outgrowths called haustoria, and feed through these connections on the host tissues. Although the small flowers of *Cuscuta* look very different from the large, showy ones of the familiar bindweeds of the family Convolvulaceae, a close inspection reveals that they are structurally related. *Cuscuta*, then, looks like a flowering plant that has started off, like the Convolvulaceae as a whole, as a twining plant using a 'host' merely as a support, and later taken to the parasitic habit.

Wild dodder is not uncommon on heath and moorland in the north and west of the British Isles in the form of the species *Cuscuta epithymum*, which frequently parasitises gorse *Ulex*, and heather *Calluna*, sometimes almost smothering the host bush. The larger *C. europaea*, however, commonly parasitic on nettles *Urtica*, and found throughout much of Continental Europe, is a rather rare plant in the British Isles, and most of its occurrences are in lowland England south of the Severn-Wash line (Plate 24). This could be a climatic limitation, and it may be significant that some recent records for this rare British plant are in the hot summers of 1989 and 1990. It looks like another candidate for spread if we get the promised global warming.

Gardeners do not, in my experience, grow dodders, or even tolerate them in their gardens, and since they are annual they can easily be controlled. In the Cambridge Botanic Garden, however, *Cuscuta europaea* has been for many years a regular parasite on various Compositae in the Systematic Beds, and has also been recorded (1967) on nettles on the bed devoted to the Urticaceae. Moreover, in 1956 it was successfully transferred on to its correct family bed, the Convolvulaceae, where it still (1989) happily parasitises the vigorous *Calystegia* plants; indeed in some seasons it comes to dominate and severely damage the host plants. On a world scale, nearly 150 species of *Cuscuta* are known, occurring through tropical and temperate regions. Distinguishing the species is by no means easy, and Feinbrun's account in *Flora Europaea* (1972) gives 17 species, three of which are American plants that have become naturalised. One of these American dodders, *C. campestris*, has been recorded in recent years in Britain and may be spreading: it is usually parasitic on medicks *Medicago*, and clovers *Trifolium*, and easily distinguished from our native dodders by its yellowish, not reddish, stems and, more surely and technically, by its capitate, not linear, stigmas.

The other group of parasitic flowering plants native to Britain are the broomrapes *Orobanche*, and the rather similar toothworts *Lathraea*. These are utterly unlike the dodder, both in general form and in the flower structure, and are stout perennial plants attached to the roots of their hosts. The robust, erect shoots are quite devoid of chlorophyll, and have a pale or brownish colour. Only one of them has any claim to be a garden plant: this is the very decorative purple toothwort *Lathraea clandestina* (Plate 26), native in Western Europe from Italy and Spain through France to Belgium. The purple toothwort flowers in very early spring or even, in mild winters, in February. It is normally parasitic on the roots of willows and poplars, and is becoming increasingly popular as a bizarre addition to damp woodland gardens. Introduced before the end of the nineteenth century to the Cambridge Botanic Garden, it is now naturalised outside the Garden by the river and other local waterways. There is some evidence that the main colony on willows by the River Cam was originally planted there in the early years of the present century by the then Curator of the Garden, but its subsequent spread, still continuing, is presumably a natural one.

Broomrapes have very small seeds, easily wind-borne, which explains why small colonies can appear sporadically and quite unexpectedly even in gardens. Plate 27 shows the lesser broomrape *Orobanche minor* growing in my own vegetable garden at the foot of a stand of lovage *Levisticum officinale*, and presumably parasitic on it. This plant appeared for the first time in 1989 and has flowered again, showing slight increase, in succeeding years. One mysterious feature of this parasitism is that some species of broomrape, such as the tall *O. elatior*, parasitic on *Centaurea scabiosa*, seem to be completely restricted to a single host plant, whilst others, like *O. minor*, can be found on a very wide range of host plants. The reason may be that there are different 'physiological races' of wide-ranging species which are indistinguishable to the human eye, each race being restricted to a narrow host-plant range. But the existence of such races is not proven.

A very different group of flowering plants lacking chlorophyll are the specialised orchids such as the birds'-nest orchid *Neottia* (Plate 25). These plants are characteristic of humus-rich soils, and feed by a complex association with different fungi. Although they are technically parasitic on their fungal root component, they are generally distinguished as saprophytes from the direct and obvious parasites we have discussed. Actually, most ground orchids show some degree of association with soil fungi in their root systems, but few are totally devoid of any green colour. This phenomenon of association between flowering plants and soil fungi is quite widespread and is called 'mycorrhizal'. The study of mycorrhiza, particularly in trees, has considerable economic importance for forestry, and could explain why certain plants are more difficult to cultivate than others. Its implications for specialist orchid growing, for example, are considerable.

The parasitic habit does not necessarily involve a total change of feeding pattern. The most familiar parasite of all, the mistletoe *Viscum album* is, as everyone knows, a green plant, still capable of using the energy of sunlight to synthesise carbohydrates. It is, however, unable to grow independently of a host tree, and in fact the germinated seed must quickly penetrate and attach itself to the living tissue of the host or it will die. In Britain, mistletoe is most commonly seen on apple trees *Malus*, although it has been recorded on a wide range of trees, including poplar *Populus* and oak *Quercus*. A survey of mistletoe hosts in Britain carried out in the 1970's (Perring 1973) recorded more than 50 different trees. Its frequency on apple is obviously largely due to its commercial value: apple growers in England found in Victorian times that it was a rewarding extra crop to be harvested for Christmas use and, although nowadays much Christmas mistletoe comes from Continental Europe, English-grown mistletoe can still be bought.

Other so-called semi-parasitic flowering plants in Britain include several familiar native genera of annual plants belonging to the Scrophulariaceae, such as yellow rattle *Rhinanthus* and eyebright *Euphrasia*, which grow parasitically on the roots of common meadow and pasture plants. It is perhaps significant that none of these has found a place in our gardens, since they prove to be rather difficult to propagate because of their host requirements.

Part III

Botany and Horticulture as Modern Hobbies

'The neatest definition of plant ecology is 'the study of what grows where, and why'; if we add 'and when, and how, and how much', we have a subject providing elements of interest for almost anyone – not just the dedicated botanist, but the farmer and the forester, the planner and the engineer, the weekend gardener and the country-lover.'

Charles Sinker, Preface to Ecological Flora of the Shropshire Region, *1985*

In the four remaining chapters I have endeavoured to set out what I see to be unifying themes enabling the keen amateur to enjoy both botany and horticulture. It is always more difficult to write about one's subject as it shapes and develops than to select from history those themes that seem to be relevant. If what I have included seems an inadequate account, I can only apologise and claim to have done my best.

I discuss first the impact of cytogenetics on horticulture and then the changing roles of professional and amateur. This is a dangerously broad canvas, and I have inevitably over-simplified; but since I myself, like a refreshingly large number of my botanical colleagues, have been lucky enough to enjoy as a hobby much of what, in my professional career, I was paid to learn and teach, this subject is at the heart of the book. Following on from this, I then consider the linked subjects of ecology and conservation, and how they have come to play such an important part in the way we enjoy our studies of plants. Inevitably, I conclude with a little speculation on how the study of wild and garden plants will look to the generation that follows.

9

The Science of Genetics and Horticultural Practice

Genetics and plant breeding

As we have already seen in Chapters 3 and 4, the rise of cytogenetics and its application to plant breeding are twentieth-century developments. We now understand something of the processes by which plants vary both in the wild and in our gardens, though much remains uncertain and speculative. In this chapter I want to make some assessment of the effect of this knowledge, derived from both wild and garden plants, on horticultural practice.

In one sense, much of this book is an attempt to present botanical knowledge so that it illuminates the way plants vary both in the wild and in cultivation, for there is no essential difference between these conditions. But we have not so far asked, except in very broad terms, whether cytogenetics has made much difference to what we, as gardeners, or the horticultural industry as a whole, actually practise in our hobby or profession. At the outset we have to recognise that plant breeding, incorporating the new cytogenetics, was concerned, very understandably, with the improvement of economically important plants such as cereals, vegetables, fruit and timber trees. Whole new institutions were founded, such as the Plant Breeding Institute at Cambridge, and research of fundamental importance was carried out in such specialised laboratories. The successes of cytogenetics applied to the main crop plants must be outside the scope of our book, but we can reasonably ask whether the great figures of modern genetics and the institutions they built up contributed much to our gardens as opposed to large-scale agriculture, horticulture and forestry.

This question is not as easy to answer as one might expect. 'Amenity horticulture', as it has come to be called, has only become relatively big business in recent years in our country, and even our vegetable gardens show surprisingly little radical change from the practice of our Victorian forebears, if we judge change in terms of 'improvement' of the plants we grow. Perhaps there is only one technical term from genetics that would be familiar to most amateur gardeners: the seed called 'F_1 hybrid' that we increasingly buy, especially for the vegetable garden. An F_1 hybrid is the progeny resulting from a cross between two different pure lines of the species we want to grow: it is expensive because to produce the seed the nurseryman must ensure that only the selected parents are involved in the cross, and that no 'foreign' pollen is accidentally introduced. In contrast we traditionally allow open pollination, simply collecting the seed from the parent plant. Why is F_1 hybrid seed better than open-pollinated seed? There are two different reasons, presumably of different relative importance in different cases. When we grown an F_1 hybrid *Pelargonium* (the gardener's 'geranium') from seed to make a summer bedding display, it is the *uniformity* of the resultant plants that we appreciate. In other cases, however, such as F_1 hybrid Brussels sprouts, the grower is interested in two different qualities, namely uniformity and unusual vigour. Strictly speaking, hybrid vigour or heterosis was well known to farmers and gardeners long before modern cytogenetics, and, indeed, we still have only partial explanations of what is clearly a very complicated phenomenon: but the practical importance of heterosis is clear enough.

In 1934 Crane and Lawrence published *The genetics of garden plants*, a book in which they brought together for the first time for the English reader a clear account of where our knowledge stood. The book has run to four editions, the most recent in 1977. To my generation this book became an indispensable reference work; indeed the name of the John Innes Horticultural Institution where the authors worked has since become a household word because of the soil compost pioneered there. Ironically, John Innes himself was far from being a practical gardener. He was a Victorian property tycoon who bought the estate of Merton Park, where the institution spent its first 35 years, as a development speculation – though he came to like it so much that he spent his last years there. To quote from the Institute's booklet issued to celebrate the 75th anniversary in 1985:

> "The bulk of his fortune was left for the establishment of a School for horticultural instruction or a local museum and art gallery. The horticultural training idea was considered by some to be perverse, since, apart from his liking for roadside trees, he had never shown much interest in that direction."

Nevertheless, with John Innes' money, the visionary enthusiasm of Sir David Prain, Director of Kew, and above all the scientific and cultural ability of William Bateson who was appointed first Director in 1910, the Institution has flourished.

Reading Crane and Lawrence, one soon realises that the impact of cytogenetics on our gardens must be assessed in two different ways. Most of the material in the book is concerned with explanation, in scientific terms, of what the gardener already knows or does. Most gardeners know that there is a difference between what is called 'pure' seed, and open-pollinated seed that will often give them plants showing undesirable variation. They expect their vegetable seeds to be 'pure' lines, and do not, for example, harvest next year's seed from a crop of broccoli allowed to go to seed. By experience vegetable gardeners know which of their crops they can trust as a source of next year's seed (among them are varieties of peas and beans, for example), but they rarely know the technical reasons why broccoli (a cultivar of *Brassica*) differs from, say, 'Little Marvel' pea (a cultivar of *Pisum*) in this very important way. Basically, the difference is that *Brassica* is self-incompatible, and open-pollinated flowers are almost always pollinated with pollen from a different plant, often a cultivar, whereas in the garden pea the flowers are very largely self-pollinated, so that any pure line will be accurately perpetuated by seed. Strictly speaking, this scientific explanation is not genetical, but behavioural, but I have used the example because the practice of vegetable gardeners illustrates so well the general point, namely that we now have general explanations in scientific terms of many areas of gardening practice which to Charles Darwin himself and all Victorians were largely obscure phenomena.

Peas in the history of genetics

Peas occupy a very special place in the history of genetics. As we saw in Chapter 3, Mendel used varieties of culinary peas *Pisum sativum* in the classic experiments that laid the foundations of modern genetics, and, many years later, in the early years of the present century, Bateson, Saunders and Punnett used the sweet pea *Lathyrus odoratus* as one of their principal experimental plants. In their joint paper published in 1905 they conclusively demonstrated that not all pairs of characters in a Mendelian cross necessarily segregated independently of each other. This phenomenon of 'coupling' of characters, which later became called 'linkage', eventually provided crucial evidence of the role of the chromosome in genetics – though, ironically enough, Bateson himself remained opposed to the 'chromosome theory' for several years after his discovery, preferring to look for an alternative explanation that would not involve a mechanism of chromosome pairing and exchange of genetic material.

Culinary peas and sweet peas share several important features making them especially convenient plants for genetical research. The first is that they are both annuals, easily grown from large seeds. Plant breeding is obviously easier when the generation time is short, and it is no accident that our knowledge of the genetics of the annual cereal grasses is so much more complete than that of the similarly commercially important long-lived timber-trees of forestry. In the same way, early geneticists learned quickly from experiments on many familiar annual plants of our gardens. Darwin, for example, used normal and so-called 'peloric' variants of the annual snapdragon *Antirrhinum majus*, and de Vries, one of the Continental pioneers who re-discovered Mendel's laws at the turn of the century, performed many of his experiments on familiar wild and garden plants, including white campion *Silene latifolia*, corn-cockle *Agrostemma githago* and opium poppy *Papaver somniferum*.

The second reason why peas proved to be so convenient to the early experimenters is that they have large flowers easily emasculated and pollinated artificially. There is no need for elaborate apparatus or special precautions in carrying out controlled breeding of peas: all parts of the flowers, including the ten stamens, are easily seen and identified. A third reason we have already mentioned: peas are normally self-pollinated, so that both selfing and crossing are easily arranged.

All these advantages in the use of peas experimentally must have been clear to the pioneers of genetics, as indeed they were to the specialist nurserymen who selected and hybridised them. One further advantage, however, only appears with hindsight. Both *Pisum sativum* and *Lathyrus odoratus* are diploid species, with no polyploid complications. It is in diploid species that the elucidation of the genetic structure proceeds most easily, but very many familiar garden plants are complex polyploids of hybrid origin in earlier phases of their evolution, and such plants present great difficulties to the geneticist. We realise now that there is a strong correlation between the annual habit and the diploid state, but not all annuals are simple diploids with low chromosome numbers like *Pisum* ($2n=12$) and *Lathyrus odoratus* ($2n=14$).

In their chapter on flowering and ornamental plants Crane and Lawrence show, by using the sweet pea as their example, how our knowledge of cyto-genetics can elucidate the history of a familiar garden flower. Introduced to England from Southern Europe at the end of the seventeenth century, the wild purple-flowered sweet pea soon showed in cultivation both white- and red-coloured variants. By the nineteenth century other cultivars had been selected, characterised by differences in flower shape and other characters. Purposive crossing began only about a hundred years ago, to recombine the variation and select new variants, and specialist growers began to cater for the rapidly-increasing interest in growing sweet peas. By 1900, when a great Bi-centennial Sweet Pea Exhibition was held in the Crystal Palace, the popu-lar interest in growing the 'Queen of Annuals' was rapidly spreading. Some famous plant nurseries still specialise in sweet peas, and Charles Unwin, son of the pioneer W. J. Unwin, who cooperated with the famous agricultural geneticist Sir Rowland Biffen in the Edwardian period to raise new varieties, made Unwin's in Histon, near Cambridge, one of the most famous sweet pea nurseries. This family business still flourishes, and in 1986 "on the wrong side of 90", Charles Unwin published the fourth edition of his book on sweet peas that first appeared in 1926! Now we can buy and grow either named cultivars coming true to seed, or, much more cheaply, an attractive mixture of flower-colour variants, which will to a large extent repeat in the next generation the range of colours – provided always we collect our seed from a range of different-coloured flowers.

Hybridisation

In Chapter 4 we discussed in general terms the relationship between wild species and their garden relatives, noting that very many familiar garden plants are of quite complex hybrid origin. In some cases the outline of the story has been worked out by a combination of historical and scientific study, and some elements of a common pattern emerge, in which both species-hy-bridisation and polyploidy are usually involved. In fact, sweet peas turn out to be quite exceptional amongst familiar garden plants whose outline history in cultivation we understand, in that they are strictly annual, diploid plants in which the modern range of variation is the product of artificial breeding and selection working on the basis of genetic variation within a single species.

On the other hand, hybridisation between related species at the same di-ploid level certainly underlies the development of the familiar garden poly-anthus from the wild plants we call primroses, cowslips and oxlips (Fig. 43). All these plants belong to the widespread genus *Primula* and constitute the Section *Vernales*, characterised by a uniform chromosome number 2n=22, a condition which contrasts strongly with the rest of the genus, in which many polyploid numbers are recorded, ranging from 36 to c.198. The garden polyanthus seems to have arisen in English gardens in the seventeenth cen-tury; its detailed parentage, of course, cannot now be traced, but there is good evidence that it involved the pink or purple flowered subspecies *sibthor-pii* of our familiar primrose *P. vulgaris* which came into cultivation from South-east Europe. Ruth Duthie (1984) gives a detailed assessment of the historical evidence.

Primulas related to the cowslip and the garden polyanthus provide the or-dinary gardener with one of the most familiar examples of the inter-relation-ships between wild and garden plants. It is a common experience that

populations of cowslips growing in the wilder parts of our gardens show a
range of variation greater than the wild plant, presumably because of pollination with other Vernales primulas, and it is not uncommon for wild populations to produce, for example, odd reddish or purplish flowers within a
normal yellow-flowered group. This mixing across the original barriers between the species shows signs of accelerating in recent years because of the
widespread loss of traditional unimproved pasture in our countryside, and
the consequent decline in wild cowslip populations, together with many
other 'wild flowers' familiar to our parents and grandparents as formerly
abundant in the English countryside. As a reaction, we have increased culti-

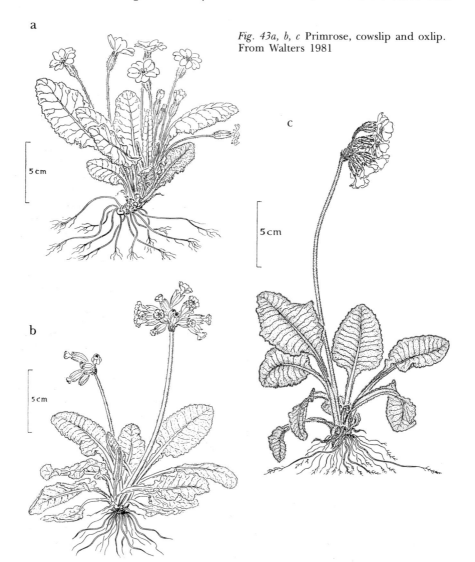

Fig. 43a, b, c Primrose, cowslip and oxlip.
From Walters 1981

vation of cowslips in 'wild-flower gardens' and in conserved herb-rich meadows as nature reserves, a modern movement discussed in the final chapter. For the present, however, we can use the familiar *Primula* example to say a little more about the significance of hybridisation in gardens.

John Ray's visit to the Oxford Botanic Garden in 1669, when he was so favourably impressed by the work of the custodian, Jacob Bobart Junior, gives us an early glimpse of the hybridisation of primulas. Bobart told Ray that he had raised seed from a "cowslip", and produced within the progeny "both primroses and oxlips" (Raven, 1950, quoted by Walters, 1981). We have no way of telling what plants were actually used, and Duthie's historical paper reminds us that the terms 'cowslip' and 'oxlip' could mean somewhat different things to different authors in the seventeenth century. Nevertheless, Ray's interest in the Bobart experiment, which contributed to his pioneer paper to the Royal Society *On Specific Differences of Plants* in 1674, emphasises how primula hybridisation has excited scientific curiosity from very early days. This interest has continued right up to the present day, and generations of Cambridge botany students are still introduced to the problems of species-hybridisation in the field by a visit to a local nature reserve in spring to see the spectacular sight of sheets of primroses, oxlips and their handsome hybrids in flower (for further information see Briggs & Walters 1984).

Against this background it is not surprising to find that these primulas were used in some of the early genetical experiments on familiar genera of garden plants. At the John Innes Experimental Station, where, as we have seen, so much important work in cytology and genetics of garden plants was carried out in the inter-war years, R. J. Chittenden (later to become the Editor of the Royal Horticultural Society's *Dictionary of Gardening*) carried out as a student a series of crossing experiments involving members of the Vernales primulas. This work had been begun by Miss C. Pellew as early as 1922. The published results (Chittenden, 1928), called rather modestly "a preliminary note", provide a wealth of information on the general make-up of these familiar plants, and throw some light on the hybridisation patterns. For example, the 'thrum' flower is dominant to the 'pin' flower, the pedunculate inflorescence (as in cowslip, oxlip and polyanthus) dominant to the single flower as in primrose, and (except in crosses involving *P. elatior*, the true oxlip) the presence of arthocyanin, producing a reddish or purplish flower colour, dominant to its absence. The fertility of hybrid seed is usually high, and F_2 and later generations can be raised. The plant used to supply purple or red colour in these experiments was *P. juliae*, a Caucasian species, which is closely related to the purple-flowered East European subspecies of *P. vulgaris* thought to have been involved in the garden polyanthus. It is most familiar in gardens as Primula 'Wanda', one of several cultivars made by crossing the Caucasian plant with other *Primula* species in the Vernales, especially *P. vulgaris*. Much further information on the genetics of the Vernales primulas is now available as a result of researches by Valentine and others on the wild British species. This work is summarised by Stace (1975, pp. 346-9).

There are many cases where a familiar garden plant has proved on investigation to be a more or less sterile species-hybrid between two wild species with the same chromosome number. One of the most familiar is the saxifrage known to British gardeners as 'London Pride', which is a hybrid between St Patrick's cabbage *Saxifraga spathularis*, a locally abundant plant in South-west Ireland, occurring also in North Spain and the mountains of North Portugal, and the Pyrenean *S. umbrosa*. London Pride, a remarkably tough Victorian garden plant which can stand up to air pollution of industrial regions, is almost entirely sterile, but is very readily propagated from offset rosettes. It is still popular as a ground cover in shady corners of gardens on poor, acid soils. The hybrid nature of London Pride has been proved by synthesising an identical plant in experimental crosses between the parent species. Like many garden plants, it is unknown in the wild because the parent species do not grow in the same region, and have been brought together only artificially in our gardens. A curious fact in this story is that gardens in Continental Europe commonly grow a similar hybrid saxifrage *S.* × *geum*, of Pyrenean origin from two species that do grow together and hybridise in nature. This plant is rarely grown in Britain, and it is very rarely naturalised anywhere in the British Isles, though it is to be found growing 'wild' in five different European countries. To complete the picture, where the Irish *S. spathularis* meets another native species *S. hirsuta*, fertile swarms are often found. Full information about this interesting group of 'Robertsonian' saxifrages can be found in Webb and Gornall (1989).

Most cases of sterile garden-hybrids have involved a sort of scientific detection work in which experimental synthesis finally clinches the argument. Increasingly, however, we have new garden plants that are made according to a more or less planned programme. *Geranium* × *cantabrigiense* is a good example. This sterile species-hybrid was synthesised in the Cambridge Botanic Garden in 1974 by Dr Helen Kiefer from two Continental cranesbills, one already a familiar garden plant in Britain, *G. macrorrhizum*, the other a much more restricted endemic native only in Albania and adjacent parts of the former Yugoslavia, *G. dalmaticum*. To quote the expert on this genus, Dr Peter Yeo: "it makes a more or less weed-proof carpet of pleasantly light green scented foliage and in some years the leaves can hardly be seen when it is in full flower." (Yeo, 1985, p.154.) This plant is becoming very popular as an easy ground cover subject, decorative both in and out of flower. Being sterile, it can only be propagated vegetatively, but this is easy, and means that new plantings accurately reproduce the characters of the parent plant.

Polyploidy

The most frequently quoted case of a new species of garden plant arising as a result of species-hybridisation followed by chromosome doubling is undoubtedly *Primula kewensis*, which we mentioned in Chapter 4. We might expect that many other examples of more or less planned hybridisation followed by polyploidy would be found amongst modern garden cultivars. It is, however, surprisingly difficult to point to more than a few cases, and we might perhaps ask why this is so. The biggest single factor seems to be that the production of 'new' garden plants remains largely in the hands of a commercial nursery trade that sees no good economic reason to change from the traditional method of open pollination yielding variable progeny, followed by selection by eye of interesting variants or, in the case of perennials, selection and propagation of vegetative mutant branches. This contrasts with the meticulously-planned breeding programmes for economically important crops carried out in the present century in the famous horticultural institutes. Amenity horticulture remains largely at the level of a hobby, and many of its practitioners would certainly wish it to remain so.

In spite of this, it is possible to point to some cases of planned allopolyploid origin amongst familiar garden plants. One of these concerns the commonly cultivated spring-flowering shrubs of the genus *Forsythia*. The only European member of the genus is the relatively little-known *F. europaea*, a very rare plant native to a small area of North Albania and adjacent parts of the former Yugoslavia, and not discovered until 1897, a plant of which Bean (1970) says: "it is the least ornamental of the forsythias and the last to flower, but is of phytogeographical interest." All our garden representatives are of East Asiatic origin, introduced into British gardens during the nineteenth century. The best-known in modern gardens is a cultivar called 'Spectabilis' selected around the end of the century from hybrids between the two Chinese species *F. suspensa* and *F. viridissima*, both diploid. Using this sterile diploid hybrid 'Spectabilis', workers at the Arnold Arboretum in the U.S.A. produced tetraploid plants by the colchicine technique in 1939, and one of these was back-crossed to 'Spectabilis' by Professor Karl Sax in 1944, who grew on a number of seedlings and studied them, selecting from amongst them tetraploid plants that have entered into commercial production. Amongst these are the eponymous 'Karl Sax', a very handsome and vigorous large-flowered forsythia that sets abundant seed and apparently breeds true (Plates 28 & 29). This cultivar appears to satisfy all the requirements of a new species of allopolyploid origin, but remains designated by its creator's name.

A good example of the wider use of polyploid breeding techniques in a familiar garden genus is found in *Lilium*, the true lilies. Gardeners and others use 'lily' to cover a whole range of flowering plants, some of them, such as the Biblical 'lilies of the field', even outside the lily family altogether. If you want to see something of the range of the plants that are called 'lilies', look at Mabberley (1987), where you will find 66 different plants listed, only 13 of which are species of *Lilium*. The genus *Lilium* itself contains about 100 species, found throughout the North Temperate region. Ten of these are European, but only one, the familiar martagon or turkscap lily *L. martagon*, is really widespread (Fig. 44). It has always found a place in British Floras, although it is uncertain whether it is a true native in any of its

Fig. 44 Martagon or turkscap lily *Lilium martagon*. From Woodcock & Stearn 1950

numerous wild localities. It is generally thought most likely to be native in woods on the North Downs, the Cotswolds and the Wye Valley. Turner was familiar with this lily in the sixteenth century, and by the eighteenth century it was quite widely grown and effectively naturalised in many park woodland sites. The only other lily qualifying for a place in the British flora is the yellow-flowered Pyrenean lily *L. pyrenaicum*, which is naturalised from gardens in a number of localities, especially in Devon.

Because of their very long association with man as beautiful and quite easily-cultivated flowers, the lilies have been extensively hybridised and selected. In recent years ambitious programmes of polyploid breeding have been undertaken, following pioneer work such as that on the structural differences in the chromosomes of *Lilium* hybrids by Richardson (1936), and some of these results, which have produced new garden cultivars of commercial importance, can be outlined here.

The chromosomes of *Lilium* are unusually favourable material for cytological study and, indeed, some of the earliest work ever done on chromosome structure used the Martagon lily (Guignard 1891). All the European wild species that have been investigated have proved to be diploids with 2n=24. The chromosomes are relatively large, and it is possible to recognise individual chromosomes in the total complement by their characteristic shape. (See Briggs and Walters 1984, pp.100-101.) The basic pattern, therefore, is relatively simple: most species-hybrids are sterile, and can be treated with colchicine to produce more or less fertile tetraploids, which can themselves be used in future breeding programmes at the polyploid level. In the Crops Research Division of the U. S. Department of Agriculture at Beltsville, Ohio, a lily breeding programme in the 1950s produced a number of commercially-important new cultivars by colchicine treatment of diploid hybrids, among them 'Tetra Mountaineer' derived from 'Mountaineer'. This new cultivar, more vigorous and with larger flowers than its diploid parent, has been used successfully in crosses to give a range of new variants. Although the colchicine method has been used effectively in such ways, the lily breeders have found an even more useful technique using triploid plants that arise not infrequently as individual progeny of diploid hybrid crosses; in particular, such triploids can be crossed with known tetraploids, when a significant proportion of the offspring are tetraploids. There is a useful review of the use of polyploid breeding methods in lilies by Thomas and Schmitzer (1989), and an earlier paper by Schmitzer (1986) discusses in particular the use of such triploid-tetraploid crosses involving 'Tetra Mountaineer'.

Whilst planned breeding involving the production and selection of artificial allopolyploids seems still to be relatively rare amongst familiar garden genera, there are many cases where our knowledge of the cytology and genetics of the group concerned can be used to understand, at least in outline, the ways in which familiar garden plants have originated from wild ancestors. A particularly good example, involving garden shrubs, concerns the groups of species that can be collectively known under the Linnaean name *Potentilla fruticosa*, and usually known to gardeners as 'the shrubby potentillas'. Some of the commonest shrubs in small suburban gardens, tolerant of limy soils and easily propagated from cuttings and from seed, these potentillas are obviously related to a famous rarity of the British flora, known since the time of John Ray, and indeed first described by him in 1671 after he had been shown the plant growing by the River Tees. This yellow-flowered shrub can still be seen by the river in Upper Teesdale: its other localities in the British Isles are in the mountains of the Lake District, and on the limestone in the Burren on the west coast of Ireland (Plate 30). On the European continent it is remarkably rare, occurring in a very few isolated localities in the mountains of the Pyrenees, the Maritime Alps and Bulgaria, and abundantly on the limestone of the Baltic islands of Öland and Gotland and adjacent parts of Estonia and Latvia. Although we now know that there are some interesting differences between different European populations, to the gardener's eye they are all rather uniform. In particular, they all have relatively small yellow flowers that are mainly produced in late spring and early summer.

In contrast, the modern cultivars we grow exhibit the kind of extended range of variation associated with the process of domestication. This affects most obviously three characters: habit, flower colour and flower size. Dwarf, semi-prostrate potentillas include 'Beesii', with greyish, almost silvery foliage and small, deep yellow flowers, suitable for rock gardens, whilst the familiar tall, bushy cultivars can be exemplified by 'Abbotswood', bearing a profusion of white flowers from May through to October, and 'Goldfinger', with very large yellow flowers. In English gardens, 'Katharine Dykes' is also very commonly grown: it has a spreading habit, somewhat blue-green foliage and small, pale yellow flowers, with the virtue of being produced throughout the summer. In recent years orange, pink or red-flowered cultivars have been selected, notably 'Tangerine' (1964), 'Red Ace' (1973), 'Royal Flush' (before 1980), and 'Princess' (1982) (Plate 31).

What can we say about the relationship between this considerable garden variation and the wild plants that were the progenitors? Here we find a problem: our knowledge of the wild variation is very incomplete. In particular, we are very ignorant of the group over its vast Asiatic range, where the plant is often abundant. What we do know, however, is that botanists who study the flora of the former Soviet Union divide the group into six species, four of them widespread and variable, and only one of these four is the yellow-flowered European and North American *Potentilla fruticosa*. We also know that throughout the nineteenth century Asiatic potentillas were introduced into European gardens, and it seems fairly certain these were responsible for the white, as opposed to yellow, flower-colour. After these early introductions, open pollination between European and Asiatic plants began to produce a range of variation that was selected by successive generations of nurserymen.

It is, of course, possible to have inspired guesses at the parentage of particular modern cultivars. For example, it seems reasonable to assume that only the European *Potentilla fruticosa* is involved in the large-flowered 'Goldfinger', whereas 'Abbotswood', with white flowers, is derived from crosses with white-flowered Asiatic plants. There is also some evidence that the red colour in 'Tangerine' and others was originally derived from plants collected as seed by Farrar and Forrest in North Burma (see Bean 1970). One of the reasons why tracing the history of hybridisation in this group is so difficult must be apparent to any gardener who has observed what actually happens in his or her own garden if several *Potentilla* bushes are grown together. The small, hard achene 'seeds' are abundantly produced on some plants and (in my experience) in most seasons, if the dead heads are not removed. Round the base of such plants appear numerous seedlings which, if grown on, will usually flower in the second year. Such open-pollinated progeny sometimes produce plants not significantly different from their parents, but not uncommonly 'new' plants arise. It is from these that nurserymen can select new and interesting cultivars. If, however, we ask what is actually happening in genetic terms, we find a set of interesting complications.

The first of these was revealed by the researches of Elkington (1969), who showed that all British *Potentilla fruticosa* is functionally dioecious, with only female plants able to set seed. It is not entirely easy to distinguish at a glance between male and female flowers because in each case there are rudimentary parts of the opposite sex. The wild populations by the River Tees have been carefully studied by Richards (1975), who has shown that the expected equal ratios of male to female flowers do not hold very well. One reason for this is that individuals can reach an age of 40 years and make, by vegetative spread, patches of up to 20m in diameter: such patches, of course, are either male or female. But there is another reason, hinted at in Richards' results. It seems that male plants predominate in open, marginal habitats with a rapid turnover, and he suggests that seedlings destined to give male plants are more able to survive in such habitats than are females. If this is true, then the apparent success of female plants over males in samples from seed may be countered by the greater viability of males. Whatever the exact picture, it is clear that the relative proportion of vegetative to reproductive spread in the wild populations would produce interestingly different situations in different conditions.

If wild British *Potentilla fruticosa* is dioecious, does this apply to other populations? Elkington was able to show that, of the European plants, those of the Baltic Islands were also dioecious. He further confirmed that British and Baltic plants were all tetraploid with 28 chromosomes, whilst the plants in the European mountains, which had hermaphrodite (normal) flowers where both male and female parts were functional, turned out to be diploid. All North American plants were also hermaphrodite and diploid. He therefore suggested that the British and Swedish plant, which was the plant known to Linnaeus, should be treated as the nominate subspecies *fruticosa*, whilst the American and South European ones constitute subspecies *floribunda*. An attempt has been made in recent years to review the whole group throughout the Northern Hemisphere (Klackenberg 1983). In this paper, Klackenberg extends our knowledge of the two subspecies (though he would prefer to give them specific rank) by showing that all Siberian plants are dioecious, whilst Caucasian and Central Asian plants are hermaphrodite. In intermediate regions, for example, the Tian-Shan mountains, both dioecious and hermaphrodite specimens are found. The other, mainly white-flowered, plants, in the south-east part of Asia (including China) he confesses are a complex requiring much further study. It is some of these plants that undoubtedly were the ancestors of many of our garden cultivars. Some at least of these white-flowered Asiatic plants which are referable to *P. arbuscula* are known to be diploid, and some cultivated plants obviously related to this species and presumably of garden hybrid origin have been shown to be triploid, hexaploid or even octoploid (Bowden 1957). We can conclude, therefore, that hybridisation in gardens has produced many polyploid derivatives, and that the process is still going on.

A final point. Klackenberg suggests that part of the explanation for the extreme complexity shown in South East Asia may be that some of the *Potentilla* there is reproducing apomictically. Neither he nor, so far as I know, anyone has conclusively demonstrated apomixis in any member of the *P. fruticosa* group, though it is well known in other parts of the genus, and is rather widespread in the family Rosaceae to which *Potentilla* belongs. Perhaps we can expect some experimental investigation of this possibility in the future.

As we saw in Chapter 4, polyploidy and apomixis are closely linked phenomena, and often both underlie complex taxonomic variation. They are difficult phenomena to investigate experimentally, which means that garden plants, which are frequently polyploids of hybrid origin, are themselves intractable experimental material. It is not therefore surprising that the genetic relationship and breeding possibilities of many familiar garden genera remain obscure. Perhaps the most remarkable of these is the genus *Rosa*, where whole books are written on the history of modern garden roses. Both the ancestral wild roses and the derived cultivars show much complex polyploid evolution, and in fact the common wild rose of our hedgerows is itself a pentaploid with a very unusual method of producing gametes (sex cells) which fuse to give the fertilised egg. In spite of the very considerable body of information, rose breeders cannot undertake the kind of controlled breeding programme illustrated by the case of *Forsythia*: their 'raw material' is already, from a cytogenetic point of view, much too complex. If we ask whether they need to, we are forced to answer 'No', for any simple crossing will produce a variety of offspring from which 'new roses' can be selected. This is a process that can go on indefinitely!

Molecular biology and biotechnology

The second half of the twentieth century has seen a spectacular growth in understanding at the molecular level of the basis of genetics. University Departments of Botany have increasingly felt it necessary to move with the times, at least to change their name to 'Department of Plant Science' or, more radically, to merge with Zoology into a joint Biology. Much of this change is due to the undoubted fact that modern understanding of genetics at the molecular level increasingly reveals the nucleoprotein DNA as the primary hereditary material, common to plants and animals alike. Not only is this development an integrating factor across the traditional teaching divide between plants and animals, but it also brings in its wake a range of powerful new techniques that can be applied, at least in theory, to all organisms. It is quite inappropriate in a book like this to attempt an account of molecular genetics but, given the public airing of aspects of this rapidly-developing area of biological science, we might at least ask the question: how much of the new look is relevant to our main topic?

One thing can be said at the outset. Most of the advances in knowledge of molecular genetics have been achieved by using micro-organisms, and have as yet had only a limited application to higher plants. To some extent, this is a matter of convenience: it has always been true that genetical advance is quicker when the experimental organism has a short life-cycle, and some microorganisms can complete their cycles in a matter of hours. But there is also a powerful economic factor. It is no accident that the prestigious unit of molecular biology in Cambridge University was set up by the Medical Research Council on the site of the new Hospital, and still flourishes there. Fundamental genetic understanding produces very quick spin-offs in human medicine, for example in the biosynthesis via bacteria of the powerful hormone insulin used in the treatment of diabetes. Having said this, we can easily point to areas where so-called 'genetic engineering' is of enormous potential significance in the quicker improvement of crop plants, and certainly aspects of molecular genetics are already altering our general understanding of the nature of variation in all organisms, though little of this has yet altered much horticultural practice.

There is one development, however, linked in the public mind to these spectacular advances, which *is* already in practical use, even in amenity horticulture. The word 'clone', which was to most people an unfamiliar technical term twenty years ago, is now commonly used, and its meaning more or less correctly understood. Looked at from the historical angle, cloning a higher plant is nothing new: it is what gardeners have always done when they have used vegetative propagation, not seed, to increase their stock. Familiar sterile cultivars like 'King Edward' potatoes or the rose 'Peace' are in fact single clones of identical genetical make-up in all individuals. The break-through has been in the development of micro-propagation as a branch of what is often called biotechnology.

Micro-propagation involves the cloning from small pieces of vegetative tissue of a large number of new individuals from a single mother plant. Of course, the possibility of doing this has been known for some years: indeed, in the case of the African violet, *Saintpaulia*, for example, the production of numerous plantlets from single detached leaves has become standard horticultural practice. We might therefore ask: when does propagation deserve the prefix 'micro-'? Perhaps when the manipulation involves very small pieces of tissue that need to be handled under a binocular microscope. The most frequently-used tissue is the actively-growing meristem or growing-point, a technique therefore called 'meristem culture'. It has become commercially important, for example, in the propagation of orchids, where there are special nutritional reasons that make the technique of micro-propagation on an agar jelly medium in test-tube culture particularly suitable. At the Royal Botanic Gardens, Kew, the micro-propagation unit is used especially to propagate nearly extinct plants and in this way quickly to reduce the risk of total extinction, and there is now an international network of research institutes and botanic gardens with its own newsletter produced from Kew. Clearly such techniques have wide application in the conservation of endangered plants. An excellent illustration of a rescue project using micro-propagation is the work of Power and Cocking (1991) on cloning the original surviving tree of the famous English cooking apple 'Bramley's Seedling' (Fig. 45).

One final point. When we say that the offspring of vegetative propagation are genetically identical, we should strictly qualify this. This statement takes no account of the occurrence of mutation and, as we saw in Chapter 3, the idea of random genetic change, or mutation, underlies all classical genetical theory. In fact, there is a great deal of evidence that the manipulation of tissue involved in micro-propagation actually increases the likelihood of mutant offspring, whose genetical constitution is *not* identical with the mother plant. We can illustrate this from some very interesting work being carried out (1991) at Wye College of the University of London on the propagation of cultivars of the garden auricula, derived more than 400 years ago from the

a

b

Fig. 45 Micropropogation
rescues the original Bramley
apple. (a) the original,
160-year old tree: (b) cloned,
self-rooted Bramley trees
before their transfer to soil.
From Power & Cocking 1991

Alpine species *Primula auricula* and crossed with related species. In this study, which is particularly directed at 'rescuing' rare auricula cultivars, they find that the "risk" of mutation is very small in plants developed directly from leaf tissue, but where the technique involves regenerating from callus tissue formed on very small pieces of a single leaf, "mutation is always a possibility." They further discuss the relative merit of leaf tissue and meristem culture for cleansing the cultivar stock of harmful viruses, and confirm the expected result that meristem culture is much more efficient in regenerating a virus-free stock. Whether the mutant plants are seen as 'good' or 'bad' depends, of course, on the ultimate user: in amenity horticulture, any new variety is potentially interesting and can be assessed according to any imposed criteria but, if the aim is to rescue and perpetuate a near-extinct auricula cultivar, mutation is an undesirable complication.

10

Botanists, Gardeners and Social Change

Herborising

In recent years, a number of writers have turned their attention to the history of natural history studies, and some have very helpfully condensed their material into semi-popular accounts and published them. Outstanding amongst them is David Allen, one of the best amateur botanists of the post-war generation, in his book entitled *The Naturalist in Britain* and subtitled 'a social history' (Allen, 1976). This is compulsory reading for anyone whose interest may be sparked by what I have to say in this chapter, and I shall allow myself the luxury of quoting liberally from it. Ten years later (1986) he produced a sesquicentennial history of the Botanical Society of the British Isles: entitled *The Botanists*, this beautifully-researched study of the varied fortunes of the Society which unites British and Irish field botanists across the amateur/professional divide is a great source of further relevant information.

It is tempting to go back, as Allen's book rightly does, to the seventeenth century to begin the story of the organised study of wild and garden plants in Britain. Indeed, we could defend a decision to go back even further, and start with those remarkable pioneer figures who preceded the deservedly famous John Ray (1627-1705): men like William Turner, the Northumbrian naturalist whose *Herball* was the standard work of the sixteenth century, or John Parkinson who published in 1629 the first English gardening book with that extraordinary title incorporating a pun on his own name: *Paradisi in sole Paradisus terrestris* (The Park on earth of the Park in sun). If the reader is moved to do so, Charles Raven's two outstanding erudite biographies (Raven 1942, 1947) are the obvious sources to consult. For my purposes, I shall limit my enquiry to the theme of my book, and at the outset ask the question: were the early pioneer students of plants botanists, gardeners or both?

There is little doubt what the answer to our question should be. Throughout the history of European civilisation, a knowledge of plants and their properties has been a necessary part of man's development. But in one very particular area, namely, medicine, the use of plants has meant that their cultivation has gone hand in hand with their collection from the wild. From classical times onwards until quite recently, the training of medical students involved recognition of European wild plants and, increasingly from late Mediaeval times, their cultivation in 'Physic Gardens'. It is not surprising therefore to find that most of the seventeenth-century botanists in London learned their plants in the field on excursions organised by the Society of Apothecaries, an ancient livery company. As Allen explains: "The study of plants had obvious practical application for the infant science of medicine and, as a result of this, alone of the various branches of natural history, could count at this time on organised support from a professional quarter." Nowhere is this link more obvious than in the history of the famous Chelsea Physic Garden, established by the Apothecaries in 1673, and still on its original site today. Another recent book illuminates our subject: Hazel le Rougetel's study (1990) of *The Chelsea Gardener, Philip Miller (1691-1771)*. Under this famous man, the Physic Garden's collections grew and achieved renown, not just in Europe, but throughout much of the rapidly-expanding British colonial empire. In the successive editions of Miller's *Gardeners Dictionary*, published between 1731 and 1768, we can trace the extraordinary growth of botanical and horticultural knowledge through these middle years of the eighteenth century, at a time when in the two ancient Universities science – and indeed all learning – was at a relatively low ebb. Although Miller's main interests were clearly in the cultivation of plants, especially those new to botany which presented a special challenge, he showed no sign of a rigid division between his enthusiasm for wild and garden plants. On a tour of Holland in 1727, for example, he not only admired the cultivation of pineapples in the famous garden at Meerburg, but botanised in the Dutch countryside, making notes on interesting plants such as the sweet flag *Acorus calamus*, and collecting *Circaea alpina* from a wood near the Hague to grow back in England. After his return he prepared a paper on the Dutch method of growing hyacinth bulbs in water, and wrote a full description of the culture of hyacinths and tulips in the *Gardeners Dictionary*. Thomas Martyn, the fourth Professor of Botany in Cambridge, and a contemporary and childhood friend of Philip Miller's son, Charles, in the Preface to his two-volume edition of the *Gardeners Dictionary* (1795-1807) says of Miller: "His objects were not confined to exotics, few were better acquainted with indigenous plants of Britain, of which he successfully cultivated most of the rare species."

Reverting to the educational and training role of the Apothecaries' Physic Garden at Chelsea, we must remember that it was an important part of the instruction of the apprentices, who normally began at the age of thirteen or fourteen and were 'bound' for seven or eight years. These were the future apothecaries, men whose role was not dissimilar to that of the general practitioner today, and it was considered essential that they should be able to recognise in the fresh state a wide range of common and less common plants used in medicine, if only to detect fraud or error in the identification of herbs supplied by professional herb-gatherers. Accordingly the 'Demonstrator of Plants' – a paid official of the Society of Apothecaries – "was required to take up his stand in the Garden every last Wednesday in each summer month ... to expound the names and uses of the more important plants." Inevitably, human nature being what it is, such occasions – especially the 'herborisings' or excursions to collect the 'simples' in the field – tended to get out of control. Anyone who has conducted modern student excursions will know the problem! Allen quotes a passage written in 1767 by a Freeman of the Society who said that he and others were deterred from sending their apprentices "to the Lectures and Botanik Walks, so often as they would have done, by the Irregularity and indecent Behaviour of some Persons who have frequented those Walks, fearing their own apprentices might be corrupted by such Examples."

These early field trips were clearly professional, but inevitably they attracted men of calibre who were pursuing their natural history interest without any obvious pecuniary or career value. They therefore provided, for the more securely-placed middle classes, occasions for cooperative, convivial groups of like-minded enthusiasts to meet, often in inns or the newly-popular coffee houses of the rapidly-growing cities. In this way they fostered the amateur-professional link that has been, and still is, a remarkable feature of both the present-day Botanical Society of the British Isles and the Royal Horticultural Society.

Collecting and herbaria

One of the big differences between the field botanist and the gardener is to be found in their attitudes to the pressed specimen. Indeed, some aspects of this difference remain to the present day as a bone of contention between the two, one side accusing the other of being obsessed with the herbarium method to the neglect of the living plant, the other retorting with a counter-accusation of slipshod methods of naming and recording garden plants. It is certainly true that nowhere is there more need for each side to learn from the other, if only to be more tolerant.

Although it is wrong to see the rise of botanical herbaria as a Victorian phenomenon, it is certainly true that the Victorian collecting mania gave an enormous impetus to the growth of the 'herbarium industry'. But before we look at this phenomenon, we should see what lay behind it in the previous two centuries, and where better to start than with this aspect of the Chelsea Physic Garden's activities?

The making of herbaria – ordered reference collections of pressed specimens of plants – seems to have originated back in the fifteenth century in the earliest Botanic Gardens attached to the Italian Universities, such as those still surviving in Padua, Pisa and Florence. In these early years, the pressed and dried collection was called a *Hortus Siccus* or 'Dry Garden', the very name emphasising its garden origin. By the eighteenth century, making a herbarium was a long-established practice, and provided a standard procedure for the recording and exchange of important information. As an example, there are historically important herbarium sheets still in the University Herbarium in Cambridge which provide evidence of the closeness of the link between Chelsea and Cambridge forty years before the establishment of the first Cambridge Botanic Garden, a garden that was explicitly modelled on the Chelsea Physic Garden. For Chelsea itself, we have a unique record of the plants in cultivation in the form of 3,750 numbered specimens collected in the Garden, at a rate of fifty specimens a year, over the period 1722-1796; this collection, which was given to the Natural History Museum in 1862, can still be consulted there. These so-called 'Royal Society' plants are the subject of a recently-published study (Stungo 1993). In Chelsea at any rate, the herbarium method provided, both at the time and, even more importantly, to future generations, incontrovertible evidence that the written claim to have been growing a particular species in a particular year was correct. To take a familiar example: there is a specimen of coffee *Coffea arabica* grown by Miller in Chelsea in 1728 (Fig. 46). Coffee was cultivated in the Amsterdam Botanic Garden, where Richard Bradley, first Cambridge Professor of Botany, had seen it growing in 1714. It was an obvious new plant for Miller to bring into cultivation at Chelsea.

Not only can herbarium specimens be used to verify the dates of introduc-

Fig. 46 Specimen of the coffee plant *Coffea arabica* growing at Chelsea Physic Garden in 1728. Photo Ruth Stungo

tion of familiar exotic crops, but also to clarify the history of groups that the taxonomic botanist calls 'critical' – ie. plants constituting wide aggregate species, but with modern knowledge seen to be divisible into several taxa with interestingly different histories. An excellent example comes from my study of *Alchemilla*, the lady's mantle, a familiar plant both in the wild (at least in Scotland and northern England) and in our gardens. Because of its supposed medicinal, even magical, qualities, the common lady's mantle was obviously familiar to generations of herbalists in Northern Europe from Mediaeval times onwards. It was known as a wild British 'herb' to Parkinson, and Ray collected both the common species, and later the more local alpine lady's mantle *A. alpina* in the North of England during his 'simpling' excursions in 1658 and 1671. The very name *Alchemilla*, which can be traced back to a Herbal published in 1485, derives from the use in the potions of alchemists of the drops of dew forming on the leaf surfaces. The modern Swedish name for the plant is 'daggkåpa' or 'dew-cape', which draws attention to the same quality.

Such a plant, much used in both alchemy and medicine, and easy to cultivate, would obviously be represented in the early Physic Gardens, both by the common species, to which eventually Linnaeus gave the binomial *A. vulgaris*, and the easily-distinguished *A. alpina* (Plate 32). We can in fact trace both these plants back in garden cultivation to the middle of the seventeenth century, because of surviving herbarium material of plants collected by Antoni Gaymans, a Dutch pharmacist, almost certainly in the famous Botanic Garden in Leiden around 1661 (Sosef et al. 1987). But the particular interest of these early 'pre-Linnaean' specimens of *Alchemilla* arises from the fact that, whereas to all the early botanists up to and including Linnaeus himself, there were in effect only two different species, and the variation shown by *Alchemilla* was hardly appreciated, we now know that a great deal of variation arises from the apomictic mode of reproduction of *Alchemilla*, and that '*A. vulgaris*' actually includes several hundred microspecies that can be distinguished from each other on a combination of slight but constant characters of size, leaf shape, hairiness, etc. Under *A. alpina* in the wide Linnaean sense a similar but less numerous group of microspecies can be described, mostly in the Alps (Fig. 47). No historical record of '*A. vulgaris*' or '*A. alpina*' can be safely assigned to a particular microspecies in the absence of a herbarium specimen. Furthermore, the apomictic reproduction ensures that, unlike most plants which can, and often do, promiscuously cross-pollinate in garden cultivation, in *Alchemilla* any spread by seed produces individuals genetically identical with the mother plant. It is for this reason possible to trace with some accuracy whole lineages in cultivation back to very early times. In this way we know, for example, that not one, but three quite distinct species of 'alpine lady's mantle' were in cultivation before the end of the eighteenth century. Using their scientific names as in *Flora Europaea* (1968) these are: *A. alpina* of Linneaus, widespread in N.Europe and in the Alps; *A. plicatula* Gandoger, the Alpine plant already in cultivation in Leiden as early as 1661, and much easier to grow in lowland Europe than *A. alpina* (Fig. 48); and finally *A. conjuncta* Babington, a handsome plant, native in the Jura and Western Alps, very easily cultivated and sometimes (as in Glen Clova in Scotland) quite permanently naturalised from early garden stocks. Without the historic

Fig. 47 Leaves of six *Alchemilla* microspecies, ranging from 1. *A. fulgens* (a *'vulgaris'* type) to 6. *A. alpina*

herbarium specimens we could not elucidate the cultivated history of these plants.

We can also support from herbarium specimens the remarkably recent arrival in our gardens of the plant that most gardeners call correctly by its Latin name – *Alchemilla mollis* (Plate 33). Given its extreme abundance in our gardens as a hardy herbaceous plant, we may find it difficult to believe that until the 1960's this species was relatively unknown. Its popularity owes much to its value in supplying long-lasting sprays of massed small yellow-green flowers from June onwards, ideal for the very popular art of the flower-arranger. The earliest specimens of this very distinctive garden plant to be found in reference collections go back to the turn of the century in a few

Above Plate 30 *Potentilla fruticosa* on the Burren limestone, Co. Clare, Ireland. (See p. 149). Photo Andrew Gagg.

Below Plate 31 Individual flowers of cultivated shrubby potentillas to show range of variation in colour and size. Top, left to right: 'Abbotswood', 'Katherine Dykes', 'Tangerine', 'Red Ace', 'Princess'. Middle, left: *P. fruticosa* subsp. *floribunda*; right, *P. fruticosa* subsp. *fruticosa*. Bottom: 'Goldfinger'. Scale in cm. (See p. 149). Photo Martin Walters.

Plate 32 Alpine lady's mantle
Alchemilla alpina on the Storr,
Isle of Skye. (See p. 159).
Photo M. C. F. Proctor.

Plate 33 *Alchemilla mollis* (See pp. 62
& 160). Photo Andrew Gagg.

Plate 34 Common
lady's mantle *Alchemilla
xanthochlora* cultivated
on a garden patio.
(See p. 161). Photo
Martin Walters.

Plate 35 Notice outside a cottage garden, Foxton, Cambridgeshire in 1992. (See p. 186). Photo Martin Walters.

Plate 36 Buddleia and young ash at edge of chalk pit, Cherry Hinton, Cambridge, July 1989. (See pp. 181 & 188). Photo Martin Walters.

Plate 37 Slender speedwell *Veronica filiformis* and daffodils in orchard, March 1992. (See pp. 105 & 174). Photo Martin Walters.

Left Plate 38
Fiddle dock *Rumex pulcher* in churchyard, Grantchester, Cambridgeshire. (See p. 185). Photo Andrew Gagg.

Below Plate 39
Wild flower meadow in churchyard, Great Evenden, Northamptonshire. (See p. 185). Photo F. H. Perring.

Fig. 48 Specimen of *Alchemilla plicatula* in Herb. Gaymans, in National Botanic Gardens, Glasnevin, Ireland. This herbarium sheet is more than 300 years old.

botanic gardens. Its native haunts are the mountains of south-east Europe and Turkey, from where it was first described in 1874; its subsequent spread via the botanic gardens of Europe seems to have been quite slow, in spite of its robust habit and effective seed spread. Indeed, in Victorian botanic gardens its relative *A. speciosa* seems to have been equally common, and proves on cultivation side by side with *A. mollis* to be equally vigorous and productive from seed. Why *A. mollis* triumphed and *A. speciosa* languished in botanic gardens is not at all clear. There are in fact four quite distinct microspecies of the *mollis* group, any of which may be growing in an English garden: I have recently succeeded in making a survey of these via the membership of the RHS, who responded well to a request for voucher material made through the columns of the Society's Journal *The Garden* (Walters 1991).

What of the native '*Alchemilla vulgaris*'? In Britain we have only three common microspecies, not one of which makes an attractive garden plant, though two of the three, *A. glabra* and *A. xanthochlora* (Plate 34), turn up not uncommonly in cultivation, and both can be traced back to the eighteenth century in Botanic Gardens. A final, oddly unexpected, observation: the only microspecies at all widespread in lowland England, *A. filicaulis* subsp. *vestita*, is surprisingly difficult to keep in garden cultivation, being subject to heavy mildew attack.

To return to our main theme: the growth of herbaria can be seen as but one facet of the fashionable hobby of the study of natural history which spread very rapidly amongst the leisured classes during the eighteenth century. This movement, parallelled by the Romantic period in literature and art, is beautifully described by Allen in the second chapter of *The Naturalist in Britain* (1976). It produced, amongst many other manifestations, some of the largest collections of natural objects ever amassed by private individuals. For example, Lady Margaret Cavendish Bentinck, who married the second Duke of Portland in 1734, devoted most of her fifty years of married life to forming an immense collection, certainly, according to Allen, "the largest in Britain, quite possibly the largest in Europe", in her great house at Bulstrode in Buckinghamshire. She employed a range of gifted collectors, amongst them James Bolton, a Halifax man, who collected lichens in the north of England, and painted beautiful illustrations of them, and John Lightfoot, eventual author of the *Flora Scotica*, who was dispatched to remote areas in the Highlands to collect rare plants. King George III and Queen Charlotte, both genuinely interested, were frequent visitors.

In the middle of this period came the impact of Linnaeus, the Swedish naturalist, and his 'sexual system' for the classification and arrangement of plants. Linnaean methods were eventually accepted rather readily in Britain, unlike in France where Buffon's monumental *Histoire Naturelle*, which took him and a group of naturalists fifty-five years to complete in forty-four volumes, captured the imagination and the loyalty of the Parisian intelligentsia. Again, Allen: "When, within a decade, much of the world was converted to Linnaeus, the French stayed faithful to Buffon ... In their approach to natural history they put entrancement before utility: Buffon wrote like a dramatist; Linnaeus, for all the efficiency of his method, like some icy, impersonal machine." Many would say that the British and the French are still effectively separated, even in aspects of modern science, by attitudes not fundamentally changed since the eighteenth century! The story of James Edward Smith and the purchase of the Linnaean collections is perhaps too familiar to need retelling: but here is the outline. Smith was the son of a rich Norwich merchant; whilst still a student in Edinburgh, he succeeded in buying the Linnaean library and collections, and around this prestigious hoard he founded, with a group of naturalist friends, the Linnean Society of London in 1788. Amongst these collections is the herbarium of Linnaeus, now world-famous mainly because of its importance in the interpretation of Linnaean names for plants, and visited by botanical experts from all over the world.

Condensing the history of field botany and horticulture into a small number of themes is ludicrously inadequate for the eighteenth century, but even more so for the Victorian period. But so far as herbaria are concerned two great developments must be mentioned. The first was a natural extension of the collectors' mania out of the limited – though very powerful – circle of the rich and famous to infect what those people would undoubtedly have called 'the lower classes'. During the nineteenth century hundreds of private herbaria, sometimes the property of the new natural history societies, sometimes amassed by ordinary men and women enjoying a relaxing hobby in the countryside, came into being and expanded. In those expansionist days, when few naturalists foresaw any conservation problems in collecting and killing wild plants and animals, knowledge of the detailed distribution at least of the rarer species grew very rapidly indeed, as 'voucher specimens' labelled with date and place of collection were pressed and mounted on stiff sheets. Remember that photography was a specialised and expensive hobby until towards the end of the century, and not readily available as an alternative verification method.

On top of this passion for collecting especially the rare and the bizarre, and only tenuously linked with it, was the growth of natural science as we know it now as a professional subject. The effect of this was to create new herbaria and zoological collections in connection with the rapidly-expanding main institutions whose roots go back into the previous century at least, but who now took on a new role as part of the nation's scientific stock-in-trade. Moreover, as the problems of preservation of dried specimens became more and more obviously a burden to the many private herbaria, these were increasingly bequeathed or transferred on 'permanent loan' to these national institutions. In this way the vast collections now kept at Kew and the Natural History Museum in London and in several other key centres grew and took their present shape. The wealth and scientific value of some of the large provincial collections are still, incidentally, relatively little appreciated: in Manchester, for example, there is one of the largest (mainly European) herbaria in existence, largely of nineteenth-century origin, and estimated (Holmgren et al. 1990) to contain a million specimens!

Educating 'the common people'

The rise of local societies of enthusiasts devoted to the study of aspects of the natural sciences is one of the most characteristic social phenomena of the early nineteenth century. It can be considered as part of a general drive for education and self-improvement which developed as the traditional agricultural communities declined in social and political importance, in the face of the steep rise in urban populations no longer tied to the land and often motivated by strong independent drives. This new educational movement is very relevant to our theme. I have chosen to illustrate it from an area, part of which I knew well as a child, namely the vast conurbation, as it now is, of Manchester and the surrounding countryside. Similar examples could be used from other cities.

The 1820's saw the formation in the young rapidly-developing manufacturing town of a Manchester Society for the Promotion of Natural History in 1821 and six years later the Manchester Botanical and Horticultural Society, which founded its own Botanic Garden in Old Trafford. The earlier of these Societies was founded by 'a number of Manchester gentlemen' who subscribed £10 each; they were the 'nouveaux riches' who saw education as part of their social improvement, and who eventually (1839) admitted as subscribing members 'strangers' of the lower classes. The master-servant relationship, so firm and traditional in the still largely 'feudal' countryside, had nothing like so strong an inhibiting effect in these brash new industrial towns. Indeed, some of the most remarkable field botanists were initially illiterate artisans who through sheer enthusiasm and force of personality edu-

cated themselves and their fellow-naturalists. As Shercliff says in his delightful study of the social history of these groups entitled *Nature's Joys are Free for
All* (1987), perhaps the most famous in the Manchester area was Richard
Buxton, born in 1786, who "had a very poor schooling and taught himself to
read in his teens working from 6 am till 8 or 9 making childrens' leather
shoes". Together with keen botanists such as John Horsefield, a weaver, and
others working as gardeners in local estates, they scoured the surrounding
countryside, walking "hundreds of miles agreeably together" and learning
the local flora, immeasurably richer in those days before the main industrial
pollution. To these marvellously self-taught men Linnaean Latin names and
the Linnaean classificatory system presented no insuperable difficulties, and
eventually Buxton was persuaded to publish in 1849 his *Botanical Guide to the
flowering plants, ferns, mosses and algae found indigenous within 16 miles of Manchester*. In the introduction Buxton hopes that despite the huge increase in
population since his youthful days there will continue to be delightful
streams, green woods and meadows within 16 miles of Manchester "where
the flowers are superior to the artificial creations in the rich men's gardens."
Here is an early emotional expression of field botany versus horticulture.
But we should beware of drawing the conclusion that all the pioneers of the
new natural history shared the same view.

Leo Grindon, who published his own *Manchester Flora* in 1859 (Fig. 49) and
whose considerable herbarium, containing more than 20,000 specimens, is
now part of the Manchester Museum collection, was a dedicated botanist
with a foot in both camps. Son of a solicitor Joseph Grindon, who was Re-
corder of the City of Bristol, young Leo derived his early interest in botany
from his mother, an intelligent and cultured woman. Leo came to Manchester
in 1838, found work as a cashier in a firm of cotton spinners, and began a long
and successful life in which field botany must have played a very important
part. Together with his friends he made the acquaintance of older men who
knew the local flora, and began regular excursions and meetings to study botany. Tensions arose between the field naturalists like Grindon who delighted
in their outdoor hobby and the more scientific and professional members of
the Literary and Philosophical Society, which were brought to a head by Grindon's application for membership in 1862. Such tensions had undoubtedly
played a part in the founding by Grindon and his friend Joseph Sidebotham
of the Manchester Field Naturalists Society in 1860, a Society "for ladies and
gentlemen who are specially interested in natural history", also open to those
"who mainly delight to ramble in the country and find pleasure in the contem-
plation of its loveliness". This Society, satirically named by some of Grindon's
critics as 'The Manchester Field and Flirtation Society', flourished in the second half of Victoria's reign, with, at its heyday, a membership of several hundred men and women, and an energetic programme of excursions and
remarkable, well-attended winter soirees. In 1859 Grindon had published his
Manchester Flora as a companion to his *Manchester Walks and Wild Flowers*
(1858). Unlike Buxton, he showed no inhibition about cultivated plants, and
the field meetings were equally likely to visit, with appropriate permission,
some private estate as to concentrate on the wild moorland areas or the 'natural' woods. In fact he explicitly states in the Preface to his text-book *British and
Garden Botany* (1864) that "those who love plants are seldom found asking

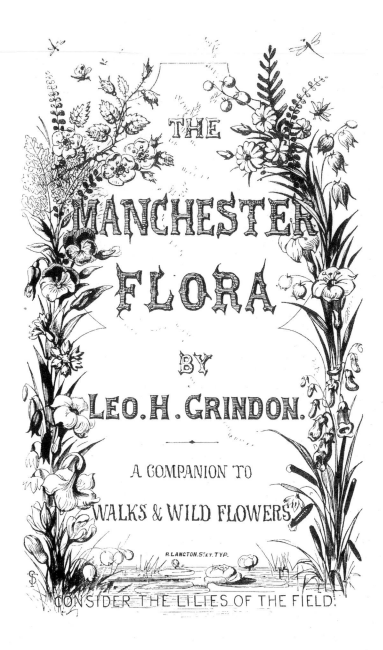

THE

MANCHESTER

FLORA

BY

LEO. H. GRINDON.

A COMPANION TO

WALKS & WILD FLOWERS

R. LANGTON. S?ET. TYP.

CONSIDER THE LILIES OF THE FIELD.

Fig. 49 Title-page of Leo Grindon's *Manchester Flora*, 1859

whether a given flower be indigenous or exotic; they wish to know what they have got, and care little for its birth-place."

Grindon's catholic tastes reflect not only his middle-class origin and early education, but also the fact that 'Field Naturalists' were themselves likely to be at least of 'respectable' origin, if not actually owners of country houses. One root, therefore, of the split between field botany and horticulture seems to be class difference, reflected in education and opportunity. In practice, Richard Buxton, a humble shoemaker, would not have had easy access to the private estates or country houses even if he had seen any need to seek it.

One final point before we move on. When Grindon began his botanising, there were no railways. Whilst this in no way prevented energetic naturalists from enjoying their hobby, the advent of the railway undoubtedly opened up the countryside around the industrial towns to mass invasions by day trippers. Grindon sees this as sheer gain. As he puts it in *Manchester Walks and Wild Flowers*: "The railways, penetrating every nook and corner ... now enable us to reach the very heart of the country not only in a very little while, but fresh and nimble for our enjoyment ... Honoured for ever be the name of Stephenson!"

The rise of professional science

Undoubtedly the most important change affecting the relationship of botany and horticulture in the nineteenth century was the rise of professional science. Any proper analysis of this phenomenon and its effects is beyond the scope of this book, but Allen provides us in *The Naturalist in Britain* with an excellent review of Victorian natural history in its social context which we can use for our purposes. He introduces us, with choice examples, to the remarkable industriousness of many naturalists of the early nineteenth century: "work for such men was more than just an interest that absorbed them; it was a compulsive discharge of sloth, recreation for them could never mean relaxation". Further: "the idea of work for work's sake also introduced a new note of fervour into the hitherto rather inconsequential pastime of collecting. As with books, the very size of a collection came to be regarded as worthy in itself, implying the strong-minded devotion of many hours of loving toil and effort ... Collecting, in short, received religious sanction".

From this background of single-minded devotion to the pursuit of nature in all its manifestations arose the new professional science in the second half of the century, and institutions came into being like the Natural History Museum in South Kensington, whose 'Victorian Gothic' building, hailed by *The Times* as "a true Temple of Nature showing, as it should, the Beauty of Holiness", has welcomed generations of school-children since its completion in 1881. The Museum's rich botanical collections (estimated at nearly 2,000,000 herbarium sheets in 1900) were, of course, only a small part of the total, and were, in fact, the subject of great and lasting controversy during much of the nineteenth century, as the pre-eminence of Kew in the study of systematic botany caused many people to ask whether a single large national herbarium should not be created and centred at Kew. The extraordinary story of this rivalry between Kew and the 'British Museum' can be read in William Stearn's very erudite book published in the Natural History Museum's Centenary Year (1981). To pursue this by-way too far would take us away from our main theme, but I cannot resist recounting Stearn's explanation of the inconvenient fact known to all taxonomists who in the course of their studies find themselves consulting these two famous Herbaria: namely, that the size of the standard herbarium sheet is quite different in the two Institutions (a fact, incidentally, used to defend the 'B.M.' Herbarium against threatened Kew take-over bids!). Stearn explains this as a historical accident, reflecting the fact that "Joseph Banks, being a rich man, could afford to buy larger sheets" and created the Banksian Herbarium, the nucleus of the B.M. collections, whilst the young William Hooker housed his own, smaller private herbarium in a small cabinet made for him locally in Norwich. Hence, even today, the 'B.M.' size is 44.5 x 28.6 cm, whilst that at Kew (and throughout the British Commonwealth) is 41.9 x 26.7 cm!

The establishment of the great national museums and herbaria was, of course, only part of the expansion of science education in Victorian times. Even the two ancient Universities were finally moved to take science seriously, so that, for example, in Cambridge the pioneer John Stevens Henslow was able, only a few months before his death in 1861, to examine candidates in Botany for the new Natural Sciences Tripos. By the closing years of Victoria's reign, professional botanists were being produced in quantity by the Universities for careers in teaching, museum curation and, of course, a very wide range of applied botanical research posts in agriculture and forestry, with the consequence that membership of the Botanical Society of the British Isles now divided clearly into amateur and professional, and still does to the present day. This cooperation, undoubtedly one of the great strengths of the British botanical tradition, reached a high point in the Distribution Maps Scheme run by the Society in the 1950's which produced the standard *Atlas of the British Flora* (Perring & Walters 1962). As Allen warns us in his discussion of the recent development of the BSBI, we should not assume that the distinction between amateur and professional is always black-and-white. "Many of those who work in the major taxonomic institutions, for example, have traditionally been as close, if not closer, to the amateur world as they have to the world of the universities".

This dramatic rise in science education in Victorian Britain must also have had its effect on the Royal Horticultural Society and the shape of horticultural study, though this effect is less clear-cut. In particular, the study of cultivated plants has never lost its severely professional side because the nursery trade has a continuous history, and indeed flourished in Victorian Britain as never before or since. The new professionals, however, were often very different from the old commercial ones: they included the 'high priests' in the taxonomic institutions whom the gardener and nurseryman viewed with some suspicion, not least because of their high-handed way of changing familiar Latin names for garden plants! This irritation and tension is still with us today, as the pages of the gardening press show clearly enough.

How far do the great national or regional Herbaria such as those at Kew and Edinburgh house important horticultural collections, and to what extent is present-day amenity horticulture based on such collections? Neither of these questions is easily answered. The Royal Horticultural Society's own Herbarium at Wisley is certainly important, and could, if present plans come to fruition, be even more important as the movement for well-documented National Collections grows (see Chapter 12); but we still lack any proper survey of the range and value of horticultural herbaria. Any standard revisions of the taxonomy of garden plants, such as are to be found in the recently-completed *New*

Royal Horticultural Society Dictionary of Gardening (Huxley et al. (eds) 1992), certainly depends heavily on the main taxonomic herbaria but, as any specialist will know, more for the essential basic information on the wild species to which all our garden plants are related than for the (much more difficult) study of the cultivated variants. For most garden genera there is still surprisingly little adequate study using traditional herbarium techniques.

One final point of importance. Most professionals are men, but most active members of the Royal Horticultural Society and the Botanical Society are women. This pattern arose in the nineteenth century and obviously has several causes. But one of these is perhaps peculiar to the study of plants: this is the widely-held view that botany was (and still is) a gentle pursuit, suitable for 'the fair sex' and really quite different from the 'hard sciences' of physics and chemistry.

11

The Rise of Ecology

Wild nature and cultivated garden

The roots of modern amenity horticulture can be traced back to the enclosed gardens made by the rich and powerful in ancient civilisations, an origin made evident by our use of the Persian word 'paradise' with all its otherworldly and religious overtones. Such enclosed gardens, as in ancient Mesopotamia or in Pharaonic Egypt, could flourish only where there was a supply of fresh water and effective protection from human and animal predators, and inevitably their owners must have felt them to be opposed to, rather than any part of, the harsh world of nature outside the perimeter walls. Nature does not looks so implacably hostile to the modern Englishman, but the basic opposition of 'wild' and 'cultivated' remains very deep in the way we see the world. The owner of many a small suburban house guards his privacy behind an impenetrable evergreen hedge of quick-growing 'Leylandii', and the outside world, though no longer full of dangerous wild beasts, retains some of its real or imagined hostility.

In one very important way the rise of Victorian scientific and technological education must have contributed to this feeling of man against nature. Inside the garden, the Victorian owner could create his own ordered version of nature tamed, even distorted, by his powerful skills. Allied to the Protestant work ethic, science and technology were harnessed to the service of the garden just as they were so ruthlessly allied to commerce in the great manufacturing cities. Of course, for the favoured few owning large estates it was always possible to see 'nature' as benign or at least not seriously hostile, and modern England has many treasured monuments to the ingenuity and good taste of eighteenth-century landowners. In our more egalitarian society, the two million members of the National Trust can enjoy landscapes created and clothed according to the designs of Bridgeman, Brown and Repton, and share something of the beauty made by the few for their private enjoyment. Indeed, we cannot tell the history of gardening without giving an important place to the changes in fashion affecting garden and landscape design in the seventeenth and eighteenth centuries, involving, as it did in England, the initial acceptance of the formal French tradition, and its eventual replacement by informal English styles. To the Victorians, then, both formal and informal traditions were available, and could both be incorporated in their gardens. The big change was in scale, for although some wealthy manufacturers could and did buy large country estates well away from the noise and dirt of the cities, the growth of gardening was mainly in smaller units, especially in the new suburban communities which followed the great expansion of the railways. Inevitably, protagonists of the regimented, formal style of gardening that we would still today associate with town parks came into conflict with the advocates of 'natural' styles, and in this controversy one figure stands out above all other – William Robinson, author of *The Wild Garden*, published in 1870, and the best-selling *The English Flower Garden* which appeared in 1883 and went through 15 editions in the author's lifetime. In that classic *History of British Gardening*, Miles Hatfield devotes one whole section to "the Robinsonian world": as he puts it, by 1883 there were in England already gardens which exemplified "the triumph of the 'natural' style of gardening evolved by Robinson and his school, which is in general the style that has been maintained – perhaps only under the force of economic circumstances – ever since."

William Robinson was a combative, even polemical, writer. His main enemy was the architect-designer, whom he saw as subordinating gardening to architecture – and, though his own opinions changed over a long and influential life (changes revealed in the successive editions of his best-selling book), he championed to the end the idea that the *plants* are what matter, not the statuary or the formal design. It is not too much to claim that the vast majority of English gardeners would broadly agree with him today, although, as happens with many battles of ideas, later generations, used to the happy combination of plantsman and designer seen *par excellence* every year at the Chelsea Flower Show, may well wonder what the fuss was all about.

The science of ecology

Robinson may have pioneered the idea of the 'wild garden', but he was totally ignorant of the word 'ecology', a word now so familiar that it is in grave danger of being overworked. In my own professional career spanning roughly half a century, I have seen 'ecology' change from being a technical term of restricted circulation amongst biologists to its present status. In the first edition of the Royal Horticultural Society's *Dictionary of Gardening* (1951) the entry under 'ecology' consists of a terse, 14-word definition: "the study of the habits and life of plants in relation to their environment." In contrast, the new, second edition (1992) devotes one and a half pages to an elegant essay on the science and especially its relevance to horticulture, finishing with the sentence: "in recent years it has grown up to become a widely respected discipline, which should play a full part in the world of gardening and horticulture".

Though the term 'ecology' was invented in the nineteenth century, the science is essentially a twentieth-century one. From the Greek *oikos*, a house, it is concerned with the relationships of plants and animals to each other and to their environment. Much of the progress of Victorian biology depended upon the detailed study of individuals, and even the fundamental Darwinian revolution found its main force in the idea of natural selection, which in its crudest form could be presented as the 'survival of the fittest'. It was perhaps inevitable that biology should develop in this way, for no general methods could emerge to study the interactions of organisms with each other in communities until the essential bricks had been laid in terms of separate understanding of how an individual plant or animal grows, reproduces its kind and dies. To many nineteenth-century botanists, their science consisted of comparative study of individual species – what we can call systematics, morphology and anatomy – and experimental study of the function of individual plants, which we call physiology. Indeed, even the latter found it hard to break into the traditional interpretation; as late as 1860, for example, the Cambridge Professor of Botany, C.C.Babington, entitled his new British

Flora *A Manual of British Botany* as if only the systematic study and classification of the higher plants existed! Ecology, as the study of interactions between individuals and between species, involved a very fundamental change
of perspective that resulted, for example, in the formation of the British Ecological Society in 1910. Like that other largely twentieth-century development, genetics, ecology embraces both plants and animals, cutting across the
traditional barriers between academic disciplines. Some knowledge of ecological principles undoubtedly helps the present generation to break down
the traditional rigid division between 'wild nature' and the ordered garden,
the theme that underlies the whole of this book. Stefan Buczacki, a popular
writer and broadcaster on horticultural matters, represents the new generation of gardeners who embrace ecology as a valuable contribution to their
hobby; his book *Ground Rules for Gardeners* (1986) is subtitled "a practical
guide to garden ecology" and provides an excellent review of the ways the
new science can help in the garden. Buczacki's acknowledgements in this
book conclude with this tribute: "... I must record my indebtedness to Joyce
Lambert, an outstanding British ecologist who, twenty years ago, first
showed me 'what grows where, and why'." Another outstanding recent book,
which would surely have delighted Robinson, is by Chris Baines (1985); entitled *How to make a Wildlife Garden*, it has become almost a text-book for a
new generation of gardeners who, like Chris himself, have only "a quarter of
an acre of garden" round their house. More overtly embracing nature conservation as an aim, Baines clearly belongs to an English tradition of all-
round naturalists to whom the garden is as valid a place 'to enjoy nature' as
is the wild sea-coast or mountain-top.

The concept of 'weeds'

Over centuries, during which man saw, at least in our Western culture, his
environment as largely hostile, wild plants which were effective competitors
with those cultivated were understandably seen as enemies. The Biblical
parable of the tares helped to fix the idea of a harmful 'tare' or 'weed'
throughout Christian Europe and has indeed persisted in our urban societies right up to the present day. Yet the very ambiguity of both words 'tare'
and 'weed' – for in both cases the word can be used to mean in particular contexts a harmless or even positively attractive plant – suggests that throughout
our history we have been aware that a weed is only a plant in what we per-
ceive as the wrong place. The Victorian gardener, brought up to treat his task
as involving a continual battle with 'weeds' and 'pests', naturally saw the
problem in black and white terms. In this he was undoubtedly assisted by the
widespread belief that, at least for 'the lower classes', dull repetitive work
such as hand-weeding provided desirable training and discipline, and this
belief dies hard.

   The 'Robinson revolution' certainly helped to break down the rigid division between garden plants and weeds. Robinson's flowery prose makes good
reading today. Here is a sample (from *The Wild Garden*, ed.4, 1894): "Our
wild flowers take possession of the hedges that seam the land, often draping
them with such inimitable grace that half the conservatories in the country,
with their small red pots, are poor compared with a few yards' length of the
blossomy hedgerow verdure." The inset illustration he chooses (Fig. 50) may
well, however, cause the modern gardener's eyebrows to rise. *Calystegia sil-*

Fig. 50 Robinson's illustration
of the 'Large White Bindweed'
Calystegia silvatica in *The Wild
Garden*

vatica, which he calls 'the Large White Bindweed', is commended in the caption as "the type of nobler climbing plants, with annual stems, for hedgerows and shrubberies" – though a reference on the following page to the large Hungarian Bindweed (the same plant) is more circumspect: it "would be best in rough places, out of the pale of the garden, so that its roots might spread where they could do no harm."

Here we see the pragmatic approach tempering the romantic vision – a feeling familiar to every plantsman-gardener today! Actually, *Calystegia silvatica* provides an excellent example of a very special phenomenon. To become an acceptable garden plant, any introduced perennial must be hardy but not too invasive: if it refuses to be 'tamed', no matter how spectacular its flowering show, it is likely to finish up as a 'weed' and outcast. In my own experience, Robinson's advice is very sound: in our garden we have by accident found the perfect position where it can be tolerated and even allowed to show its paces – coexisting with hens and the 'Himalayan blackberry' *Rubus procerus* along the field-side fence.

Reproducing wild plant communities

As William Robinson himself would have admitted, at least in his later writings, some garden communities are much easier to treat like 'wild nature' than are others. The two contrasting 'natural' features which can quite easily be reproduced in a small modern garden are open water with reed swamp in the pond, and mountain vegetation in the rock garden. A visit to the Chelsea Flower Show will soon convince the sceptic of this for, given money and enthusiasm, it is possible to create literally in a week an attractive garden with water, rocks and carefully-chosen plants. Brought down to the practical restrictions which would operate in an ordinary suburban garden, it would still be true that both pond and rock garden could be made in a single season. Whether the upkeep is quite so straightforward, of course, is another matter. Ponds in particular present interesting 'weed' problems which could be facetiously summed up in the question "When does a pondweed become a pond weed?" As many a primary school biology teacher is learning, the colonisation of small artificial ponds newly made in the 'nature area' can be surprisingly rapid (see p. 189).

Other plant communities we commonly create in our gardens are much less natural, of course. Perhaps the suburban lawn offers the most extreme example. Obviously related to pasture grassland, with the lawn-mower taking the place of the grazing animal, it can be a manicured, bright green patch consisting almost exclusively of one or two selected lawn-grasses such as the fine-leaved forms of red fescue *Festuca rubra*. Such a monocultural lawn is both expensive and time-consuming to maintain, and most people settle for some compromise, in which fairly regular cutting and occasional chemical application stabilises a grassland in which up to six species of grass and, say, a dozen 'weeds' are present. What are these persistent lawn weeds? Ecologically they belong to close-grazed pasture and reproduce largely (in some cases exclusively) by vegetative spread. The common daisy *Bellis perennis* is the most traditional and familiar of all these lawn weeds. Truly native daisies are probably rare, found, for example, in damp mountain grassland communities or in dune slacks on the coast. The familiar lowland plant is a more vigorous variant with larger flower-heads which, we assume, has been selected over centuries of intensive grazing in the British countryside. White clover *Trifolium repens* is a similar case, though here we normally prevent flowering more effectively than with the daisies, and notice only the bright green 'shamrock' leaves.

Because lawn weeds can survive in the non-flowering state, we may occasionally discover plants we never knew were in the lawn. This tends to happen in hot, dry summers, especially if there is a hosepipe ban in force and the lawn goes parched and brown. In the famous drought summer of 1976, when over much of England there was hardly any rain for three months, deep-rooted perennials drawing water from lower soil levels often showed up as green patches on brown lawns and sometimes, because grass-cutting ceased, actually revealed themselves by flowering. On the Front Lawn of King's College in Cambridge, for example, there were a few flowers of harebell (the Scottish 'bluebell') *Campanula rotundifolia* showing in August of that notorious drought year. Harebells are not frequent in the Cambridge area and are, moreover, almost impossible to detect in turf in the non-flowering state because (in spite of the specific name *rotundifolia* which refers to the early leaves only) the leaves are small and very narrow, and quite lost among the grass leaves. The harebell has apparently disappeared again on the King's College lawn, but it is quite likely still to be there in its non-flowering state.

So far the lawn weeds discussed have been native plants, all of which we assume were around, though probably much less commonly, before agricultural grazing began. Our prettiest lawn weed in England today, however, was first introduced into Europe as a garden plant: this is the slender speedwell *Veronica filiformis*, a plant native in the Caucasus and the Turkish mountains, whose history in Britain we discussed in Chapter 7 (Plate 37). Daisy and speedwell both make impressive contributions to the spring flowering of lawns, and increasingly gardeners are coming to see them as attractive garden plants that are assets rather than liabilities.

Most English gardens, even the smallest, can show some small patch of lawn, but we need a larger garden to afford the possibility of other grassland communities related to the traditional hay meadows of the English countryside. Robinson was a great champion of such 'wild' grasslands. In *The Wild Garden* he devotes a whole chapter to the subject with his customary conversion zeal: "Mowing the grass once a fortnight in pleasure grounds, as now practised, is a costly mistake. We want shaven carpets of grass here and there, but what nonsense it is to shave it as often as foolish men shave their faces! There are indeed places where they boast of mowing forty acres! Who would not rather see the waving grass with countless flowers than a close surface without a blossom?" Much has changed in the century since Robinson advocated the 'wild garden'. For one thing, he assumed that his client garden owners had the estates, and the man-power to run them, but by the end of the World War I mowing large areas of grass had mostly ceased to be a standard unquestioned practice, and by the end of World War II even the gardeners who knew how to use a scythe were few and far between. 'Wild gardening', then, became more and more a social and economic necessity, to which taste and fashion no doubt adapted itself. Fashion in recent years has changed again, as we shall see in the final chapter when we consider the impact of the green movement in general and ideas of nature conservation in particular on the way we see our gardens.

Ecology and field botany

Many professional ecologists reading this chapter might well object that the movement towards wild gardens, in which the distinction between weeds and garden plants is far less rigid than before, has little to do with their science. Indeed, they often deplore what they see as a misuse of the term ecology to give a spurious scientific respectability to a wide range of 'green' ideas which have sprouted in recent years. Whilst this reaction is understandable, it is in danger of alienating the professional scientist from the amateur gardener at a time when some rapprochement is particularly easy. The popularity of some presenters of gardening programmes on radio and television owes much to this very genuine desire of many amateurs to understand in scientific terms aspects of the hobby they so much enjoy. Of course, ecology is only one of the many modern scientific developments whose findings may be relevant to amenity gardening, but it is nevertheless an important one. To take a very simple case. The attitude of many Victorian gardeners to butterflies in the garden was crudely negative. The cabbage white butterflies were pests, enemies on which war was waged, and the host plants, brassicas, on which their caterpillars fed had to be protected. Victorian gardening books had little to say about the wide range of other, harmless and often beautiful butterflies that frequent our gardens. They belonged to 'wild nature', and their presence in gardens was thought of as mildly interesting but unimportant. This apartheid was reinforced by the semi-popular literature on butterflies, which was explicitly designed for the collector, and concerned with little other than identification; even the information about host plants of the larvae was remarkably sketchy, except for the rarer species confined to specialised habitats. Contrast this with Baines' very readable chapter entitled 'Over the garden wall', (1985) in which he supplies a concise and informative list of what he calls "caterpillar plants for garden butterflies" and from his own experience discusses the ecological requirements of a range of attractive butterflies in his town garden, relating, for example, the occurrence of the common blue *Polyommatus icarus*, to a patch of bird's-foot trefoil *Lotus corniculatus* on which the caterpillars feed. He also stresses the importance of the complex of wildlife habitats that abut on all town gardens, and the role of 'waste ground', as planners usually call it, in supplying both food plants for larvae and nectar-flowers for adults, exhorting us for example, to be tolerant of nettles *Urtica dioica*, the food plant of the commonest large brightly-coloured summer butterflies, the small tortoiseshell *Aglais urticae* and the red admiral *Vanessa atlanta*.

The butterfly example illustrates how knowledge of what can be called the autecology of individual species can greatly increase both our enjoyment of field biology and our understanding of the interrelationships between organisms. Indeed, the investigation of plant-animal relationships in pollination, predation, and even mutual protection seems to be a growth industry in modern field studies, and is clearly stimulated by the fact that ecology, like genetics, transcends the traditional boundaries between the plant and animal sciences. We might therefore ask where that leaves the traditional field botanist. Do members of the Botanical Society of the British Isles, the British Ecological Society and the Royal Horticultural Society cooperate in joint projects? Briefly, the answer is "Yes, but not much". Anticipating our final chapter, we can say that most keen field botanists, however committed they are to the conservation of nature, do not change the way they enjoy their hobby except in the matter of collecting specimens. In this respect there is a real revolution. We still collect, but have very largely sublimated our acquisitive instincts by the use of colour photography or, more generally, by refined recording methods. We are still, however, recording presence or absence of particular plant species in particular sites, a game whose rules were largely laid down in the nineteenth century. I see no reason why we should be ashamed of this, any more than we should deplore the fact that most gardeners want little more from the professional scientist than a stable name for the plant they like to grow. It may be inconvenient for the professional to find, for example, that the field botanists can tell us where a particular species is at what date, but cannot supply a hint of how much there is, or what it is growing with. Most naturalists, like most gardeners, do not want their hobby to become a burden of responsibility, and it is unfortunately true that even making a decent list of associated species is a good deal more time-consuming than recording a single specimen of the plant in question. The effect of this is greatly to limit the number of field recorders who are prepared to collect reliable habitat data.

One tradition that is understandably resistant to much change is the local

Flora, usually a book dealing with the wild vascular plants of a particular County. Since John Ray published his famous Flora of the Cambridge area in 1660 Britain has had an unbroken succession of County Floras, and there is no sign of any significant interruption to this remarkable literary output. In recent years, however, such Floras have begun to recognise that the description of vegetation types could greatly improve the interest of the detailed recording of individual species. John Dony's *Flora of Bedfordshire*, published in 1953, was one of the pioneers: it included 86 habitat studies of sites selected throughout the county to illustrate the range of vegetation types, and for each species in the traditional systematic part reference was given to particular habitat studies in which they were present. Several other Floras appeared with similar ecological content; some, such as the multi-author *Ecological Flora of the Shropshire Region* (Sinker et al. 1985) are very impressive cooperative works proudly offering a range of local expertise.

In recent years the learned societies have given increasing support to field projects with an ecological bias, both by making grants to amateur workers and by sponsoring collective surveys. The mistletoe survey already mentioned in Chapter 8, which showed that, contrary to popular opinion, more than 60 different trees and shrubs act as host to mistletoe in Britain, is a good example of a 'network research' project carried out by members of the BSBI and the RHS which goes beyond the mere recording of the plant studied (Perring 1973). So far as the BES is concerned their long-running *Ecological Flora*, a series of papers on the autecology of British plants, has now (1992) covered about 200 species and is still in active production. Undoubtedly the concern for nature conservation, and the popularity of 'green' issues in general, is a powerful force in favour of ecological study and research, from the highly technical to the simple local field study, and the naturalist has never had such a rich published literature to stimulate and educate an appreciation of plants and animals. Our final chapter looks at some of the implications of this 'green' concern.

12

Late Twentieth Century Attitudes

The 'Green movement'

As the twenty-first century approaches, all our politicians pay lip-service to environmental concerns, and interest in the natural world, strongly encouraged by television programmes of impressive technical brilliance, has never been so widespread. At the same time, gardening as a hobby has an enormous following, especially among the new leisured classes of the retired, whose life expectation is now some ten years longer than that of their parents. It is not surprising, therefore, that 'green' attitudes increasingly influence both natural history and gardening as hobbies. In this final chapter, some of these changing attitudes are illustrated and discussed, and a few tentative predictions made about how the ideas and interests of our successors might shape themselves.

One fundamental change, which really underlies the whole of this book, is that we no longer see the environment as starkly differentiated into natural and artificial. This change of attitude has crept upon us, but is now so important that it needs a careful examination. Of course, we can still see the extremes, and our television screens can bring them all too vividly into the living room – the devastation of the landscape by burning oil-fields in Kuwait, or the drab, polluted devastation of inner city decay, contrasted with the prosperous green English countryside carefully presented as a tourist attraction, or the overwhelming richness of tropical rain-forest. But this generation at last understands that man is part of nature and cannot ultimately survive by continued senseless opposition to it. Whether we like it or not, we must cooperate, both with nature and with each other.

It is no part of this book to pursue any of the great global political, social and religious problems such a change of attitudes must produce. Our theme is a very restricted one, but our starting-point must be this new attitude, for how we pursue our leisure activities must reflect to some extent these changes. 'Green' thinking has in recent years altered our daily lives and, although we may not always realise it, our attitude to much in the outside world. It would be surprising if these attitudes had not penetrated into the popular view of the plant world.

National Collections and Plant Directories

Following an international conference of botanists held at Kew in 1975, which was the starting-point of much effective cooperation to prevent widespread depletion or even extinction of the plant resources of the world, the Royal Horticultural Society took the parallel initiative for garden plants in 1978. From this conference arose the organisation called the National Council for Conservation of Plants and Gardens (NCCPG), and under the aegis of this body the National Collections scheme came into being. Holders of

NCCPG National Collections may be private gardens, large or small, public authorities owning parks or amenity gardens, botanic gardens or commercial nurseries. In each case the owner or representative undertakes to hold a living collection of a particular group (usually a genus) of horticultural interest, and make the material reasonably available to bona fide students. Jane Taylor's book *Collecting Garden Plants*, published in 1988, gives an excellent, readable and beautifully illustrated account of National Collections, listing all the collections registered by 1988 and describing 39 of them to illustrate the range: trees, shrubs, perennials and rock plants, and bulbs. At the time of writing (July 1992) there are more than 500 National Collections, and the success of the scheme has been such that parallel schemes are being set up in other countries, including France, Australia and the USA.

There is no doubt that the British tradition of gardening is particularly suitable for the development of the National Collections scheme. For one thing, gardening is often a cooperative, even a collective enterprise, and the British are good at committees. But there is more to it than that. We like to have our expert areas in which we feel reasonably confident: and setting up or expanding a National Collection introduces the gardener to the botanists and vice versa in a particularly satisfying way. It does in fact much to break down the traditional divisions, for most National Collection holders aspire to hold stocks of the botanical parent species, if possible of known wild origin, and to relate them to the horticultural varieties and hybrids. To be frank, there are inevitable disappointments and areas of disillusion involved. For example, the amateur gardener soon discovers that named cultivars for which some unique distinction is claimed may be quite undistinguishable when grown together and carefully compared. The professional horticultural taxonomist has always been aware of this problem, but many amateurs are certainly not, and it comes to many as a shock to find that no-one can authoritatively decide whether cultivar X is the same as cultivar Y. In fact, the very existence of National Collections undoubtedly brings some order out of the chaos of cultivar names in many groups, and so gradually contributes to an understanding of what we actually have in our gardens.

Parallel with the growth of National Collections in recent years has been the growing influence of *The Plant Finder* (Philip 1987) a remarkable publication initiated by the Hardy Plant Society, updated annually, and now a standard reference work for many keen gardeners. The aim of the book is to provide a 'plant directory', arranged alphabetically under generic name (from *Abelia* to *Zizia*) and containing under Latin or cultivar name more than 55,000 garden plants (1922/93 edition) that are offered in current British nursery catalogues, together with a coded reference to the nursery concerned. With this directory the keen gardener can trace suppliers of both common and rare amenity garden plants – with the proviso that there can be no guarantee that the plant supplied is correctly named. As the Preface to the current edition puts it: "Some (nurseries) still cling to old names that are obsolete, obsolescent or, worse still, figments of their imagination. There are far too many plants on sale under confusing and inaccurate names." Although this is true, it is also the case that the publication and widespread use of *The Plant Finder* is leading to a gradual improvement of nursery plant names. Nurserymen are increasingly aware that the correct name is desirable, not least because their customers are more discriminating and often show a strong interest in growing the less commonly available garden plants.

One of the intractable problems about plant names arises from the fact that gardening has a long documented history and therefore an enormous literature of variable value and accuracy. Names can be seriously out of date because the reference works themselves are out of date. Perhaps a small example will illustrate the kind of problem. In the genus *Alchemilla*, most gardeners know *A. mollis*, and many nurseries sell this plant under its correct name. The current *Plant Finder* lists sixteen species, however, including '*A. splendens*' offered by nine nurseries. I have never seen in any garden in Britain true *A. splendens*, which is a relatively rare wild plant of the European Alps, and can almost guarantee that a plant bought under this name is incorrectly named. Yet the name persists, partly, one suspects, because it is an attractive name that might help to sell the plant to which it is attached! Similar incorrect names must lie around in the nursery trade in almost any garden genus one cares to investigate. One of the aims of the *Plant Finder* is to reduce gradually the number of such wrong names, to the benefit of all concerned. Undoubtedly an area of tension between botanists and gardeners is inevitable in the attempts by specialists to 'find the correct name', which produces in its train a series of name-changes sometimes affecting familiar garden plants. Gardeners often accuse the professional botanist of being insensitive to their need for stability of names, and there is some justification in this charge, yet the creation of an internationally agreed system of naming plants remains the aim of all the specialists, to whom a reasonable stability is essential. A very remarkable ambitious project towards this desirable end for gardeners was launched in 1989, when Piers Trehane published the first volume of his projected three-volume *Index Hortensis*, subtitled "The Authoritative Guide to the Correct Naming of our Garden Plants". Trehane's starting-point, like the *The Plant Finder*, is the nursery catalogue, but his aim is more ambitious and less severely practical. From "some 2,800 nursery catalogues from Northern Europe over the years 1984-87" he has assembled a basic list of garden plant names which has been refined into this first volume covering herbaceous perennials.

The European Garden Flora Project

The completion in 1980 of the five-volume *Flora Europaea*, in which were named, classified and described all vascular plants wild in the whole European continent, naturally stimulated botanists and horticulturists to consider the possibility of a similar project to cover the garden plants of Europe, and in 1984 the first volume of the *European Garden Flora* was published (Walters et al. (eds) 1984→). There are now (1992) three published volumes of this standard work, and a fourth volume is ready to go to press and two more volumes are planned. Designed to provide the gardener with an authoritative account of every vascular plant genus in cultivation in European gardens, the Flora includes practical keys for identification and black-and-white illustrations of selected groups. Of particular interest to our theme of wild and garden plants is some comparison of the content of *Flora Europaea* and the *European Garden Flora*. Here are some statistics for three selected genera that are reasonably well represented in our wild and garden floras.

Genus	No. of species in *Flora Europaea*	No. of species in *European Garden Flora*	No. of species common to both Floras
Arenaria	51	8	7
Salix	70	79	41
Tulipa	11	32	10

For *Arenaria*, a genus with rather few attractive garden species (mostly 'alpines' for the rock-garden), nearly all the ones we grow are native European plants. In the case of the willows *Salix*, only about half of our garden species are of wild European origin; here gardens have been enriched with a range of non-European plants, mostly from Asia, though the most important species are European natives. Finally, when we choose a very familiar garden plant, *Tulipa*, we find that we cultivate nearly all the relatively few European species, but that the great development in our gardens has been from species from the near and middle East.

Note that the *European Garden Flora* tells us about the botanical species, subspecies and hybrids from which our garden flora is derived. It does not try to give an account of the named cultivars unless, as sometimes happens, one or two are particularly common or important in gardens. Where a genus or family contains many cultivars, however, the Flora indicates where more detailed accounts can be found.

The Royal Horticultural Society's *Dictionary of Gardening*, a four-volume standard work published in 1951, has long been recognised to be in need of revision. As I write, the Society has succeeded in publishing the totally rewritten successor, also in four volumes, which will undoubtedly become an essential reference work, though its price may mean that it remains largely a book to consult in libraries. A more popular single-volume work, profusely illustrated in colour, appeared in 1989 at a reasonably modest price: the RHS *Gardeners' Encyclopaedia of Plants and Flowers*, and has already found its place in the libraries of amateur and professional gardeners alike. Many other semi-popular gardening books have appeared in recent years, and a visit to any large bookshop will soon reveal that amenity gardening is still, in spite of economic recession, a growth industry in Britain.

The spread of aliens of garden origin

The word 'alien' is highly emotive, with its overtones of immigration policy and racist bias. Some of the popular press would even extend these overtones to their reporting – usually in the 'silly season' of July and August – on the 'threat' of giant hogweed, giant rhubarb or Japanese knotweed spreading and replacing our harmless, inoffensive native vegetation. But, as we saw in Chapter 1, the British flora as a whole is recent and re-immigrant, so that there has been no time since the final retreat of the ice, some 15,000 years ago, when no 'new' plants were arriving in what are now the British Isles. Although immigration is a continuous process, the speed of immigration and consequent change is of course variable. We have good reason to think that the opportunities for immigrant plant species to 'escape', as we tend to say, and hold their own or expand in wild vegetation are greater now than ever before in Britain. There are several reasons why this might be so. The first must be that we are introducing new foreign species from the wild at an accelerating rate to satisfy horticultural demand for novelty. What is now available through the nursery trade in Europe draws on the whole world for its source material, a rich assortment increasingly well documented in the new Dictionaries, Encyclopaedias and Floras we have been discussing. Moreover, new garden plants undergo very rapid selection, often consciously at the hands of the horticultural trade itself, who can rapidly popularise some 'strain' of an exotic species and dignify it with a cultivar name. But this is by no means the only selection: the very fact that a new species becomes widely grown means that the stock, whether propagated vegetatively, as with most hardy perennials, is quickly subjected to a range of environments presenting contrasting conditions of soil and climate, and the weakest plants will go to the wall. Hardiness, the ability to stand winter frost and cold, which we discussed in Chapter 1, is perhaps the most familiar of all these environmental constraints. It is entirely understandable that relatively few garden plants grow well throughout the whole area of the British Isles from the cool, exposed uplands to the hot, drier sheltered lowlands, and most gardeners know this from hard experience. What is less expected, however, is to find that predictions about garden hardiness based upon knowledge of the original native distribution of 'new' garden plants are by no means reliable. As we saw in Chapter 5, some of our most successful trees, introduced from very restricted native habitats, prove to be quite remarkably hardy and adaptable to most parts of Britain.

Who would have predicted such overwhelming success for that rare Chinese shrub *Buddleia davidii*, when it was first introduced into European gardens in the nineteenth century? Its name commemorates the French missionary Père David, who first discovered the plant in 1869. The first specimens introduced into western gardens came via Russia, and presumably from seed originally brought by the early Russian plant collectors, but these plants, according to Bean, were "an inferior form, being of comparatively weak, low, semi-prostrate habit, poor in colour of flower." They were superseded by a much more vigorous and horticulturally attractive variant raised in Paris in 1893 by the famous nursery firm of Vilmorin. But all the rich range of colour-varieties we now have apparently derive originally from Wilson's seed collections in Hupeh and Szechuan in the early years of the present century, and many modern cultivars have been raised in the past half-century in the U.S.A. This plant is now very widely naturalised indeed on waste ground over much of England and Wales, where its lilac flowers are such an attraction for butterflies in late summer (Plate 36). Undoubtedly the fact that the small, winged seeds are abundantly produced and widely dispersed by wind has aided its rapid spread. So, from being a local speciality of Central China, this plant we now call the butterfly bush has achieved via our gardens an astonishing success, and still seems to be spreading. What makes for success in one case, and not in a hundred others? We have to confess that we do not know. Nor do we know why the naturalised plant is predominantly lilac in colour, whilst our gardens present a fine range of colours from white to deep purple or red. All we can say is that the natural selection which is acting on the species in the wild seems to favour the wild type which is lilac-coloured, although, of course, other colour variants can occasionally be found in wild habitats. The ubiquitous butterfly bush and its ecological requirements would make a fascinating study, easily conducted in most of our English cities and towns, for anyone interested in the themes of this book.

With hindsight we can appreciate the success of some garden escapes in establishing themselves as members of the British flora. It does not seem to be possible to predict success, however. Which of the more than 55,000 garden plants stocked by British nurseries and listed in *The Plant Finder* are likely candidates for the twenty-first century? We can, of course, rule out whole groups of plants as non-starters. For example, the best a half-hardy annual like the familiar garden lobelia *Lobelia erinus*, a native of South Africa, can hope to achieve, even in a long hot summer, is 'weed' status in pavement edges outside urban gardens. So the next real success story is to be sought among hardy perennials rather than annuals or biennials. If we look at the few cases that have become notorious, they seem to divide into two groups: one, including *Buddleia* and the giant hogweed *Heracleum mantegazzianum*, are perennials with little or no power of vegetative spread, whilst others, such as the Japanese knotgrass *Polygonum cuspidatum*[1] are tough, long-lived perennials with very vigorous clonal spread and, indeed, very limited seed production in Britain.

How we judge success, of course, is very subjective. One criterion might be that the erstwhile garden plant can be found throughout much of the British Isles in wild habitats. On that criterion Japanese knotgrass is certainly successful: since it was first recorded wild in 1886 it has spread on waste ground, railway banks, riversides and most other disturbed habitats throughout the British Isles. *Buddleia*, on the other hand, is mainly in England, Wales and Ireland, and rare or absent over much of Scotland. Perhaps this is a question of time: a hundred years is not long for a new plant to find its natural range.

Of course, not all successful aliens that find a niche in the British flora come via gardens. Traditionally, seaports were, and to some extent still are, the point of entry for a whole range of foreign plants, and members of the Botanical Society have long enjoyed botanising on waste ground where commercial detritus produces an impressive alien flora. Nowadays airports are increasingly important, and the opportunities afforded by rapid air travel are considerable, though perhaps less obvious. Casual, unrecorded colonisation must be responsible for many successful alien weeds of earlier times such as the American pineapple weed *Matricaria discoidea*, first recorded in 1871 and now ubiquitous throughout the British Isles. The recording of new alien plants, many of them of garden origin in Britain, has until recently been handicapped by the absence of any easy method of identification. The *New Flora of the British Isles*, by Professor Clive Stace, published in 1992, sets out to remedy this deficiency. It includes some 3000 species of vascular plants covering, in addition to the 1500 or so undoubtedly native species, all naturalised plants and all recurrent casuals. To give some idea of the effect of this change of policy: the third edition of the standard *Flora of the British Isles* by Clapham, Tutin and Moore (1987) includes under the genus *Cotoneaster* only the single native species and six species naturalised from gardens. Three other garden species are mentioned by name as garden escapes. In Stace's

---

[1] I have elected to retain the name *Polygonum cuspidatum* for this plant, partly because there is as yet no consensus among modern Floras and reference works about what generic name to use if the large genus *Polygonum* is divided.

Flora there are no fewer than 45 species (or hybrids) of *Cotoneaster*, all but one escaped from gardens and recorded somewhere in the wild in Britain. For further comparison, the *New RHS Dictionary* includes 78 species and hybrids as garden plants. Botanists not infrequently find single bushes of *Cotoneaster* on rock faces in old quarries far from gardens: now we can attempt to identify such presumably bird-sown plants with confidence.

Concern about climatic change which may be caused by the so-called 'greenhouse effect' on the atmosphere has undoubtedly focussed interest on the evidence of changes in our flora in response to periods of relative warmth. Meteorologists warn us that we should not argue too much from a succession of hot, dry summers, but gardeners faced with hose-pipe bans or farmers feeling the effects of restrictions on crop irrigation can be forgiven for wondering whether some irreversible shift of climate is already taking place. Our gardens are full of evidence that short-term changes can have very rapid effects. Thus, a selection of warmer-than-average summers and relatively mild winters has enabled many people to grow *Eucalyptus* species in sheltered gardens in south-east England, but we know from long experience with this Australian genus that the next hard winter will kill back all garden *Eucalyptus* over much of England. Some, particularly *E. gunnii*, will probably shoot again from the base, but they will never make a large tree. Evidence of northern extension of range of southern species is less impressive in plants than in birds and insects (especially some butterflies), but claims have been made for particular species. The reverse situation, when a plant retreats to the north, leaving a scatter of extinct records along the southern fringe of its range, is also known: in the case of the oyster plant *Mentensia maritima* (Fig. 51) it is not easy to explain the retreat except as climatic response (Perring 1974). For a sober and authoritative assessment of the impact of climate change on British vegetation, the paper by J. P. Grime (1991) can be recommended[1].

The countryside as a garden

Outside our garden, as I write this in July, we have a wide strip of grassland, colourfully splashed by wild flowers. It adjoins a public footpath, and beyond it on both sides of the old bridle-way, now provided with a concrete surface to take agricultural machinery, there are weed-free arable crops of cereals ready for harvest. The grassland strip was also arable until last autumn, when a grass seed mixture was sown, and six months later it was greening over, a process aided by two or three cuts with a powerful tractor and cutter-bar. Last week I conducted a 'wild-flower walk' which spent a very productive afternoon immediately inside and outside what is legally the boundary of the garden, and took in the footpath and 'meadow' flora, yielding without difficulty some fifty species of flowering plants. Many of these are weeds, ranging from the pineapple-weed *Matricaria discoidea*, through the common poppy *Papaver rhoeas*, to the sow-thistles (*Sonchus*) and nettles *Urtica dioica* of our bonfire area, but taking in also the large bindweed *Calystegia silvatica*, originally a garden plant from Central Europe, and undoubted natives such as self-heal *Prunella vulgaris*, and dog's mercury *Mercurialis perennis*, on a damp

[1] The proceedings of a joint symposium of the British Ecological and Linnean Societies, which considered 'Global Change and the Biosphere', have now been published (*Ann. Bot.* **67** Suppl. 1). Several of the papers deal with aspects of climatic and vegetational change.

Fig. 51 Distribution of
the oyster plant *Merten-
sia maritima* showing
retreat northwards.
● recent records (post-
1950); ○ old records
(pre-1950). From
Perring 1973

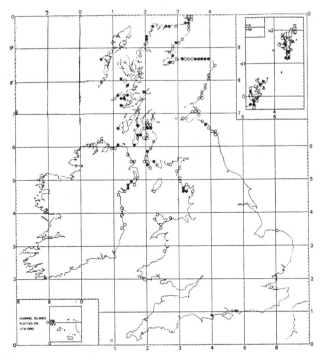

shady bank. Both visually and scientifically (in terms of variety of flowering plants) this is an attractive site, and could of course be parallelled in thousands of places throughout the British countryside. Moreover, the new grassland strip represents a process now rapidly transforming much of the lowland English countryside, namely the shrinking of intensively-farmed arable areas and the creation of plant communities ranging from temporary set-aside, through golf-courses and grazing meadows, to hedgerows, copses and woodland. In Britain, as in much of the European Continent north of the Alps, the ruthless spread of mechanised chemical agriculture is relaxing its hold, and 'nature' is being restored. This period of relaxation is, of course, driven by economic forces, and could be reversed as quickly as it has begun. It is, as we all know, a local phenomenon of agricultural over-production in a world in which many people starve and millions are under-nourished. Nevertheless, its effect on how we see and enjoy the British countryside is increasingly evident, and administrators, owners and tenants of land are all affected by the 'green' ideas we have already discussed. Let us look at a few examples of these radical changes.

Churchyards have always had a special interest for naturalists, as also for historians, novelists, poets and artists. Indeed more than 150 years ago the famous horticulturalist J.C.Loudon wrote: "Churchyards and cemeteries are scenes not only calculated to improve the morals and the taste, and by their botanical riches to cultivate the intellect, but they [also] serve as historical records." Partly, no doubt, this wide interest derives from the fact that the country churchyard was, and often still is, a very special site in the village, and its upkeep and use was a matter of general concern, not just to the Vicar himself but to all his parishioners. To some extent, old churchyards can be thought of as public gardens and, like gardens in general, they show a great range of management styles, from complete neglect – the fate of many a remote churchyard around a closed country church – to fussily manicured lawns, weed-free gravel paths, and neat flower beds. In the 1960's, before the present green concerns developed, many churchyards were 'rationalised', old gravestones removed and much historic and wildlife interest lost. Nowadays, stimulated especially by Francesca Greenoak's very timely and beautiful book entitled *God's Acre* (1985), the Church of England officially, and very many of the clergy, are much more aware of the intrinsic interest of the churchyard, and the importance of some practical management policy for the whole church and churchyard complex. Excellent advice on the management of churchyards to promote their wild-life interest can now be obtained, both from the County Trusts themselves and from the Church of England's own Church and Conservation Project (see Appendix for details). Nowhere is the Anglican tradition of compromise more obviously relevant than in the management of the churchyard, where, for example, the architect may strongly recommend the ruthless removal of all ivy from buildings and walls, whilst the entomologist and ornithologist advocate its retention as a valuable wildlife habitat. The tension between botanists and gardeners is also evident. In my own experience, defending the old grassland in the churchyard because it contains interesting local species such as the fiddle dock *Rumex pulcher* (Plate 38) is by no means easy, though the English tolerance of eccentric naturalists does really help! After all, one of our most influential naturalist authors, Gilbert White, was an eighteenth-century country parson, and his village, Selborne, has become a national shrine to the English naturalist tradition.

Botanically, there are two main kinds of habitat of special interest in churchyards. To the botanist interested in higher plants only, it is usually the un-improved grassland amongst the gravestones that has most value, for many species formerly common in traditional pasture meadow, such as cowslip *Primula veris*, or hay meadow, such as ox-eye daisy *Leucanthemum vulgare*, are now much reduced in the countryside in general, but can still survive in the churchyard (Plate 39). For the specialist in ferns, mosses or lichens, however, it is the buildings, walls and gravestones that provide the rich flora, and many rare and local mosses, liverworts and lichens, often with very special habitat requirements, are known from old churchyards.

From churchyards we may extend our view to take in land managed for recreation or sport. Here the borderline between 'wild nature' and managed garden is rapidly becoming blurred, and the conservation organisations themselves are faced with a range of questions about planting and management that they, with the best will in the world, may find it very difficult to answer. The purists among us, alarmed at what they see as irresponsible planting or sowing of alien species in the countryside, try to advocate rigid policies that neither the general public nor, often, the authorities concerned, feel they can strictly adhere to. Nowhere is this tension more obvious than in the attitude to tree planting. The native British tree flora is, as we saw in Chapter 5, very restricted indeed, and our gardens, parks and woodlands are now much enriched, in terms of different kinds of trees, by centuries of largely planned introduction of exotic species. The gardener in us, to whom the range and variety of plants has always been intrinsically interesting, still feels, like the eighteenth-century landowners often did, that success in growing exotic trees is a wholly desirable achievement. What is wrong with an English countryside where the village on the skyline shows a group of wellingtonias towering above the other trees? Are we not forced to the conclusion that some, at least, of our concern about aliens is illogical? Perhaps, as in architectural styles, all that is needed to change public perception of the new and the exotic is the passage of time. We do well to remember that, when Dutch engineers introduced windmills and wind pumps to Britain in the seventeenth century, these contrivances were severely criticised for their deplorable intrusion into the English countryside. Now we lovingly restore and preserve them.

There is, however, another side to the question, revealed with such admirable clarity by Oliver Rackham in his writings on English woodland and the shape of the countryside (eg Rackham 1976). It is possible for ecologists to distinguish with considerable conviction between ancient woodland, whose direct continuity with the original 'wild-wood' is certain, and secondary woodland of all kinds, including, as the extreme case, commercial forests of exotic conifers. No-one needs persuading that ancient woods need protection, not only from felling and clearing, but also from re-planting with exotic species, which was the fate of many woods in the 1950's and 1960's. Inevitably, many surviving ancient woods will become nature reserves, in practice if not in designation, as our management of the countryside becomes more and more a matter of conscious policy. Such reserves have, of course, a great educational and recreational potential, as many County Wildlife Trusts have realised.

The English countryside, then, is rapidly becoming a managed one, in which the overwhelming dominance of efficient agriculture is no longer determining all change. Much of the rural scene is diversifying, but in the process we find ourselves increasingly thinking of management for recreation or 'wildlife'. Inside our gardens, once jealously secluded, a parallel change is taking place, and the pressure of manicured tidiness relaxes (Plate 35). To the European tourist much of rural England already looks like a garden. Is this what we want? Even if it is not, can we define and carry through any alternative policy? These are debatable questions for the twenty-first century.

Greening our Cities

For my generation, Richard Fitter's New Naturalist volume *London's Natural History* (1945) opened up new vistas of interest, especially with its fascinating final chapter reporting on surveys of the 'bomb-site' floras which sprang up in London following the destruction of the Second World War. As Fitter explains: "The effect ... has been to produce extensive areas of open ground throughout the most heavily built-up parts of London", so that "there is more open ground today within a mile of St. Paul's Cathedral than there has been since the early Middle Ages". Keen botanists, among them J.E. Lousley and Edward Salisbury, meticulously recorded the return of nature as the wild flowers covered the bomb sites, noting, for example, that the rose-bay willowherb *Epilobium augustifolium* was by 1945 probably the commonest plant in Central London. Rose-bay was in fact a rare plant in lowland England throughout Victorian times, being recorded by Trimen and Dyer's *Flora* (1869) for only eight localities in the whole County of Middlesex, one of them being Paddington Cemetery. Indeed, Victorian botanists probably thought of it only as an attractive garden plant, especially since some old garden forms seem to be relatively sterile, and therefore more amenable to control in the herbaceous border. Even more noteworthy to the botanists was the phenomenal spread on city waste ground of the Oxford ragwort *Senecio squalidus* first recorded, presumably as an escape from the Botanic Garden, in Oxford in 1794. The spread of this alien species northwards in Britain is still continuing: its colonisation of waste ground in Edinburgh and Glasgow, for example, has taken place mainly in the last twenty years. Moreover, when it meets the ubiquitous groundsel *Senecio vulgaris*, radiate variants of the latter begin to appear; although the precise details are still uncertain, it seems to be the case that these newly-arising radiate groundsels are the product of hybridisation between the native weed and the invader. More remarkably still, a new, fertile species, *Senecio cambrensis*, has arisen from the crossing of these two species by the process known as allopolyploidy which we discussed in Chapter 9; this plant is known as yet only from North Wales where it was first detected, the adjacent counties of Denbigh and Shropshire, and more recently in Leith, Edinburgh. Indeed, the whole group of related weedy species of *Senecio* seems to be in active spread and evolutionary change on the open ground of our big cities, providing a wealth of material for the botanist interested in variation and selection.

With the heightened concern of recent years with the problems of inner city decay has come a new interest in bringing wildlife and green areas into the urban scene. In London itself, the movement pioneered by Max Nicholson, former Director-General of the Nature Conservancy Council (as it then was), has stimulated the growth of ecological gardens, and many City authorities now show a much greater awareness of the value of sites that previously planners have thought of only as waste ground suitable for development. The Victorian idea of a regimented public park, with formal flower beds, tennis courts and laurel shrubberies, is being superseded by a more open policy in which 'wild nature' is given more play. To some extent, this change of attitude might be thought to be a case of 'making a virtue of necessity', for the labour costs of running a weed-free Victorian park make it increasingly impractical. 'Urban wild-life areas' or 'public open spaces', whatever their designation, seem to suit both the purses and the tastes of many administrators. Such places can be very valuable, not least because they can provide a range of habitats in which a rich and diverse flora and fauna can survive, even flourish, within a city boundary. Management can be very inexpensive, and voluntary groups can often do the necessary strimming, pathmaking and scrub-clearing to retain the ecological diversity. In such city sites, the flora is usually enriched by garden escapes which become well established, and in places where botanical recording has been more or less continuous since the seventeenth century, some plants become famous rarities with a long history of recording.

Just such a site is found in a complex of chalk pits on the edge of the City of Cambridge at Cherry Hinton, just within the modern City boundary. The oldest of these pits, Lime Kiln Close (known to local people affectionately as 'The Spinney') is in a key position on a cross-roads, and was threatened with housing development in the early 1950's. The City Council, supported by the newly-formed Naturalists' Trust, opposed the development at a key public enquiry held in 1956, and won its case. The Council then acquired the site and declared it a "public open space with natural history interest", and the Trust (now the Bedfordshire and Cambridgeshire Wildlife Trust) managed the site in cooperation with the City. Thirty-five years after this timely action, as I write, plans are being made for a ceremonial declaration of the site as a Local Nature Reserve. In Lime Kiln Close, rare and local species of plants and animals, including the wild cherry *Prunus avium* itself, survive happily under pressure from human visitors, especially the generations of local children for whom the partially wooded area has provided a marvellous natural playground. Human pressure to the right degree is in fact contributing to ecological richness and species diversity here, for casual trampling and damage to young trees prevents the natural succession moving to ash woodland. Working out how to regulate and manage such areas to which people have free access is increasingly important as 'green' ideas spread and are applied to our towns and cities. Is Lime Kiln Close, as it moves into the twenty-first century, a 'garden' or a 'piece of wild nature'? Does it matter which of these we call it, provided its beauty and interest survive for future generations to enjoy? (Plate 36).

In all our great cities there are welcome signs that 'urban wildlife', as it is often called, is making the news and receiving the attention of planners and politicians alike. The recent Flora of the City of Glasgow (Dickson 1991), beautifully illustrated in colour with photographs and paintings of wild flowers done by local artists, cannot fail to increase public interest in the 'waste places', canal banks, even neglected gardens of that City. From the many examples Jim Dickson chooses to describe, none is more remarkable than the results of his team's survey of the wild helleborine orchids. The broad-leaved helleborine *Epipactis helleborine*, a widespread orchid in Britain, is normally associated by botanists with woodlands, though Summerhayes, in his classic New Naturalist volume on the *Wild Orchids of Britain* (1951, ed.2 1968), explains that it can be found in "a greater variety of situations than any other British orchid, except possibly the Twayblade and the Common Spotted Orchid." To Glasgow botanists, who probably knew the orchid only in the Bothwell Woods on the outskirts of the City, it obviously came as a delightful surprise that it grew in more than half of the ninety City Grid Squares, and was indeed among the orchids second only to the common spotted orchid *Dactylorhiza fuchsii* in its frequency. Dickson gives a breakdown of the habitats of the broad-leaved helleborine in the Glasgow area as follows: parks, cemeteries and golf-courses 35%, gardens 28%, woodland and scrub 26%, meadows 3% and roadsides 3%. He comments: "perhaps it has increased in recent decades because cheap labour is no longer available to keep gardens as tidy as they might be." How many Victorian gardener's boys assiduously weeded out the broad-leaved helleborine from the dark shrubberies of the large houses, one wonders?.

Education and nature conservation

As our ideas about wild nature change, so does our attitude to the whole teaching of biology. Anyone who has experienced the quiet revolution in primary schools, whether as a teacher, parent, relative or governor, can hardly have failed to be impressed by the spread of teaching about wild-life and the environment, and the enormous potential this holds for the future management, not just of our own land, but of the planet as a whole. The role of the Field Studies Council, which has established since World War II a network of Field Centres throughout Britain, has been of special importance in educating teachers, parents and children to appreciate the scientific importance of natural history. Many books and learned studies are now devoted to the wider implications: I merely intend to comment on those aspects which are relevant to the subject of our attitude to wild and garden plants.

The first, and most obvious, is that schools are now encouraged to make and use 'wildlife areas' in their grounds. Such areas, often created from scratch in the corner of the school yard or playing field, are certainly gardens, in that the design contains, say, a planted and managed hedge, an area of mown or strimmed grassland, and the inevitable pond. But they are also potential native habitats and therefore nature reserves. Whatever we may think of this movement, we should surely rejoice over two aspects of it. Firstly, children go out of the classroom and into the field to observe for themselves the shape, variety and habits of plants and animals, and the new National Curriculum encourages, even requires, this kind of biological learning. This, in the hands of a competent teacher, can do nothing but good. Secondly, parents can be involved, and indeed often do become involved because their children are interested, and again recent official attempts to increase the parental role in primary teaching facilitate this process.

School wildlife areas do present management problems. One of them is highly relevant to our theme : when does a weed become a wild flower, or *vice versa*? The case, discussed in Chapter 8, of the introduced New Zealand aquatic, *Crassula helmsii*, which until quite recently was a relatively unknown aquarist's garden plant, illustrates the point beautifully. One newly-constructed school pond I know was furnished with a variety of aquatics from garden ponds, and within three years was almost full of this single alien 'weed' *Crassula*. At least the experience can be the basis of a lesson on ecological balance – though some might say that this involves sophisticated ideas more suitable for secondary than primary classes. This leads on to the very general problem, on which my impression is that botanists are unable to speak with one voice. Should 'wildlife areas' try to use only native plants? It seems to be the case that County and District Councils who offer stock to schools either free or at a subsidised rate to make wildlife areas generally offer only native species, and this is a sensible policy, easily defended, for example, by the argument that our native woody plants provide food and shelter for a wide range of native animals, especially insects and birds. On the other hand, why should we exclude, for example, the butterfly bush *Buddleia*, whose flowers are so attractive to butterflies, or the introduced garden *Cotoneaster lacteus* whose abundant berries provide winter food for fieldfares and redwings from Scandinavia?

This is only part of the general concern which we have already discussed. In an ideal world, it might well be the best policy to create a habitat or group of habitats and then 'let nature take its course'. But the temper of the age is against non-interference, partly because we mostly want quick results, and filling your pond and wildlife area with sown, planted or imported wildlife means that you can get quick results and 'something for the children to see'. Professor Norman Moore, one of our outstanding nature conservationists, records in his delightful autobiography *The Bird of Time* (1986) how he constructed a new pond in a field behind his house when he retired in 1983. Norman is an expert on dragonflies, and he "stocked his pond with water-plants" throughout the following summer. To his delight, by the end of that summer "no fewer than twelve species of dragonflies had visited the pond" and he had recorded two other species nearby. Fourteen species is more than one third of the total number of dragonflies recorded in the British Isles! The dragonfly expert clearly has the best of both worlds. All he has to do is to dig the pond and wait – the dragonflies, swift and powerful fliers, will find it and colonise it. Botanists have to wait a longer time for results. Should we do so, and hope that birds (or humans) will accidentally introduce the appropriate seed? Why not help nature? Perhaps we can compromise, and do a little helping, recording the name and origin of our introductions, whilst leaving nature to do the rest.

Of course school wildlife gardens are not the only places where organised instruction at primary and secondary level is increasingly being provided. Many nature reserves are greatly enhancing their educational activities, and again the climate of opinion favours such a development. In the case of the nature reserve I know best, Wicken Fen, owned by the National Trust and used by the University of Cambridge for many years for teaching and re-search, the new policy has been to set aside and develop a special 'Educational Area' at the edge of the reserve where parties of primary school children can be instructed under supervision. When the nature reserve is large enough (Wicken covers about a square mile of territory) such a policy is entirely prac-tical, and the extremes of primary teaching and University research are easily accommodated. Nevertheless, even Wicken Fen, which in my student days was a remote piece of 'unspoilt nature', is now inevitably more and more like a wild garden in which zones are scheduled for different purposes and sub-jected to different degrees of management. Is this a development we should deplore? Or do we welcome it? The next generation must decide.

Appendix

Natural History and Nature Conservation Organisations

The following organisations mentioned in the text are normally very willing to give information about their activities. A stamped addressed envelope would be appreciated.

British Ecological Society (BES)
Burlington House
Piccadilly
London W1V 0LQ

Botanical Society of the British Isles (BSBI)
c/o The Natural History Museum
Cromwell Road
London SW7 5BD

Chelsea Physic Garden
66 Royal Hospital Road
London SW3 4HS

Church & Conservation Project
National Agricultural Centre
Stoneleigh
Warwickshire CV8 2LZ

Countryside Council for Wales
Plas Penrhos
Ffordd Penrhos
Bangor
Gwynedd LL57 2LG

County Trusts for Nature Conservation *see* **Royal Society for Nature Conservation (RSNC)**

English Nature
Northminster House
Peterborough PE1 1UA

Field Studies Council
Montford Bridge
Shrewsbury SY4 1HW

Linnean Society of London
  Burlington House
  Piccadilly
  London W1V 0LQ

**National Council for the Conservation of Plants and Gardens
(National Collections) NCCPG**
  RHS Garden
  Wisley
  Woking
  Surrey GU23 6QB

National Trust
  36 Queen Anne's Gate
  London SW1H 9AS

Nature Conservancy Council (NCC). Until 1991, the official Government organisation for nature conservation in Britain. Now replaced by three separate bodies for England, Wales and Scotland. For England, see English Nature; for Wales see Countryside Council for Wales; for Scotland see Scottish Natural Heritage.

Royal Horticultural Society (RHS)
  Vincent Square
  London SW1P 2PE

Royal Society for Nature Conservation (RSNC)
  The Green
  Witham Park
  Waterside South
  Lincoln LN5 7JR

Royal Society for the Protection of Birds (RSPB)
  The Lodge
  Sandy, Bedfordshire

Scottish Natural Heritage
  12 Hope Terrace
  Edinburgh EH9 2AS

Bibliography

Allen, D.E. 1976 *The Naturalist in Britain*, Allen Lane, London.

Allen, D.E. 1986 *The Botanists*, St.Paul's Bibliographies, London.

Babington, C.C. 1860 *A Manual of British Botany*, Gurney and Jackson, London.

Baines, C. 1985 *How to make a Wildlife Garden*, Elm Tree Books, London.

Barber, L. 1980 *The Heyday of Natural History*, Jonathan Cape, London.

Bateson, W., Saunders, E.R. & Punnett, R.C. 1905 Experimental studies in the physiology of heredity. *Report to the Evolution Committee of the Royal Society* **2**:1-55, 80-99

Bean, ed.8 1970-. See Clarke, D.L.

Bennett, J.H. 1965(ed.) *Experiments in plant hybridisation*, Oliver and Boyd, Edinburgh and London.

Bowden, W.M. 1957 Cytotaxonomy of *Potentilla fruticosa*, allied species and cultivars, *Journ. Arnold Arb.* **38**:381-388.

Bradley, R. 1716-27 *The History of Succulent Plants*. Decades I-V. London.

Bradley, R. 1721 *A Philosophical Account of the Works of Nature*, Mears, London.

Brickell, C.D. et al (eds.) 1989 *Gardener's Encylopaedia of Plants and Flowers*, Dorling Kindersley, London.

Brickell, C.D. & Mathew, B. 1976 *Daphne*, Alpine Garden Society, Wisley.

Briggs, D. & Walters, S.M. 1984 (ed.2) *Plant Variation and Evolution*, University Press, Cambridge.

Buczacki, S. 1986 *Ground Rules for Gardeners*, Collins,London.

Buxton, R. 1849 *A botanical guide .... of Manchester*, Heywood, Manchester and Longman, London.

Chittenden, R.J. 1928 Notes on species crosses in *Primula, Godetia, Nemophila and Phacelia*, *J. Genet.* **19**:285-314.

Clapham, A.R., Tutin, T.G. & Moore, D.M. 1987 (ed.3 of Clapham, Tutin and Warburg's *Flora*) *Flora of the British Isles*,University Press, Cambridge.

Clarke, D.L. (ed.) 1970- (ed.8 of Bean's Manual) *Trees and Shrubs hardy in the British Isles*, John Murray, London.

Coats, A.M. 1963 *Garden Shrubs and their Histories*, Vista Books, London.

Cook, C.D.K. 1978 *The Hippuris Syndrome* in Street, H.E. (ed.) *Essays in Plant Taxonomy* pp.163-176, Academic Press, London.

Crane, H.H. 1951 *Pansies and Violas*, Collingridge, London.

Crane, M.B. & Lawrence, W.J.C. 1934 *The Genetics of Garden Plants*, Macmillan, London.

Cuthbertson, W. 1922 *Pansies, Violas and Violets*, Jack, London and Edinburgh.

Darwin, C. 1859 *On the Origin of Species ....*, Murray, London.

Darwin, C. 1862 *On the various contrivances by which British and foreign orchids are fertilised by insects ....*, Murray, London.

Darwin, C. 1868 *The variation of animals and plants under domestication*, Murray, London.

Dickson, J. 1991 *Wild Plants of Glasgow*, Aberdeen University Press, Aberdeen.

Duthie, R. 1984 The origin and development of Polyanthus, *Plantsman* **6**:28-32.

Dony, J. 1953 *Flora of Bedfordshire*, Luton Museum, Luton.

Elkington, T. 1969 Cytotaxonomic variation in *Potentilla fruticosa*, *New Phytol.* **6**:151-160.

Evelyn, J. 1664 *Sylva, or a discourse of forest trees*, London.

Ewen, A.H. & Prime, C.T. (eds. & trans., 1975) *Ray's Flora of Cambridgeshire*, Wheldon and Wesley, Hitchin.

Fisher, R.A. 1936 Has Mendel's work been rediscovered? repr. in Bennett, 1965 (q.v.).

Fitter, R.S.R. 1945 *London's Natural History* New Naturalist No.3, Collins, London.

Friday, L. 1991 The size and shape of traps of *Utricularia vulgaris*, *Functional Ecology* **5**:602-7.

Friday, L. 1992 Measuring investment in carnivory ... in *Utricularia vulgaris*, *New Phytol.* **121**:439-445

Gerard, J. 1597 *The Herball or Generall Historie of Plantes*, London.

Gilmour, J. & Walters, S.M. 1954; ed.5, 1973, *Wild Flowers* New Naturalist No.5, Collins, London.

Givnish, T.J. et al. 1984 Carnivory in the Bromeliad *Brocchinia*, *Amer. Nat.* **124**: 479-497.

Gledhill, D. 1985 *The Names of Plants*, University Press, Cambridge.

Godwin, H. 1956; ed.2, 1975, repr.1984, *History of the British Flora*, University Press, Cambridge.

Gray-Wilson, C. & Mathew, B. 1981 *Bulbs: the bulbous plants of Europe and their allies*, Collins, London.

Greenoak, F. 1985 *God's Acre*, Orbis, London.

Grime, J.P. 1991 The impact of climate change on British vegetation, in Battarbee, R.W. & Patrick, S.T. (eds.), *The Greenhouse Effect: Consequences for Britain*, 37.

Grindon, L. 1858 *Manchester walks and wild flowers*, Whittaker, Manchester.

Grindon, L. 1859 *Manchester Flora*, William White, Manchester.

Grindon, L. 1864 *British and Garden Botany*, Routledge, London.

Guignard, L. 1891 *Nouvelles études sur la fécondation*, *Ann.Sci.Nat.(Bot.)* **14**:163-296.

Hadfield, M. 1960, repr.1985 *A History of British Gardening*, Penguin Books, Harmondsworth.

Harper, K. 1977 *Population biology of plants*, Academic Press, London & New York.

Hay, R. & Beckett, K.A. (eds.) 1985 *Readers' Digest Encyclopaedia of Garden Plants and Flowers*, Readers' Digest, London.

Hayward, J. 1987 *A new key to wild flowers*, University Press, Cambridge.

Hegi, G. 1926 *Illustriente Flora von Mitteleuropa*, **5** (2): 912. Lehmann, Munich.

Henslow, J.S.L. 1846 *Address to the Members of the University of Cambridge on ... the Botanic Garden* (pamphlet) Cambridge.

Heptinstall, S. 1988 Feverfew - an ancient remedy for modern times?, *Journ. Roy. Soc. Med.* **81**:373-4.

Hibbard, S. 1872 *The Ivy*, Groombridge, London.

Hickey, M. & King, C.J. 1988 *100 Families of Flowering Plants*. University Press, Cambridge.

Holmgren, P.K. et al. (eds.) 1990 *Index Herbariorum* ed.8, New York Botanic Garden, New York.

Hooker, J.D. 1849-51 *Rhododendrons of the Sikkim Himalaya*, Reeve, London.

Hooker, J.D. 1870 *The Student's Flora of the British Islands,* Macmillan, London.

Hubbard, C.E. 1954; ed.3, 1984 *Grasses*, Penguin Books, Harmondsworth.

Hume, H.H. 1953 *Hollies*, Macmillan, New York.

Huntley, B. & Birks, H.J.B. 1983 *An Atlas of Past and Present Pollen Maps for Europe: 0-13000 years ago*, University Press, Cambridge.

Hutchinson, J. 1969 *Evolution and Phylogeny of Flowering Plants. Dicotyledons: Facts and Theory*, Academic Press, London & New York.

Huxley, A. et al. (eds.) 1992 *The New Royal Horticultural Society Dictionary of Gardening* (4 vols.), Macmillan, London.

Jalas, J. & Suominen, J. (eds) 1988 *Atlas Florae Europaeae* **2.** University Press, Cambridge.

Jermy, C., Chater, A.O. & David, R.W. 1982 (ed. 2) *Sedges of the British Isles*, Bot. Soc. Brit. Isles, London.

Johnson, T. (ed.) 1633 *Gerard's Herball*, London.

Juniper, B.A. 1989 *Carnivorous Plants*, Academic Press, London.

Klackenberg, J. 1983 The holarctic complex *Potentilla fruticosa* (Rosaceae), *Nordic Journ.Bot.* **3**:181-191.

Le Rougetel, H. 1990 *The Chelsea Gardener: Philip Miller 1691-1771*, British Museum (Natural History), London.

Linnaeus, C. 1753 *Species Plantarum*, Salvius, Stockholm.

Lysons, D. 1795 *Environs of London*. London.

Mabberley, D. 1987 *The Plant Book*, University Press, Cambridge

McClintock, D. 1984 Bamboos *in* S.M. Walters et al. *European Garden Flora* **2***:55-65*

Marsden-Jones, E.M. & Turrill, W.B. 1957 *The Bladder Campions*, Ray Society, London.

Martyn, J. 1728-37 *Historia Plantarum Rariorum*. London.

Martyn, T. 1788 *Thirty-eight Plates with Explanations*. London

Martyn, T. (ed) 1795-1807 *[Miller's] Gardener's and Botanist's Dictionary*. London.

Miller, P. 1724 *The Gardeners and Florists Dictionary*. London.

Mitchell, A. 1974 *A Field Guide to the Trees of Britain and Northern Europe*, Collins, London.

Moore, N.W. 1986 *The Bird of Time*, University Press, Cambridge.

Morton, A.G. 1981 *History of Botanical Science*, Academic Press, London.

Murton, R.K. 1971 *Man and Birds* New Naturalist No.51, Collins, London.

Page, C.N. 1988 *Ferns* New Naturalist No. 74, Collins, London.

Page, N. & Stearn, W.T. 1974; ed. 2 1985 *Culinary Herbs*, Royal Horticultural Society, Wisley and London.

Parkinson, J. 1629 *Paradisi in Sole Paradisus Terrestris*, London.

Pennington, W. 1969 *The History of British Vegetation*, English Universities Press, London.

Perring, F.H. 1973 Mistletoe *in* Green, P.S. (ed.) *Plants Wild and Cultivated*, (B.S.B.I. Conference Report), Bot.Soc.Brit.Isles, London, pp.139-145.

Perring, F.H. 1974 Changes in our native

vascular plant flora *in* Hawksworth, D.L. (ed.) *The Changing Flora and Fauna of Britain*, Academic Press, London.

Perring, F.H. & Walters, S.M. (eds.) 1962; ed.3 1982, repr. 1990 *Atlas of the British Flora*, Bot.Soc.Brit.Isles, London.

Philip, C. 1987- *The Plant Finder* (annual editions), Headmain, Whitbourne, Worcs.

Power, B. & Cocking, E. 1991 How we saved the Bramley, *The Garden* **116**:90-94.

Proctor, M.C.F. & Yeo, P.F. 1973 *The Pollination of Flowers* New Naturalist No.54, Collins, London.

Rackham, O. 1976 *Trees and Woodland in the British Landscape*, Dent, London.

Raven, C.E. 1942; ed.2 1950, repr. 1986 *John Ray: naturalist*, University Press, Cambridge.

Raven, C.E. **1947** *English Naturalists from Neckam to Ray*, University Press, Cambridge.

Raven, J. 1971 repr. 1992 *The Botanist's Garden*, Collins, London; repr. Silent Books, Cambridge.

Raven, J. & Walters, S.M. 1956 *Mountain Flowers* New Naturalist No.33, Collins, London.

Ray, J. 1660 Flora of Cambridgeshire. See Ewen, A.H. & Prime, C.T.

Richards, A.J. 1975 Notes on the sex and age of *Potentilla fruticosa* in Upper Teesdale, *Trans.Nat.Hist.Soc.Northumb.* **42**:85-92.

Robinson, W. 1870 *The Wild Garden*, John Murray, London.

Robinson, W. 1883 *The English Flower Garden*, John Murray, London.

Rose, P.Q. 1980 *Ivies*, Blandford Press, Poole.

Rosser, E. 1955 A new British species of *Senecio. Watsonia* **3**:228-232.

Rowley, G. 1954 Richard Bradley and his History of Succulent Plants. *Cactus and Succulent Journal of Great Britain*, **16**:30-31, 54-55, 78-81.

Rushforth, K. 1987 *Trees for small gardens*, Royal Horticultural Society, Wisley & London.

Schmitzer, E. 1986 Breeding with Triploid and Tetraploid Lilies *Yearbook N.Amer.Lily Soc.* **39**.

Shercliff, W.H. 1987 *Nature's joys are free for all*. Published by the author, 2 Hazel Drive, Poynton, Cheshire.

Slack, A. 1986 *Insect-eating Plants*, Alphabooks, Sherborne.

Sinker, C. et al. 1985 *Ecological Flora of the Shropshire Region*. Shropshire Trust for Nature Conservation, Shrewsbury.

Sosef, M.S.M. et al. 1987 *Catalogue of the Herbaria of Antoni Gaymans (1630-1680)*, Riksherbarium, Leiden.

Stace, C.A. 1975 (ed.) *Hybridisation and the flora of the British Isles*. Academic Press, London.

Stace, C.A. 1992 *New Flora of the British Isles*, University Press, Cambridge.

Stearn, W.T. 1981 *The Natural History Museum at South Kensington*, British Museum (Natural History), London.

Stungo, R. 1993 The Royal Society Specimens from the Chelsea Physic Garden 1722-99. *Notes Rec. Roy. Soc. Lond.* **47** (2).

Summerhayes, V.S. 1951; ed.2 1968, *Wild Orchids of Britain* New Naturalist No.19, Collins, London.

Taylor, J. 1988 *Collecting Garden Plants*, Dent, London.

Thomas, D. & Schmitzer, E. 1989 Polyploidal Lily breeding simplified, in *Lilies and Related Plants* (RHS Lily Group1988-9) ed. D.Reed, Royal Hort. Soc., London, pp.69-77.

Thomas, G.S. 1983 *Trees in the Landscape* Jonathan Cape, London.

Trehane, P. 1989 *Index Hortensis*,Quarterjack Publishing,Wimborne, Dorset.

Trimen, H. & Dyer, W.T. 1869 *Flora of Middlesex*,Hardwicke,London

Tutin, T.G. et al. (eds.) 1964-1980 *Flora Europaea* (5 vols.), University Press, Cambridge.

Unwin, C.W.J. 1986 (ed.4) *Sweet Peas*, Silent Books,Cambridge.

Walters, S.M. 1970 Dwarf variants of *Alchemilla, Fragm.Flor.Geobot.* **16**:91-98.

Walters, S.M. 1981 *The Shaping of Cambridge Botany*,University Press, Cambridge.

Walters, S.M. 1986a The name of the rose ...., *New Phytol.***104**:527-546.

Walters, S. M. 1986b *Alchemilla*: a challenge to biosystematists, *Acta Univ. Ups. Symb. Bot. Ups.* **27**:193-198.

Walters, S.M. 1989 Obituary of John Scott Lennox Gilmour *Plant Syst. Evol.* **167**:93-95

Walters, S.M. 1991 *Alchemilla* Update, *The Garden* **116**:62-3.

Walters, S.M. et al. (eds.) 1984-1990 *European Garden Flora* (3 vols., incomplete), University Press, Cambridge.

Webb, D.A. 1978 Flora Europaea - a Retrospect *Taxon* **27**:3-14

Webb, D.A. & Gornall, R.J. 1989 *Saxifrages of Europe*, Croom Helm, London

Woodcock, H.D. & Stearn, W.T. 1950 *Lilies of the World*. Country Life, London.

Yeo, P.F.1985 *Hardy Geraniums*, Croom Helm, London.

Index

All page references to plants are given under their Latin names. With few exceptions, English names are indexed under the name of the group (eg 'Italian alder' as 'alder, Italian'), and are followed by their Latin equivalent under which page references will be found. Books are indexed under authors, not titles. Place names and geographical regions have not been indexed unless the references are unusually important (eg Breckland). References to figures are indexed as page references: the plates are not indexed. Page numbers followed by 'f' indicate a footnote.